149 Ways to Profit from Your Divorce

Lucinda Pennington

The Bobbs-Merrill Company, Inc. Indianapolis/New York

To my husband, Bill Welsh–
a partner chosen with my head
whom my heart adores.

Published by The Bobbs-Merrill Co., Inc.
Indianapolis/New York
Manufactured in the United States of America
First Printing
Designed by MARY A. BROWN

Library of Congress Cataloging in Publication Data

Pennington, Lucinda.
149 ways to profit from your divorce.

1. Divorce—Economic aspects—United States.
I. Title. II. Title: One hundred forty-nine ways to profit from your divorce.
HQ834.P45 1983 332.024'02 82–17789
ISBN 0–672–52744–8

I'd like to extend a special thank you to:

Commissioner Richard Denner for his generous gift of insight and guidance,

Dr. Gerry McCormack, for sharing those attributes that make her an outstanding role model,

Attorney Ronald Supancic for his humor and experience, and my mother, Laura Williams, for her unflagging love and support throughout this project and so many others.

None of the people discussed in this book are based on any one client or individual. All names are fictitious and all case histories are of the author's creation, based on the composite of her professional experience.

—Lucinda W. Pennington
Counselor at Law

Contents

1

A Full Year's Worth of Good Advice

DECIDING whether or not to end your marriage is one of the most difficult determinations you will ever make. Being told that your spouse wants a divorce may be even worse. The very thought of divorce can make emotions soar and logic head for the nearest fire door. Yet, amidst anger, frustration, disappointment, and guilt, you *must* concentrate on learning legal rights, allocating assets, and dissolving your "marital partnership." In the process, you will negotiate one of the most important business deals of your life.

You and your mate have acquired property, accumulated savings, invested in assets, and gathered about you a wide variety of furnishings, property, and even intangible rights. All of these must be divided or allocated between the parties in a way that is fair to both—all at a time when you may feel incapable of apportioning the remaining postage stamps.

Recognize that you will probably suffer ambivalent feelings about taking many of the steps suggested in this book. If divorce is a real possibility in your relationship and you do nothing, you will probably lose valuable rights and property if your marriage ends. On the other hand, if you begin now to prepare for a possible divorce, will you trigger the very parting you dread? Will your actions undermine any chance at a better marriage? Will tending to your self-interest push you closer to the divorce that you would like to avoid?

Every assertive (not aggressive but assertive) action risks a negative outcome. Despite this, you *must* act in a way that promises the best chance at a positive result for you. If you feel that a brief separation, individual therapy, marital counseling, more emotional sharing, or another course of action could reknit your unraveling relationship, *do it!* If you've sincerely tried to improve your marriage without success, and you realistically see no possibility of continuing together, then admit that you've done all you can to nurture your partnership, and recognize that you now must shift your concerns to caring for (and protecting) yourself.

Emotional pain can cripple the common sense and survival instincts of *both* spouses during divorce, but for the mate who is less financially sophisticated, or less well informed about the family assets, even a temporary "fade-out" can mean a dramatically unfair division of commonly owned property.

In fact, once a parting seems inevitable, it is wise to begin setting out your goals as quickly as possible. The sooner you begin to plan this "business" of divorce, the more beneficial the final result will be. As much as a full year before the actual separation, you will want to consider the following advice concerning assets, money, the house, and the children. Use this "final year" to orchestrate a leaving that will be less traumatic and more profitable for each spouse — but especially for you.

Assets by Any *Name . . .*

. . . can smell as sweet. But it is important to know *whose* name each asset bears. For example, if *you* brought property to the marriage, try to retain title in your name alone. If you received gifts during marriage (even from your spouse), these, too, can be considered your separate property. Assets received by inheritance or intestate succession should also carry only your name. ("Intestate succession" means property passes on to you when a relative dies without a will, and you are in the line of inheritance.) In addition, if you and your mate have a written agreement that your earnings, the chiffonier, or the stocks belong only to you, take title solely in your name.

You're getting the idea, but don't stop now. Remember that all earnings and profits flowing from these assets are separate property as well. So are the proceeds if such an asset is sold. Clearly, it is crucial to keep such funds in an account showing only *your* moniker.

Once the title to an asset seems clear, *preserve* your rights by acting as though the property is yours alone. People often set out on the right legal foot by segregating property, or reaching a property agreement with a spouse, but over the years, or in a sentimental moment, that separate intention blurs into sharing acts. These actions *can* speak louder than previous understandings, and courts will determine each asset's status by studying your actions toward it, and toward each other, in the months or years since the initial determination of ownership.

Consider this example. When Bill T. married for the second time, he wanted to give his new spouse, Monica B., a special wedding gift. So Bill altered the deeds on his photography studio and his home to read "Bill and Monica, Joint Tenants, as Husband and Wife." When Monica sought a divorce seven years later, Bill's attorney informed him that Monica's net worth had headed for the stars with that single, long-ago stroke of Bill's generous pen.

Other couple's actions do not shine so clear, but the effect can be the same. While Sally F. was married to Jim, she received a small inheritance when her mother died. Sally always *intended* to visit their bank and open an account in her own name, but she only managed to cash the check one busy day while running errands. Upon arriving home, Sally stuffed the bills into an old flour container on the pantry's top shelf. Over the ensuing months, Sally often talked with Jim about what they might do with "their" new funds. From time to time, they discussed taking a cruise, and they mentioned before several friends that they were intending to use "their new money" to finance the trip. Once or twice, when small shortages arose in the household budget, Sally donated cash from the flour tin to tide them over. By the time Sally filed for divorce some months later, Jim had ample evidence that Sally's *actions* showed an intention to change her separate property into cash now owned equally by both of them.

In short, if you hold the mountain retreat in your own name, decline to rename it "Binky and Dick's Hideaway." If you are contemplating divorce, do not add your mate's name to the registration on the Jaguar. Overlook adding your spouse's name to any of your "own" bank or savings accounts. This is not the time to tell your broker that spouse's sell order is as valid as your own, nor to announce before dinner guests, "Darling, you have as much right to these antiques from my Uncle Harry as I do." In other words, unthinking behavior can deprive you of ownership interests worth thousands to you when divorce arrives.

About this time you may well be thinking, "Gee . . . this sounds awfully cold and calculating . . . maybe even hostile. I've always thought of us as a team; we've always shared everything. How can I say now that some things are mine and mine alone? How can I turn against my mate this way?"

It's unfortunate that divorce must be faced alone, for it's a time when we could most use a capable, supportive, willing partner to see us through. Since a marital breakup can trigger such needs, it is especially difficult to shift gears from being a duo to playing a solo act during divorce. Still, it is crucial to take sensible steps at this time. Staying practical is necessary, and here's why.

First, you *were* a team. Whether you are seeking the divorce or your mate has sought one, your "twosome-ness" is in the past tense. It may be months or years before you find another companion to help you survive economically. You may never find such a partner again. In the years ahead, you will have to provide for yourself. If your marketable skills are weak and your earning ability is shaky or low, you will need all the head start on a new life you can muster. If the law in your state *wants* you to keep certain assets as your separate property, does it make sense to give those rights away?

Second, keep in mind that nothing suggested here asks you to hate your spouse. These strategies merely ask you to care for yourself and your financial welfare. An enlightened self-interest need not mean that you dislike your mate, only that you consider yourself worthy of some planning and effort. Following these guidelines only means that you are ready to rely—from now on—primarily on *you*.

Third, if you are likely to be the custodial parent (or the spouse with physical custody of the minor children most of the time), you are "strategizing" for others, too. There has probably never been a support award that matches the *real* cost of raising a child. Any property advantages that you can gain for yourself will also benefit others depending on you.

Keeping these factors in mind, consider the following additional suggestions for preserving your rights in separate property. If you are still using your own separate funds to pay household expenses, ask your spouse to agree in writing that you will be reimbursed. Courts tend to find that such transfers are "gifts" contributed to the marital community. Without an agreement, there may be little chance of ever seeing those funds again. If it is unlikely that your mate will sign such an agreement, be sure at least to repay yourself from household expenses for your loans. Keep the balance in your separate account at its starting level.

If, during the marriage, you receive property that you *agree* will belong to you (earnings, for example), treat that asset as yours alone. Have your spouse sign a simple written agreement in which he concurs in your sole ownership, and put all those earnings into a bank account bearing only your name. If you later decide to make an investment with those funds, put title in your name only and be prepared to demonstrate the source of the purchasing funds in your solely owned account. Taking title to real property with your own money? Be sure you have your spouse sign a quitclaim deed. Such a document (available in any stationery store) can transfer to you all of your mate's interest in a particular parcel of real estate.

By including a "legal description," you eliminate any chance of later confusion about exactly which property you mean. Some legal descriptions appear mysterious: The SW ½ of the SE ¼ of Township 32, Range 21. Other legal descriptions look quite straightforward: Map Book 329, Page 020, Parcel 029, Tract 0037. Finally, a few may appear more colorful than helpful: All of Lot 12, Bluebird Point, a subdivision located on Star Route Two, Red Bluff Point, Lampe, Missouri.

However it reads, copy your legal description carefully onto your quitclaim deed where indicated on the form. This formality will serve as extra insurance to make your sole ownership complete. It should describe the property with a street address *and* a legal address, and make clear that your mate transfers to you any and all rights he/she may have in that piece of property by virtue of being your spouse. Record the quitclaim deed so that clear title will be proved every time a title search is undertaken when you wish to transfer, sell, or borrow against this property.

In addition, consider drawing up a list of your separate property—all those goodies received as gifts, by will, or through inheritance when an antecedent dies intestate—without a will or without a valid will. Separate property also includes assets that either of you brought to the marriage, or that you and your spouse agree will remain yours alone. Ask your spouse to sign this list, with you, before a notary public. Put the list in a safe spot known only to you—probably *outside* your home, in case you later lose access to the family residence.

If you and your mate currently have approximately equal separate property, but you realize that you will shortly be receiving more separate property assets that he/she will receive, offer to "sign off" on spouse's separate property in exchange for his/her signature on your list—and on the additional paragraph where it states that all other property coming to you by gift, inheritance, or intestate succession will remain only yours.

Of course, if your marital roommate is about to acquire substantial property via any of these methods, the last thing you want to see is such a list presented for *your* signature. As soon as the property comes into your spouse's possession, begin to encourage a change in title to "Terry and Troy, husband and wife, as Joint Tenants"; to a jointly held bank or savings account, or to some other status that illustrates your mate's intention to convert the property to a commonly owned asset.

Remember that only eight states—Arizona, California, Idaho, Louisiana, Nevada, New Mexico, Texas, and Washington—follow community property rules in determining the ownership characteristics of all assets acquired during the marriage period. In other words, courts in these states *presume* that a piece of property gained while married is owned equally by both marital partners, whether one contributed financially or not. Even in community property states, however, assets received by gift, by will, or by intestate succession come to you or your mate as separate property—an asset over which only one owner can exercise control. If your spouse receives such separate property, promptly urge a change of title to include your name. Even in community property forums, appearing on the title as an asset's owner can ensure a handsome bonus for you.

In America's remaining states, title to an asset can prove especially important, because in these common-law-governed jurisdictions, the person earning, acquiring, or holding a particular asset is often declared its sole owner by the courts during a divorce. Even in these forums, however, an approach to property division known as "equitable distribution" is gaining ground.

In fact, 47 states now follow equitable distribution guidelines in dividing assets, but don't relax and hope that Uncle Judge will take care of you. Help that person on the bench allocate a hefty share of the marital property to you by providing evidence like a shared title, records of your financial contribution, a binding agreement between your spouse and you about ownership rights, etc.

Finally, note that arriving at division of property through out-of-court negotiations with your spouse does not require that you adhere to state laws about asset allocation. So long as you do not hide assets or purposely under or over value property, either one of you can receive—with the full knowledge and approval of the other—60, 70, even 80 percent of your commonly owned property. Such an agreement, if freely made between two adults represented by independent counsel, will probably receive the court's okay, regardless of whether you live in a community-property, equitable-distribution, or common-law jurisdiction.

But what to do when a spouse appears to hold all the property cards? When your mate has most of the assets in his/her name? If your marriage partner has received gifts or inheritances during the marriage, brought certain assets into the marriage, or thinks that all the earnings and other property acquired during your time together should be his/hers alone, you have your work cut out.

Naturally you'll want to encourage any tendencies your spouse has shown to transmute, or change, the separate property into a joint tenancy, tenancy in common, tenancy by the entirety, or other form of co-ownership arrangement. Funds that formerly belonged to your spouse alone should be placed in a joint financial account; deeds should be changed to reflect the shared ownership. Creating any joint tenancy requires a writing, and that that writing should be recorded in the county where the real property is located, so that your ownership rights are known to all. In some states, one mate's transfer of separate property to the other spouse as his/her separate property requires a written instrument as well.

In addition to recording all new common ownerships in real property (land, houses, apartment buildings, condominiums, etc.), notify the department of motor vehicles so that both names can appear on the registrations of all cars and other vehicles. Inform all banks and savings and loans associations that the accounts should bear two names (or open one or more new joint accounts equally accessible to you as the lower-earning or unemployed spouse) Make sure that the stockbroker changes company records to reflect your name on your mate's trading account.

If the asset is one not easily labeled or to which co-ownership interests cannot be recorded or otherwise "announced," start collecting evidence of your spouse's donative (gift-giving) intent. *Now* is the time to rename your spouse's sailing skiff "Jeff & Mandy's Pride." Start a scrapbook of all the cards you receive with gifts from your spouse; note the occasion, the guests, if any, and any special toasts. Arrange celebrations to announce the gift, if suitable, and take photos to include in your "evidence album." Once you get the idea, your imagination and creativity may set the only limit to bringing your partner's separate property under the community umbrella for your coming rainy day.

In fact, increasing your ownership rights—by writings, by name changes, or by actions alone—will also benefit you well before a potential separation: a joint owner cannot alone sell an asset, borrow against it, pledge it as security for a separate loan, or lease it for (usually) more than one year.

Finally, let's consider the last scenario for acquiring property during the marriage years—buying stuff together. If you purchase assets as a pair but *you* put up the down payment from your separate property funds, get a writing delineating your contribution and determining what proportion of the profit you would realize in any ultimate sale. Arrange your agreement so that you share *pro rata* in the sale proceeds (in ratio to your contribution). It is not profitable merely to recover your monies when the property is sold. If you've bought wisely, and the market for this asset rises, your share of the profits could prove most attractive at escrow's close. (Remember that the formal process of an escrow protects all the parties involved in your transfer or sale. Escrow periods can last from 30, to 60, to 180 days. During this time, the buyer obtains any remaining financing, and the seller pays for a title check to ensure that clear ownership will pass, that the property is free of termites, and that there are no outstanding liens or debts against the property except those owed to mortgage lenders or acceptable to the purchaser. While the parties are finding financing or paying for reports, the escrow officer holds title to the property and any funds already paid. If such a company completes the title transfer without complying with your requirements, and you suffer damages, you can hold the firm liable for your loss. Before you hand over title to real estate (or to some other valuable asset), open an escrow with a company offering such services, or count on a trusted third party to ensure that your buyer or seller meets all your demands and conditions before an ownership change occurs.) Let's study the following example to see exactly how such an arrangement might pay off for you.

> Jennifer and Jack had often talked about starting a small but potentially profitable modern art collection, but three children arrived within their first five years of marriage, and the two art lovers had to postpone buying the lithographs they often admired on Sunday strolls through their local

galleries. Then Jennifer's cousin died unexpectedly; the young mother received a small inheritance. At last the two could begin acquiring a few prints, but Jennifer was concerned about losing track of her separate funds. She felt that the ownership rights in the new artworks should reflect her contribution. Since they expected their lithographs to rise in value, Jennifer wanted a comparable portion of the profit on an ultimate sale to be her separate property. The two agreed that Jennifer's contribution (the down payment on three works) equaled a one-third share in the total purchase price. When Jack and Jennifer decided to divorce, seven years later, they reviewed their simple agreement about Jennifer's ownership rights. The three pieces involved had more than tripled in value on the date they had the works appraised. While Jennifer's dollar contribution had represented about $2,500, her final *proportionate* share in the works' value totaled $7,500. If their agreement had reflected merely that Jennifer would have been repaid the dollars contributed, her share on evaluation date would have been only the $2,500 originally put in. And of course, with inflation she would have actually lost money on the joint investment. In addition, Jennifer could claim her other property rights in the joint assets after her $7,500 was paid off the top when the works were sold. While Jack was free to purchase Jennifer's share in the lithographs, he was as bound by their agreement as a third-party buyer would have been, and Jennifer would have received the same amount of cash.

The larger your joint purchase (a house or apartment building, for example), the more crucial the need for such a writing, spelling out the proportionate ownership rights of each investor.

On the other hand, if your spouse has used his/her separate property to buy something for both of you, *do not* suggest documenting any separate interest. If there is no separate writing, the court is more likely to assume that the asset is equally held and that your mate intended a gift of that separate property when he or she contributed to its purchase.

While these suggestions may be entertaining to read about, you may hesitate to take some of the steps suggested so far. It's quite natural to feel uncomfortable about orchestrating the facts about property and ownership in order to prevail at a later time, when you plan to end your relationship. Setting the stage for a more profitable departure can seem pretty sneaky—or worse. You may well have invested a great deal of energy in trying to make your marriage work; now you're being asked to invest that energy for your benefit alone—to the possible detriment of your spouse.

To help yourself decide whether to take such steps, weigh some weeks of discomfort against possible years of anger, frustration, and low self-esteem deriving from diminished resources over all the years ahead. Once you are in a position to bargain effectively for support and property rights, you may *choose* to trade some of these gains for other concessions important to you. Or you may concede points to effect a more friendly, swift settlement. The point is that if you have little to trade, you may find yourself leaving even a long marriage with few material possessions and few chances to bargain for adequate support. In other words, the mate with numerous assets and/or much property can afford to compromise; the other often faces a drawn-out, costly, usually traumatic fight for a sufficient share of the property to finance a new start. Which spouse would you rather be?

Now let's consider money, moola, or bucks. No matter what you call it, liquid assets are a valuable plus, so start economizing *today* for an adequately financed bargaining period. Why is immediate cash so crucial in achieving the kind of out-of-court settlement you need? Because the spouse with money "muscle" can afford to refuse to negotiate, can delay court appearances, and can sabotage settlement conferences—all for the purpose of driving the less well-heeled mate to accepting a less-than-fair share of property, or an inadequate amount for child or spousal support.

In fact, the lower-earning or unemployed spouse often has a difficult time making ends meet in the months (and even years) that may pass before all the issues in the case are resolved by negotiation or trial. In the meantime, the higher-earning mate persists in offering a share of the property and a figure for support that are often very low. The months drag on. The needy spouse uses up the limits on the available charge cards, puts off or neglects family bills, and begins to borrow from relatives and friends. Since all these obligations are incurred after separation, many are likely to be allocated solely to the borrowing spouse. Before long, the penniless and in-debt partner is viewing even a puny settlement offer with bright and desperate eyes. This "dance of the dollars" has a common and predictable outcome—one that the unprepared mate often regrets for many years after the final decree.

So, back to the most effective way to ensure that you have immediate cash when you are ready to separate. First, draw up a family budget and follow it for these positve results:

- There will ultimately be more money to divide.
- There will be more funds available to pay *you* over the course of this year (more about this later).
- You will have a clear and convincing outline of family expenses to support your request for adequate child and/or spousal support.
- Finally, better money management *may* cure the marital rift, making divorce unnecessary.

The benefits of the first suggestion are obvious.

As to the second, once you've got control of (or at least a voice in) the allocation of family funds, get spouse to agree that you, as the lower-earning or homemaker spouse, should receive a monthly "pension plan" allotment. Teamsters build retirement benefits for their later years; you can do it, too. Call it a housekeeping fee, an allowance, a mad-money contribution—anything that will help your spouse understand that you need some spending money of your own. Of course you do *not* spend it; rather, you open an account *in your name only,* using a bank where your spouse has no contacts and no accounts. Make sure that you both understand that the funds are an outright gift to you. Each month, put these monies faithfully into your new account. To this account, add other cash gifts from your spouse, gifts or inheritances from friends or relatives, and any windfalls that come your way because Aunt Bessie forgot to draw up a will (or drew up an invalid will). Also, deposit your salary *if* you and your mate have an agreement (preferably in writing and signed by both of you) that what you earn remains yours alone.

Now, keep this account *off limits* to community creditors and your own spending sprees. The balance is your "blast-off bread," so don't mess with your escape hatch. When the time comes, this money will provide you with the financial muscle to support yourself and to hold out for a settlement or judgment favorable to you. Your share of other assets will, of course, be payable to you over and above the sum you have saved in your separate property account.

The third advantage to becoming a more active financial partner in the remaining months is that you will have a clear and convincing outline of family expenses to support your request for adequate child and/or spousal support. Eventually, you will have to establish your spouse's *ability* to pay the support you and the children require, but you can begin immediately to prepare proof of your living costs. In general, the better the life-style you enjoy before the separation, the more funds a court is apt to grant you to maintain that life-style. You will need objective evidence to show what it costs you to live and to boost the support dollars you wish to receive. Therefore, begin *now* to gather standard-of-living evidence like canceled checks for the gardener, pool person, landscaper, housecleaner, maid, or live-in help; for child-care assistance, skin-care specialist, masseuse/masseur, horseback-riding instructor, tailor, and Junior's tutor. Don't forget proof of country club or health club memberships; car payments; pet or horse board and feed bills; hobby costs; dental, orthodontia, dermatology, podiatry, manicure, hair-styling, doctor, and chiropractic bills. Include programs from plays and shows, wine labels, restaurant menus, ticket stubs to sporting and cultural events, copies of your social calendar (including entertaining at home), adult education costs, and so on. Other often-forgotten living expenses include·

- Special or favorite foods.
- Gourmet and esoteric food preparation or serving appliances.
- Gifts to charity.
- Insurance premiums (dental, medical, life and home and car coverage as well).
- Club or association dues and fees.
- Private-school costs (including tuition, uniforms, books, sports participation, room and board).
- Lessons in tennis, sailing, skiing, and other sports.
- Vacations.
- Adult toys (dirt bikes, dune buggies, racing boats, and other diversions like video recorders or electronic games).
- Sports equipment and related costs.
- Boat expenses (including taxes, upkeep, slip fees, maintenance and repairs, insurance, registration).
- Therapy or psychiatric bills.
- Surgery (the more elective or cosmetic surgery, the higher the standard of living implied).
- Wardrobe costs (purchase *and* maintenance, dry cleaning, and storage, if applicable).
- Furs and jewelry (purchase, maintenance, storage, insurance, extra security or lock box if necessary, cleaning and repair).
- Security systems (home, boat, camper, cars).
- Gifts to you (pattern, frequency, the approximate cost, the quality of gift).
- Gifts to others from you and/or your spouse. (A wide range of recipients indicates lavish discretionary income; frequency, quality and caliber are all useful clues.)

- Charge accounts (is the credit limit especially high? Are the stores expensive, the boutiques of an unusual or esoteric nature? Include credit accounts maintained at quality restaurants or other retail or service outlets).
- Pets (including food, housing, grooming, veterinarian costs, insurance, breeding, and any special costs).
- Automobiles (style, model and year; leased or purchased? The latter shows more financial stability. Price, insurance, costs to run, maintenance and repair bills can all indicate a more-lavish-than-average life-style).
- Other transportation (taxi, bus, or limousine).

If a large payment or cost occurs only once a year, divide the sum by 12, so that you will have an accurate monthly total of all expenses. Wherever possible, make copies of canceled checks, bills, credit statements, and other written documentation of the family's life-style and your mate's apparent ability to underwrite those costs.

While collecting such material, take over paying the family bills to get the following:

- An intimate knowledge of *real* family income.
- An overview of *all* his/her income sources and how they might be expanded or improved upon (crucial for later evidence of an ability to pay healthy support).
- An inside peek at what investments are stashed where, and how much he/she has salted away.
- A feel for increasing the yield of various currently nonproductive assets that could generate more support dollars.
- A complete look at what it takes to maintain your life-style.
- An accurate idea of how much the kids cost.
- Financial savvy.
- An increase in and more control over the discretionary cash available (from this fund will come your present "pension" payments and your later support monies).

Because you will now know where all the canceled checks are, what or who received the funds, and why, it will appear natural for you to prepare (or have an active role in preparing) this year's joint income tax return. If your household pays taxes on a quarterly (or more frequent) basis, list your name and social security number first on the joint tax return. Any overage on such tax accounts is usually refunded to the first Social Security number appearing on the return. Even if the refund check bears both names, there is little to prevent a determined spouse from forging your name, collecting the cash, and dissipating the funds. Even if you must obtain your mate's signature to cash the refund check, keep the document in your possession until you both visit the bank—together—and endorse it only before the same teller. The funds can then be split, apportioned, or allocated to one party alone, as you agree. Because immediate cash gives a spouse negotiating muscle and hold-out power, don't risk letting a tax refund check of *any* size be delivered to your spouse, if you believe that you will be living apart at the time the refund is due and you suspect your mate will finagle possession of all the funds. Consider which party you would rather put in charge of this sometimes substantial amount.

If *you* have possession of the check, and your spouse agrees to sign it without receiving a share at that time, *take all the funds!* It will help you finance the mortgage, raise the children, pay the bills, hire legal advice, uncover all the assets, and, most important, survive possibly drawn-out negotiations or await a distant trial date without settling for less than your fair share (or more) of the communal property. You can even the financial score at a later date during final settlement negotiations or during trial.

Home Sweet "Real Estate Account"

Many married couples' largest asset is the family home. Knowing how title is held to this asset is the first step in preserving your share in this property. If your spouse alone owns your living quarters, or has recorded only his/her ownership rights, try to have the deed put in co-ownership as soon as possible. Remember to record the new deed.

Why fret so much about how title is held? Because a joint tenancy, tenancy by the entirety, or a tenancy in common says to the court and to the world that you both want the house to be owned by both of you. In fact, in California, a joint tenancy deed raises the strong presumption, in the event of a separation or divorce, that the residence is community property. So strong is this "legal conclusion" that the mate wishing to prove a separate property ownership or interest must produce evidence of an agreement or "understanding" between the parties that both agreed to an uneven balance in ownership rights.

If you find that title should be altered to protect your interest, don't dawdle! If you separate, or announce your divorce plans too soon after orchestrating a change in the form of property ownership, your spouse may contest your right to the property, arguing that you planned to defraud him or her. In other words, he/she might say to the court, "Your Honor, if I had known that my spouse was planning to divorce me, I never would have altered title to the house. I only changed title because I thought that our marriage would last, and that she/he intended to stay with me. Instead, he/she was plotting to gain an ownership interest at the very time that he/she was trying to get me to change the wording on that deed!" He/she may also balk at sharing in other property if a large interest in the family home has only recently been transferred to you.

Now Just Don't Mess Things Up . . .

Once an asset has been named partially or wholly yours (by agreement, by taking title, or by the sharing actions of your spouse), act as though the property is yours alone, or yours, too. Take an active interest in its operation, improvement, and maintenance.

If an asset has been allocated to you alone, avoid seeking the other party's active management or participation. Don't use the proceeds or profits for household expenses (unless you have a written agreement to ensure repayment). Don't discuss "our" original Picasso—particularly before witnesses.

In short, once you have title and ownership rights arranged in your favor, treat that piece of property *in a manner consistent with its title* to preserve your asset rights.

If you're still thinking that it's selfish to spend so much energy gaining and retaining assets and property, and that the ending of a marriage shouldn't necessarily prove profitable, consider this. Your partnership with your mate required a great deal of time and emotional commitment—energies you would have devoted to yourself alone if you had not wed and perhaps started a family. During this married period, you may well have given up several career plans, or chosen not to pursue some personal goals . . . all of which would probably have made you more wealthy than you are today. Your energy, time, commitment, and loyalty were instead invested in the business of marriage, a going concern that has accumulated an inventory, fixtures, equipment—even "accounts receivable," the salaries due one or both of you for your efforts while wed. If you had chosen to start a small business of your own instead of marrying your spouse and had devoted as much time, energy, and skill to its success, would you walk away without getting the best price you could from a sale? Of course not. In this case, you will take some assets with you, you will sell some to other parties (as though you were dismantling your small company), and you will trade or sell other property (or your interest in other property) to your "business partner," your mate.

Though emotions will play a large part in the divorce process (and probably wouldn't run as high in a normal business dissolution), emotions should not be allowed to prevent you from making sensible, self-enlightened decisions that will repay you for all the work you have done. In other words, when your emotions urge you to walk out without your fair share (or more) of the joint property, channel those emotions into talks with a therapist or friend. Emotional reactions can cause costly mistakes that you will live with for years to come. It may feel good for a short period of time to give in and give up important asset rights for a quick resolution to the issues involved. Try not to let the promise of fast relief cheat you of your share. Remember that you are the equivalent of a business person in this instance; make a good business deal.

Every Little Asset Has a Value All Its Own

Now that you've solidified your separate and community property rights, it's important to itemize and compare the worth of what you actually own, together and separately. The checklist on the following pages will help you uncover *all* of your property, and determine your approximate interest in each asset.

While filling out the columns, remember that the fair market value is what a stranger would pay on the open market for the asset involved. Obligations include *all* debts attached to the particular property: mortgages, liens, debts, first, second, and even third trust deeds; and any other promises to repay that have a *connection* with that property. The difference between what that asset would *sell* for today and the debt *owed* on that asset is the amount that is to be divided between you.

What, exactly, does all that mean? Once you have arrived at the amount that is up for grabs, you must decide or negotiate how it is to be split between you. The law usually does not require that every piece of property be divided. It may also not demand that a single large asset be sold and the net proceeds apportioned between you. So long as the bottom lines on your individual property lists are approximately equal (or at least equitable), you should have no problem gaining the court's approval of your marital settlement agreement. Now what do I mean by equitable? Once the separate property has been given to the spouse who owns it, all of the remaining assets will be those in which you *both* have a share. In some cases, it will be fairest to split the property equally and give half to each spouse. Stocks, for example, can easily be allocated equally by giving each mate an even number of shares. In other cases, a particular asset needs to go to just you or your partner. Woodworking tools, for example, may prove a burden to Marcia but a delight to Dan. There is no sense in splitting these up, or in selling them (at a loss) and dividing the cash. However, if Dan gets the saws, drills, and hammers, then Marcia is entitled to an asset (perhaps the antique sideboard) of equal value. Once the special interest assets are divvied up between you, consider what amount of property or money it will take to make an even total for each of you. The rest of the assets, then, will have to be allocated or parceled out between you to make those totals equal.

It is only in community property states (Arizona, California, Idaho, Louisiana, Nevada, New Mexico, Texas, and Washington) that the split must be fifty/fifty if the court divides all the community property. But keep in mind that even in these states, *there is nothing illegal or wrong with both spouses' agreeing that one should receive more than half of the community property!* We will cover this concept in more detail in later chapters.

Almost every other state operates on principles of equitable distribution. This means that many factors must be considered when a piece of property is allocated to one spouse, or the assets are apportioned, or a single asset is divided unequally. The final division in these cases needs to reflect contributions of a particular spouse, the source of the payment for the asset, the earning ability of each mate, who has the custody or support of the minor children, and other factors that make an unequal division of the common assets right or "fair." So long as you both agree, the ultimate division of property can be unequal. In all three kinds of states, you may want to consider the advice given in Chapter Six ("Ways to Gain Assets During the Split") to maximize your allocation of property in your asset-division sessions.

Before dividing *anything*, however, we must know the value of what we own, the amounts we owe, and the actual size of the net amount under discussion. To reach that goal, complete the assets chart on pages 20-34. In some cases you will need to obtain appraisals from experts to learn the fair market value of an asset. This topic will be covered in Chapter Four ("Final-Weeks' Insurance for a Profitable Divorce"), but you may wish to glance at that information now.

When you feel ready, start working on the chart. If you and your spouse have openly discussed divorce, get him/her to help you fill in the figures. In this case, it is wise to involve as many knowledgeable people as possible to fix accurately the values involved. One thing you do not want to do, however, is take your mate's word on the value of an asset. Unless you have personal knowledge, based on facts, that the figure quoted you is true, *verify every assessment* by consulting with a recognized expert in the field. You will learn some inexpensive, easy ways to obtain such valuations in Chapter Four; the energy expended in getting good evaluations from *disinterested* sources can pay worthwhile dividends.

But enough cautionary warnings; let's proceed to make you feel pleasantly surprised when you see how many assets this "business" of marriage has generated. (When you review Chapter Three, "The 90-Day Treasure Trove," you may well uncover items of unexpected treasure lurking in your marital business. These assets and their values will have to be added in to the lists that follow *before* effective negotiations can begin between you about property allocations. But for right now, the following list will provide an excellent overview of your partnership assets and their values.)

A few final notes: You may use any evaluation date that the two of you agree upon, and it need not be the same for all the assets, but you may wish to skim Chapter Six ("Ways to Gain Assets During the Split"), before tackling the following chart. No separate property is to be included in the computations on the next few pages. Lastly, consider all other factors that would make a certain allocation or division of an asset a *fair* solution, rather than an absolutely legal one.

Asset Insurance—Are You Really Married?

This question raised in seminars always garners a lot of giggles, but your right to share in the common marriage property depends upon a valid marriage. Better double-check your asset insurance—your spousal right to receive. The problem of an invalid marriage is more common than you might suppose, and it is a serious one. If your relationship does not fall under family-law provisions in your state, you may be forced to rely only on contract principles—promises of your partner to share property with you or take care of you after a breakup—in order to recover any asset or property share or to receive any support.

In most states, a formalization of the marriage commitment *must* occur. Did you

—obtain a license?
—complete any necessary blood tests, counseling, waiting period, or other actions required by your marriage state?
—attend and make suitable vows at a ceremony presided over by the proper official or licensed person?
—have your marriage license and forms completed and filed by the official performing the ceremony?
—obtain a final decree of divorce or annulment before marrying your present spouse?
—perform any necessary acts to "finalize" the marriage, as required by your state (sexual consummation, cohabitation, etc.)?

Even if you have only lived together as unofficial husband and wife, do not give up hope. You may qualify as a "putative spouse." This is a mate who believes in good faith that he or she is indeed validly married to the partner involved. Sometimes the lack of a necessary requirement results from a mistake or oversight. Other times it is the intention of one party to stage a make-believe marriage whose validity the other spouse relies upon. In either case, an innocent spouse is a deserving one in the eyes of the law. While you may have to seek to have your rights upheld in another section of the courthouse (in a civil rather than family-law forum), your status should be considered worthy of protection in allocating and dividing the property.

If you must admit that there has not been even the semblance of a wedding ceremony, you may still qualify as a common-law spouse. Alabama, Colorado, Georgia, Idaho, Kansas, Iowa, Montana, Ohio, Oklahoma, Pennsylvania, South Carolina, Rhode Island, Texas, and the District of Columbia all recognize common-law marriages. Each state has its own standards about the type of behavior that will convert simple cohabitation to a common-law marriage. Check the rules in your state if you feel you may qualify. The requirements will be

Asset Evaluation Chart

Community, Marital, or Jointly Owned Asset	A — Fair Market Value on Evaluation Date	B — Total of All Obligations and Debts Connected with This Asset	Difference Between A and B	Factors Affecting Allocation or Division	Proposed Allocation or Division	
					Husband	***Wife***
Real Estate						
House, condominium, cooperative, mobile home, or other primary residence	$ ________	$ ________	$ ________		$ ____	$ ____
Second Home	$ ________	$ ________	$ ________		$ ____	$ ____
Third Home	$ ________	$ ________	$ ________		$ ____	$ ____
Income property	$ ________	$ ________	$ ________		$ ____	$ ____
Unimproved property	$ ________	$ ________	$ ________		$ ____	$ ____
Cemetery plots	$ ________	$ ________	$ ________		$ ____	$ ____
Interest in any real estate	$ ________	$ ________	$ ________		$ ____	$ ____
Trust deed, amounts owed to you	$ ________	$ ________	$ ________		$ ____	$ ____

Long-term leases	$ ______	$ ______	$ ______	$ ____	$ ____
Joint tenancies held with other parties					
1. ______	$ ______	$ ______	$ ______	$ ____	$ ____
2. ______	$ ______	$ ______	$ ______	$ ____	$ ____
3. ______	$ ______	$ ______	$ ______	$ ____	$ ____
Total	$ ______	$ ______	$ ______	$ ____	$ ____
Personal Property					
Furniture and furnishings in primary residence	$ ______	$ ______	$ ______	$ ____	$ ____
Furniture and furnishings in second home	$ ______	$ ______	$ ______	$ ____	$ ____
Furniture and furnishings in third home	$ ______	$ ______	$ ______	$ ____	$ ____
Outdoor furniture	$ ______	$ ______	$ ______	$ ____	$ ____
Pool equipment	$ ______	$ ______	$ ______	$ ____	$ ____

Community, Marital, or Jointly Owned Asset	A — Fair Market Value on Evaluation Date	B — Total of All Obligations and Debts Connected with This Asset	Difference Between A and B	Factors Affecting Allocation or Division	Proposed Allocation or Division	
Personal Property					***Husband***	***Wife***
Gardening or maintenance tools and supplies	$ ________	$ ________	$ ________		$ ____	$ ____
Works of art	$ ________	$ ________	$ ________		$ ____	$ ____
Antiques or heirlooms	$ ________	$ ________	$ ________		$ ____	$ ____
Collections						
Clocks, sea shells, knives, guns, bottles, glassware, coins, comic books, first editions or rare books, stamps, other	$ ________	$ ________	$ ________		$ ____	$ ____
________	$ ________	$ ________	$ ________		$ ____	$ ____
________	$ ________	$ ________	$ ________		$ ____	$ ____
________	$ ________	$ ________	$ ________		$ ____	$ ____

Workshop tools	$ ______	$ ______	$ ______	$ ____	$ ____
Hobby equipment and supplies	$ ______	$ ______	$ ______	$ ____	$ ____
Boat	$ ______	$ ______	$ ______	$ ____	$ ____
Plane	$ ______	$ ______	$ ______	$ ____	$ ____
Trailer	$ ______	$ ______	$ ______	$ ____	$ ____
Camper	$ ______	$ ______	$ ______	$ ____	$ ____
Camper shell	$ ______	$ ______	$ ______	$ ____	$ ____
Truck	$ ______	$ ______	$ ______	$ ____	$ ____
Motorcycle	$ ______	$ ______	$ ______	$ ____	$ ____
Dune buggy	$ ______	$ ______	$ ______	$ ____	$ ____
Vehicles	$ ______	$ ______	$ ______	$ ____	$ ____
1. ______	$ ______	$ ______	$ ______	$ ____	$ ____
2. ______	$ ______	$ ______	$ ______	$ ____	$ ____
3. ______	$ ______	$ ______	$ ______	$ ____	$ ____
4. ______	$ ______	$ ______	$ ______	$ ____	$ ____
Jewelry (purchased as investments, not gifts)	$ ______	$ ______	$ ______	$ ____	$ ____
Animals or pets	$ ______	$ ______	$ ______	$ ____	$ ____
Personal papers, photographs, or memorabilia of value to a library, institution, or museum	$ ______	$ ______	$ ______	$ ____	$ ____

Community, Marital, or Jointly Owned Asset	A — Fair Market Value on Evaluation Date	B — Total of All Obligations and Debts Connected with This Asset	Difference Between A and B	Factors Affecting Allocation or Division	Proposed Allocation or Division	
					Husband	*Wife*
Personal Property						
Artworks in progress	$ ______	$ ______	$ ______		$ ____	$ ____
Editorial work in progress	$ ______	$ ______	$ ______		$ ____	$ ____
Photographic work in progress	$ ______	$ ______	$ ______		$ ____	$ ____
Recording work in progress	$ ______	$ ______	$ ______		$ ____	$ ____
Videotaping work in progress	$ ______	$ ______	$ ______		$ ____	$ ____
Other work in progress	$ ______	$ ______	$ ______		$ ____	$ ____
Property in third parties' hands	$ ______	$ ______	$ ______		$ ____	$ ____
Savings accounts						
1. ______	$ ______	$ ______	$ ______		$ ____	$ ____
2. ______	$ ______	$ ______	$ ______		$ ____	$ ____

Checking accounts					
1. ________	$ ________	$ ________	$ ________	$ ____	$ ____
2. ________	$ ________	$ ________	$ ________	$ ____	$ ____
Certificate of Deposit					
1. ________	$ ________	$ ________	$ ________	$ ____	$ ____
2. ________	$ ________	$ ________	$ ________	$ ____	$ ____
Safe-deposit boxes					
1. ________	$ ________	$ ________	$ ________	$ ____	$ ____
2. ________	$ ________	$ ________	$ ________	$ ____	$ ____
Deferred salary now due husband	$ ________	$ ________	$ ________	$ ____	$ ____
Deferred salary now due wife	$ ________	$ ________	$ ________	$ ____	$ ____
Uncashed traveler's checks	$ ________	$ ________	$ ________	$ ____	$ ____
Cash emergency funds	$ ________	$ ________	$ ________	$ ____	$ ____
Treasury bills	$ ________	$ ________	$ ________	$ ____	$ ____
Savings bonds	$ ________	$ ________	$ ________	$ ____	$ ____
Stocks	$ ________	$ ________	$ ________	$ ____	$ ____
Bonds	$ ________	$ ________	$ ________	$ ____	$ ____
Mutual fund shares	$ ________	$ ________	$ ________	$ ____	$ ____

Community, Marital, or Jointly Owned Asset	A — Fair Market Value on Evaluation Date	B — Total of All Obligations and Debts Connected with This Asset	Difference Between A and B	Factors Affecting Allocation or Division	Proposed Allocation or Division	
					Husband	*Wife*
Personal Property						
Money market shares	$ ________	$ ________	$ ________		$ _____	$ _____
Annuity payments or lump sums	$ ________	$ ________	$ ________		$ _____	$ _____
Personal promissory notes owed to husband and wife	$ ________	$ ________	$ ________		$ _____	$ _____
Trust interests (only if jointly owned)	$ ________	$ ________	$ ________		$ _____	$ _____
Individual retirement account of husband	$ ________	$ ________	$ ________		$ _____	$ _____
Individual retirement account of wife	$ ________	$ ________	$ ________		$ _____	$ _____

Husband's Keogh account	$ ______	$ ______	$ ______		$ ____	$ ____
Wife's Keogh account	$ ______	$ ______	$ ______		$ ____	$ ____
Husband's profit-sharing rights	$ ______	$ ______	$ ______		$ ____	$ ____
Wife's profit-sharing rights	$ ______	$ ______	$ ______		$ ____	$ ____
Husband's pension plan	$ ______	$ ______	$ ______		$ ____	$ ____
Wife's pension plan	$ ______	$ ______	$ ______		$ ____	$ ____
Credit union accounts						
1. ______	$ ______	$ ______	$ ______		$ ____	$ ____
2. ______	$ ______	$ ______	$ ______		$ ____	$ ____
Interests in any limited partnerships	$ ______	$ ______	$ ______		$ ____	$ ____
Interests in any close corporations	$ ______	$ ______	$ ______		$ ____	$ ____
Interest in any family business	$ ______	$ ______	$ ______		$ ____	$ ____

Community, Marital, or Jointly Owned Asset	A — Fair Market Value on Evaluation Date	B — Total of All Obligations and Debts Connected with This Asset	Difference Between A and B	Factors Affecting Allocation or Division	Proposed Allocation or Division	
					Husband	*Wife*
Personal Property						
Right to income from royalties, patents, license fees, permits, drilling rights	$ ______	$ ______	$ ______		$ ______	$ ______
Other						
1. ______	$ ______	$ ______	$ ______		$ ______	$ ______
2. ______	$ ______	$ ______	$ ______		$ ______	$ ______
Tax-loss carry-forward	$ ______	$ ______	$ ______		$ ______	$ ______
Stock option rights of husband	$ ______	$ ______	$ ______		$ ______	$ ______
Stock option rights of wife	$ ______	$ ______	$ ______		$ ______	$ ______
Joint tax refunds due	$ ______	$ ______	$ ______		$ ______	$ ______

Contracts for personal services of husband	$ ______	$ ______	$ ______	$ ____	$ ____
Contracts for personal services of wife	$ ______	$ ______	$ ______	$ ____	$ ____
Investments Diamonds, silver, gold, precious metals, precious stones, commodities					
1. ______	$ ______	$ ______	$ ______	$ ____	$ ____
2. ______	$ ______	$ ______	$ ______	$ ____	$ ____
3. ______	$ ______	$ ______	$ ______	$ ____	$ ____
4. ______	$ ______	$ ______	$ ______	$ ____	$ ____
5. ______	$ ______	$ ______	$ ______	$ ____	$ ____
Life insurance policies (cash value only)					
1. ______	$ ______	$ ______	$ ______	$ ____	$ ____
2. ______	$ ______	$ ______	$ ______	$ ____	$ ____
3. ______	$ ______	$ ______	$ ______	$ ____	$ ____
Lawsuits or actions pending on your behalf	$ ______	$ ______	$ ______	$ ____	$ ____

Community, Marital, or Jointly Owned Asset	A — Fair Market Value on Evaluation Date	B — Total of All Obligations and Debts Connected with This Asset	Difference Between A and B	Factors Affecting Allocation or Division	Proposed Allocation or Division	
					Husband	***Wife***
Personal Property						
Husband's second business (Amway, Avon, etc., including goodwill, accounts receivable, and inventory)	$ ________	$ ________	$ ________		$ ____	$ ____
Wife's second business (see above)	$ ________	$ ________	$ ________		$ ____	$ ____
Husband's "sideline" income-producing interest — car repairs, photography, woodworking,						

lecturing, writing, consulting, counseling, etc., including tools of the trade					
Office supplies					
Inventory					
Work in progress					
Accounts Receivable					
Orders to be filled					
Goodwill	$ ______	$ ______	$ ______	$ ____	$ ____
Other					
1. ____	$ ______	$ ______	$ ______	$ ____	$ ____
2. ____	$ ______	$ ______	$ ______	$ ____	$ ____
Subtotal	$ ______	$ ______	$ ______	$ ____	$ ____
Wife's "sideline" income-producing interest including tools of the trade					

Community, Marital, or Jointly Owned Asset	A — Fair Market Value on Evaluation Date	B — Total of All Obligations and Debts Connected with This Asset	Difference Between A and B	Factors Affecting Allocation or Division	Proposed Allocation or Division	
					Husband	***Wife***
Personal Property						
Office supplies						
Inventory						
Work in progress						
Accounts receivable						
Orders to be filled						
Goodwill	$ ______	$ ______	$ ______		$ ______	$ ______
Other						
1. ______	$ ______	$ ______	$ ______		$ ______	$ ______
2. ______	$ ______	$ ______	$ ______		$ ______	$ ______
Subtotal	$ ______	$ ______	$ ______		$ ______	$ ______
Husband's company, practice, sole proprietorship, or partnership interest, including*						
Inventory						

Accounts receivable					
Tools and equipment					
Office equipment					
Office supplies					
Goodwill					
Subtotal	$ ______	$ ______	$ ______	$ ___	$ ___
OR					
Appraised sales value on the open market, considering all of the factors listed above*	$ ______	$ ______	$ ______	$ ___	$ ___
Wife's company, practice, sole proprietorship, or partnership interest, including*					
Inventory					
Accounts receivable					
Tools and equipment					
Office equipment					

Community, Marital, or Jointly Owned Asset	A — Fair Market Value on Evaluation Date	B — Total of All Obligations and Debts Connected with This Asset	Difference Between A and B	Factors Affecting Allocation or Division	Proposed Allocation or Division	
					Husband	*Wife*
Personal Property						
Office supplies						
Goodwill						
Subtotal	$ ________	$ ________	$ ________		$ ____	$ ____
OR						
Appraised sales value on the open market, considering all of the factors listed above*	$ ________	$ ________	$ ________		$ ____	$ ____

*In either estimate, a professional evaluation or appraisal of this interest is *strongly* advised.

listed in that state's law codes; any law library reference clerk should be able to help you find them. Ask yourself:

- Did I satisfy *all* the requirements laid out by my state for forging a common-law marriage bond?
- Do I have evidence (in addition to my word) that I have met those requirements? Evidence might include mail addressed to both of you as Mr. and Mrs., witnesses who could describe your marriagelike life-style, joint accounts or other property held as husband and wife, or filing joint tax returns.

If you previously lived together in one of those 14 states, and if you qualify as a common-law spouse under that jurisdiction's requirements, then you will be regarded as a legal mate in other states as well.

If, however, you *know* you're not married and cannot really claim to be wed under any of these principles, then hurry up and tie the knot—legally. After the wedding, remember to heed all the advice given earlier in this chapter about putting the assets in both names, changing the car registrations, adding your moniker to the stock-brokerage account and other assets. Don't dawdle in making these "alterations in ownership." In case of divorce your spouse may argue that you have practiced a form of fraud and persuade a judge to take all your newly acquired property away.

Even if your spouse is willing to change title to certain assets, it would be wise to orchestrate a move to a community property state, if at all possible. In California, for example, there is a strong presumption that assets held jointly and/or accumulated during the marriage years are to be considered owned by both mates regardless of where the asset was originally acquired. You may recall that current community property states are Arizona, California, Idaho, Louisiana, Nevada, New Mexico, Texas, and Washington.

But it is not enough merely to move to a community property state; it is necessary to show the court that you intend to remain there. To give the court jurisdiction (power) over you *and* your common property, you must provide evidence that you intend to make the new state your home. How can you do this effectively? Move in all the furniture and personal belongings, buy or rent property, open local bank and savings accounts, notify the local department of motor vehicles to change your license and re-register your cars, and mail change-of-address cards to creditors, friends, and periodicals. Try to arrange a sale of your property in other states, but don't worry too much if your spouse balks at this move. At least in California, a concept called "quasi-community property" may allow you to share in the value of out-of-state assets. Check to see if such a concept exists in your community property state. If it does, remember to obtain an accurate appraisal of the out-of-state property (how much is the farm in Foggy Bottom really worth?) *in writing,* before you leave your former home. If several months or more elapse between the time of the appraisal and the date that you and your mate actually part, remember to update the estimate—Foggy Bottom may have dramatically risen in value.

Because you give a court power only by meeting its residency requirements (six months in California), don't rush to file for a dissolution of your marriage bond the week that you arrive. Each state's residency requirements differ, so check with your reference librarian at the local law library or school.

There is *nothing wrong* with "helping" a state's legal system—set up for the protection of *all* its residents—to give you a fair share in assets that you helped a mate acquire.

In the case of your "marital business," your contribution may have been one of funds, professional expertise, amateur assistance, or "sideline support." In most states, it matters little whether or not you actually worked in the business itself (or shared your spouse's executive position). It *is* sufficient and valuable if you provided the home environment that helped your mate to earn, acquire, and succeed. Whether you served as husband or wife, consider the lunches you packed, the business associates you entertained, the company dinners you endured, the home crises you handled so that they wouldn't drain your spouse's energy, and the five o'clock troubles, wails, and whimpers you've assuaged. No one can say that you have not earned—in equal measure—the right to share in every asset accumulated during your time together.

Waits and Means

In order to *ensure* that fair share, you may have to time, and even delay, your scheduled departure date. Here are some tips relating to a separation date that can help you avoid a few of the major pitfalls costly to many parting partners.

1. If yours is a nine-year marriage, stick it out for the tenth-anniversary party. A ten-year-or-more marriage entitles you to

apply, when eligible, for derivative benefits under your mate's earning record in the Social Security system. Either side can often file for the final decree, once your state's requisite waiting period after the date of service of the divorce petition and accompanying form on the other party has elapsed. In other words, even *starting* divorce proceedings before the ten-year mark could cut off your later benefits if it provides time for your spouse to request the final judgment within the ten-year span. Banking derivative benefits will not reduce your spouse's Social Security funds, as your mate's receipts merely set the framework within which you can apply. Your benefits under the derivative rights can reach 50 percent of the amount your spouse is entitled to receive. It is especially important to preserve these rights if you have never worked, cannot work, or do not choose to build up a Social Security earnings record of your own. In this manner, you can collect derivative benefits even if you have never been employed.

2. If you and your spouse gave another person the right to use or inhabit real property until that tenant's death, you have given another a life estate. If that tenant appears about to escape from this mortal coil, hang on with your spouse until all the property interests revert to the marriage community. It's a good deal easier to set a value on an asset in hand and to determine your share in it than it is to appraise and divvy up the value of a property that may not "return home" before the separation day.

3. If you and your mate hold a life estate in someone *else's* property, wait until that right to occupy or use it is put in print and recorded, in joint tenancy form, of course, or via a title that reflects that you hold it as husband and wife. The right to use another's property (especially at below-market rates) is an asset that has a value. If your mate is going to stay, and you plan to leave, have that value appraised and obtain your share. If *you* will be the staying spouse, hope that your mate will not consider such an intangible in listing your common property and sharing it equitably.

4. If your spouse was the plaintiff (filing party) in an action for personal injuries and is about to obtain a money judgment against one or more defendants, stay until payment arrives. Personal injury awards received after separation are more likely to be considered separate property and to be allocated entirely to the harmed spouse with no offsetting compensation to a mate. If you cannot delay your departure until after the receipt of such funds, ask for a reimbursement of one half of the funds that the community expended to care for the injured party. In other words, you want to be repaid your half of the commonly owned monies that the marital community expended for the sole benefit of your injured spouse. Repayable costs can include hospitalization, nursing care, medications, rented equipment, and other therapeutic aids. This reimbursement is provided for in some state codes and, if not, worth asking for repayment as a gesture that is "only fair."

If *you're* the injured party, ask your attorney to arrange to delay payment to you until after you've split.

5. If your spouse injured *you*, the payoff (if your state recognizes such recovery rights between spouses) should be your separate property *whenever* received. *But don't let your mate pay off the obligation or damages from community or marital property, which is up to half yours to start with.* Have any payment drawn from your partner's separate property first, and from insurance proceeds second. Remember that you do not have to give a compensating offset for pocketing these funds.

Now, a consideration of the last topic, children, that for some will rank first in motivation and concern. If you are not a parent now, make sure that you are not pregnant (or that your partner is not expecting a child) before finalizing your asset division and any support rights.

If you already have offspring, you need to determine whether you are likely to be the primary custodian (responsible for most of the day-to-day care), a parent who visits seldom or frequently, or part of a parental team that will share both the expenses and the physical custody of the kids as equally as possible. Many custody-support combinations are feasible, but if you will need support dollars from your spouse for the benefit and care of the children, keep in mind the following facts.

Courts normally require only the parents of children (natural or adopted) to furnish dollars for support. Some states presume that a child born during the marriage (or for a set time afterwards) is the product of both mates if it was conceived during the marriage, the couple were cohabiting, and both were capable of conceiving offspring. But this presumption does not apply in all cases; you must ensure that a child-support obligation will be recognized and enforced by court order, levy, or execution, if necessary.

To get questionable-source children or offspring by a deceased spouse supported by *this* mate, you'll need to arrange an adoption or get the person to be assessed to "recognize" that youngster as his own. Visit the reference librarian at your local law library, law school, or university for a quick review of what is required for adoption or for "legitimizing" children in your state. This will take time to carry through, so start early. You may face the same possibility of invalidation for fraud that you do on changing ownership of an asset if the action occurs too close to the separation date.

If your child is the offspring of a current friend, but you are not married, get legally hitched, or do the necessary research to see what's needed to make your lover legally responsible for supporting his child. Often the court is eager to find a paying parent to keep minors (and their financially stretched mothers) off the welfare rolls. Therefore, a series of actions may be sufficient if they reveal the father's intent to acknowledge the child. These can include welcoming the child into the father's home, "holding out" the child as his own progeny, telling relatives and friends about "his" son or daughter, etc. Arranging such a set of facts may be easier than you think, but again, do not delay. Accomplishing the necessary "legal connection" will give you access to a support-paying parent during separation and after the divorce.

While no child support will match the true cost of raising a youngster (or even caring for it most of the time), it would hardly be fair to your children to overlook this source of financial aid—even if it means that you must design the scenario of your departure so that *both* adults are legally responsible for contributing to the welfare of their daughters and sons. If you would not take such steps to ensure your own financial well-being (and I hope that you will), do it to protect your children. This is an effective means of ensuring that living expenses can be met without actually personally involving the children as a lever or tool. Remember, too, that manipulation, coyness, and the use of guilt have little or nothing to do with this determination of obligation—it is a legal tie that the facts will (or will not) support. All you can do is try to establish, for the good of your minor children, that the bond should be forged and the monthly monies paid.

The next chapter, "Six Months from Freedom," explores why

"good" divorces occur between equals . . . and how *you* can become an equal—in knowledge, power, and communal riches—even if you *don't* have a full year to prepare. It will show you how to establish what a partner's complete income (including the most esoteric fringe benefits) is, and how to enjoy every moment of your detective work. "Six Months from Freedom" will also reveal easy ways to develop valuable skills, how to prepare for your postseparation debut while paying only half (or maybe none) of the resulting bills, and how to get more than half of the marital assets allocated to you.

2

Six Months from Freedom

EVEN IF your separation day could be months away, it's not too early to lay some groundwork for a friendlier, swifter, more profitable divorce. As a basic rule, keep in mind that "good" divorces (and they *do* occur) tend to happen between equals—people who are well matched for the rigors of parting and starting anew. To deal effectively with your mate in a fair, open way that is beneficial to you, you will need to feel as able to solve problems; as knowledgeable about income, assets and debts; as rich in self-esteem; and as fortunate in having other options and possibilities waiting for you as your spouse.

Problem-solving ability often comes from taking an active role in facing everyday affairs. Instead of waiting for others to set the beat, active-role people create their own goals, arrange schedules, pace themselves, and make profitable bargains with others by negotiating with their own worth in mind. Feeling a little helpless after measuring yourself against those skills? An active outlook *can* be learned and will grow stronger with daily homework that you can easily arrange. The next time you see someone else begin to make, alone, a decision that affects you, chip in. If you've followed the same "social map" all your married life—letting your mate be the leader—try suggesting a new course or two of your own. If you've gone out in the evening only with your spouse, venture out alone or with a group of supportive friends. Rather than always parrot your mate, propose a different point of view.

As soon as you feel a little more in charge of your life, practice your problem-solving abilities by creating scenarios and figuring out one, two, or more solutions. While you're commuting, figure out how you'd live without that extra income that your partner provides. While loading the wash, pretend you had to sell your home and work out some answers to the resulting chaos. During boring meetings or television commercials, consider ways of paying off creditors if your debts were to double overnight. You have now faced, in fantasy, the most common problems faced during a divorce. Because you've come up with valid, viable solutions in your imagination, you are forearmed in reality. More important, your problem-solving "muscles" are beginning to show some bulk—with more exercise in the coming months, you should be able to face separation, divorce, and the years afterward with a skill that will do far more than just see you through.

The next guarantee of bargaining equality flows from gaining knowledge about the assets, income, and debts of your marital partnership. This chapter will provide a detailed guideline to all the marriage's property and earning power. You must do the footwork, tracking, sleuthing, and adding up. But no other method will give you as broad or accurate view of the property and obligations to be allocated or divided during divorce.

Third, better (and less bitter) partings happen when the partners each possess a healthy self-esteem. Better bargains with better terms tend to flow from mates with comparable levels of self-worth. When each party enjoys high self-respect, it seems easier for each to make the concessions and the compromises necessary in forging fair marital settlement terms. Neither feels threatened by the other; neither feels that he or she must prevail or be diminished as a person. Final agreements often prove more creative, for such spouses can channel their energies into tailoring special terms rather than into attacking each other.

Once your partner recognizes that you have gained (or polished) a high level of self-esteem, there will be fewer attempts to push you into unfavorable terms by tactics designed to threaten your self-confidence. Self-esteem, then, sounds like a powerful aid in the divorce process, but gaining it may take some guts. You can start by standing up for little things during day-to-day activities. Be assertive, but not aggressive. Use a normal but firm tone of voice. Repeat your wishes or terms if the first delivery isn't understood. Consider group or individual counseling, or sign up for an assertiveness training class in your area. Practice by giving yourself small homework assignments: you will no longer do more than your fair share in car-pool duties; the children cannot borrow the car if they do not help around the house; you are willing to go to your spouse's employer's Christmas party only if your mate swears that you will both leave two hours after arriving. Insist on things where your rights and self-respect are at stake; bargain for a concession on bigger or less personal issues. In both cases, you may trigger surprise and hostility (you are no longer that predictable, safe doormat who puts everyone's wishes ahead of his or her own). But in time, your self-respect (and that of others) will grow and begin to show.

Lastly, partners with comparable options and possibilities awaiting them seem less interested in prolonging a divorce. A swift resolution appeals to such mates because many exciting and rewarding benefits lie ahead for them. To become one of these enviable people, remember that it is only necessary that you *believe* many attractive options will crowd your postdivorce days.

Acquiring such a conviction takes some imagination, honesty, and creativity—but the rewards make the effort worthwhile. Since your possibilities depend in part on how others view you, consider your strong (and weak) points as others would. To assess yourself in the most helpful way, pretend that you are an employer, a friend, a banker, a retailer, a prospective business partner. While playing each role, study yourself objectively to find out how salable you are to each of these people, who will all play important roles in your single life. Consider how you can make yourself more marketable or valuable to each of these types, for they can prove powerful allies or stubborn obstacles—the choice is up to you. There is still time, at this juncture, to gain more schooling, more social polish, more earning skills, a more attractive appearance, a healthier credit rating, or to develop a good new business idea that would appeal to a new partner and a wide market.

With some promising possibilities awaiting you, the process of divorce can seem a good deal less traumatic, and your options as numerous as your spouse's.

Let's deal in more detail with gaining knowledge about the assets, income, and debts of your relationship. Learning about the income and debts should flow from taking an active role, as described in Chapter One, in family budgeting, bill paying, and borrowing. To assess accurately your common assets, you will want to study Chapter Three for the hidden treasure often found in marriages. Meanwhile, the following list will help you probe every possible location of communal goods:

1. Study agreements drawn up before or after your wedding day allocating property, or specifying that acquired assets are to be considered owned by both parties.
2. Make a complete inventory of all the household furniture and furnishings. Take pictures of unusual items. Consider hiring a videotape firm (or using the family movie camera) to establish your home's contents on a given date before separation occurs. Some spouses will back a truck up to the door and remove more than their fair share; others suffer from selective recall when negotiations begin. (A Santa Barbara attorney encouraged a client's Polaroid ability. "It turned the case around," reported the counselor.)
3. Acquire copies of several years' worth of your and your spouse's tax returns, including joint, individual, corporate, partnership, fiduciary, and other forms.
4. Copy financial statements for the past several years, as well as accountants' reports, balance sheets, income statements, statements of financial conditions, profit-and-loss statements, and all footnotes explaining accounting or assessment procedures used.
5. Copy and study (with help, if necessary):

- Buy and sell agreements
- Leases for premises (business or residential)
- Partnership or stockholder agreements
- Notes payable *to* you, or payable *by* you
- Deeds, conditional sales contracts, and other documents relating to title
- Documents relating to acquisitions of real and personal property
- Retirement, pension, and/or profit-sharing plans, including plan details and statements outlining the present interest of the earning individual
- Brokerage statements

For help in establishing the true and complete value of a business or professional practice, gather five years' worth of records covering:

- Books of original entry, including all journals and general ledgers
- Accounts receivable
- Work in progress
- Work completed, but not yet billed
- Inventory
- Insurance policies
- Bank statements and canceled checks (both business and personal) and all savings account records relating to the business or the professional/owner

- Paid bills
- Contracts for present or future work
- Payroll and sales tax returns
- Corporate minute book and stock books
- Other records normally kept in that type of business or profession, like commission reports, computer assessments, appointment books, sales reports
- Accountant's or bookkeeper's paper work
- Depreciation schedules

Other financial records may be:

- Paycheck stubs
- Checkbook registers (the pages on which the check writer records the recipient's name and the purpose of the payment)
- Personal ledger or financial diary
- W-2 forms
- Savings and checking account activity statements
- Evidence of bearer bonds, Treasury bills, savings certificates of deposit, savings bonds, savings deposit slips.
- All negotiable instruments
- First, second, third or more trust deeds (owed to you)
- Insurance policies indicating the value of furnishings, collections, etc.
- Annuity, dividend, or trust payment records
- Patent applications
- License rights
- Certificates showing value of gems, coins, or precious stones
- Evidence of any deferred salary owed your spouse, but not yet paid
- Evidence of commodities like silver, gold, industrial metals, etc.
- Interests in any family business or close (privately owned) corporation
- Mutual fund and/or money market accounts
- Evidence of the right to receive income from royalties, permits, etc.
- Recent evidence of unusual value in workshop or hobby tools
- Records of contributions in an Individual Retirement Account or Keogh account, or both
- Credit Union account balances (often overlooked because the account is maintained at a spouse's place of employment)
- Tax shelter investments or packages
- Oil leases and/or drilling rights

Outside your home or your spouse's office, look for records revealing other real estate (include raw land and even cemetery plots). List all boats, planes, cars (whether running or not), trucks, campers, trailers and motorbikes. Include any valuable pets or livestock, particularly if currently pregnant by (or breedable to) another valuable animal.

If the information you seek is not now available or is incomplete, make copies of any keys you may need to reinvestigate the area where the records are stored. Don't forget that many people ferret important documents away in unusual places, like a second home, car trunks and glove compartments, safe-deposit boxes, rented storage areas, file cabinets in the attic, cellar, or garage. Having guaranteed access to information can prove crucial in these remaining months; a fair division cannot occur if assets cannot be found.

Be patient with yourself if all of this seems overwhelming . . . that's why these suggestions are proposed well before your anticipated separation day. Take the steps first that seem easiest for you, and work up to the more difficult record copying as the weeks go by.

If you know you need to get your property information together but can't seem to get motivated, consider this: an attorney will attempt to do exactly what I have outlined here in order to include all the potential common property (and to determine what, if anything, should be characterized as separate property). Your counselor may well be less effective in discovering these assets (because your mate may lie or hide property after separation), and will certainly send you a bill that can whittle down the assets that *are* uncovered in this formal discovery process. A counselor may charge $100 or more for sending your spouse a list of common questions about the earnings and property; it may cost several hundred dollars for a deposition, in which your mate is questioned under oath, and a court reporter records all his or her replies. Keep in mind that courts are less willing than in the past to assess your spouse for *your* legal fees and costs—you may well end up paying every nickel of your legal bills yourself, out of your fraction of the common property uncovered by traditional-but-often-unsuccessful means after the separation date.

There is also a final factor that you will want to consider in undertaking your own discovery of your spouse's assets, income, and debts. Turning over such chores to a stranger who will serve as rescuer presents an appealing scenario. While we wallow in our friends' sympathy, someone else does all the work. We show up only to collect the final check representing our share of those jointly owned delights. If we don't understand what is going on and emerge clutching our final decree feeling confused and somehow disappointed, we can blame our spouses. If the check is not as large as we hoped, the same friends will empathize with us about that "incompetent" legal counselor. As English poet Eliza Cook noted in her work *Love On,* "Who would not rather trust and be deceived?" Almost a century after her death in 1889, human nature still prefers the comfort of believing, and the righteous anger that follows deceit, to the discomfort of completing our own investigation, and facing sole responsibility for each asset or right overlooked.

It is not easy to resist the lure of this double bind, but once you know of its power, you can sidestep these pitfalls effectively.

While you're gathering information about income, debts, and properties, consider boosting your asset share by gaining rights in property that would otherwise belong solely to your spouse. The first situation that lends itself to this kind of treatment is the military pension, recently declared the separate property of the earning spouse nationwide. The October 1981 issue of *Money* magazine reported these developments:

> Following the suggestion of the Women's Equal Rights Legal Defense and Education Fund in Los Angeles, stockbroker Phyllis Manger and retired Navy commander Arthur Manger signed an agreement stipulating that, in the event of a dissolution of their marriage, the pension rights of Mr. Manger would be divided between the parties. Both in their mid-fifties, the Mangers have provided, in part, for a better future for Mrs. M. . . .
>
> In Alexandria, Virginia, a 34-year-old Coast Guard lieutenant commander agreed in writing to divide any future pension funds with his wife, now 30 years old. As Gayle Bolinger puts it, "Military wives spend years catering to their husband's career. When the husband retires and runs off with some young chick, the wife is out in the cold."

While states are now empowered to apply local divorce law to military pension characterization and division, ensure your right to share by obtaining such an agreement from your military mate.

Currently, Railroad Retirement Act benefits are considered the separate property of the employee spouse. But there is no reason why you cannot draw up a simple agreement stipulating that such benefits are to be considered jointly and equally owed by *both* spouses, so that you will share in your mate's benefits.

In other cases, you may want to suggest an agreement—all such "contracts" should be in writing, of course—that you will share in a separately owned property to a greater extent with each passing period of time. For example, if the primary residence or a second home is owned by one party alone, seek an agreement that you (the nonowner) will gain an additional percentage of joint ownership rights with each passing month or year. This method of earning your share can appeal to even a spouse who is a bit selfish about his or her possessions. Remember to record such an agreement with the recorder of the county where the real property is located, so that it will provide notice to anyone purchasing the land that you have an ownership right.

If you're still feeling a bit queasy about blatantly orchestrating title or ownership interests to ensure your profitable divorce, this review of legal history may help you adapt.

About ten years ago, legal scholars and professionals created and suggested the adoption of a Uniform Marriage and Divorce Act. In summary, the act provided that courts would not award property to punish one party's sexual (or most other) misconduct. Instead, the assets should be allocated as fairly as possible, regardless of whether one mate has behaved well or badly. The act and its provisions took the blame and finger pointing out of divorce actions and attempted to make them less emotional events.

How well has the idea worked? So far, only ten states have passed versions of the Uniform Marriage and Divorce Act, but recent laws and court decisions in sister states mean that another dozen forums have moved toward the fairer approach. In all, 23 states have agreed since 1970 that any assets acquired during the marriage years should be allocated or divided fairly, to effect a more equitable result. In addition, more courts are regarding marriage as an economic partnership, whose *economic* ties are to be severed as unemotionally and with as fair a result as possible. While no two states approach the dissolving of a marriage in exactly the same way, today, some 47 states try to divide marital assets either equally or equitably.

Clearly, with so much emphasis on property rights, it behooves *both* spouses to know the extent, number, and value of *all* the assets acquired since the wedding day. The law also seems strongly to suggest that both marital partners should share fairly in the common assets. Though the law cannot endorse manipulative conduct, it does approve of "self-help," and if the result you achieve is fair, your actions may merely ensure the outcome intended by your state's court decisions and civil code.

Now that you feel a bit more protected in your property rights, heed this word of caution: some states can be regarded—at least in attitude—as common-law forums. This means that the party who earned the asset or whose name appears on the property is likely to be declared the sole owner thereof, with little or no equalizing offset to the other spouse. Because the divorce law in each state is constantly shifting and because the operation of a "common-law effect" may be somewhat subtle, it would be wise to consult briefly with a divorce lawyer in your new home state if you and/or your mate plan an across-the-border move. *Before* packing, consider the following means of ensuring your property rights if your destination is a state forum less hospitable to equitable ownership shares:

1. Draw up an agreement describing the character of the property as jointly owned, and both of you sign it before a notary public.
2. Gather evidence showing the origin of resources used to make a major purchase, evidence showing an intent to hold the asset jointly, or evidence revealing your name as co-owner.
3. If the property remains in your mate's name alone, try to find evidence that the two of you intended this title form for convenience only, for a tax benefit, or for some other reason that runs contrary to your intent to hold the property communally.
4. Finally, if the property involved is divisible (shares of stock, bank accounts with similar balances, collections of items that can be parceled out), allocate equal shares to each partner before making the move; each partner holds a share as his/her own property.

Whether you move or stay, it makes sense that the larger the communal pot, and the richer the jointly-owned stew of assets, the richer you will be when all is divided, said, and done. To secure that more promising outcome, maximize the value of property you hold together during the months, weeks, or days that remain of your marriage. You're not a whiz at the current smorgasbord of investment opportunities? Look around for something familiar that you can improve and boost in value before separation day. Choose just *one* stock after thorough research, and wait for a climb. Help in the family business until the books are finally showing all the black they can. Fix up that income property and bring the rents up to par. Even home and hearth can make money for you, as they did for Sally B., who won the envy of her former classmates at a memory-laden affair. Sally B.'s story came to light one sunlit afternoon at a barbeque, when a good-looking fellow nearing forty said:

> I went through high school with Sally, and here we were at our 20th reunion. Everyone in our class thought that Sally never had a lot of

smarts; didn't seem to be playing with a full deck. But I found out she'd been divorced twice in those 20 years, and each time, she'd pocketed half the inflated value of the family home. Imagine, 50 percent commission, and she never even got a learner's permit in real estate sales!

There are two good reasons for increasing the value of the common assets in these remaining months. The first, of course, is to profit, as did Sally B. The second is so that you will have more assets of greater value to orchestrate a buy-out of the property you really want to keep.

You will want to give careful thought to which assets you will need in your new life, which are more valuable than others (more about this later in this chapter), and which assets you are willing to give up. Through effective and savvy barter and trade, you can emerge the richer spouse. To do this, you must decide which asset you want allocated to you, and which property you can give to your spouse as an offset. In short, you will be purchasing your mate's interest in the property that you wish to keep. Here's an example of how one wife accomplished her goal:

Judith was a homemaker nearing 50 when her electrician husband announced that he wanted a divorce. Though Judith was a championship bridge player, she didn't know how to play her cards in this case. "If I go into court and cry," she suggested to her attorney, "maybe the judge will give me the house." Judith thought her only liquid assets were her tears . . . . but with careful detective work, she established the value in her spouse's union pension plan, which more than compensated for the net value in the family residence. Mr. Judith got all rights to his retirement benefits; Mrs. Judith got the home's ownership transferred to her alone.

From being helpless and angry, Judith progressed to being a knowledgeable negotiator, gained what she needed, enhanced her self-esteem, and struck a profitable bargain as well—because she knew the extent and value of the common assets and arranged a tradeoff of comparable worths.

Since other future benefits will depend upon how much your mate makes in wages or salary, you may want to use this time to establish your partner's *complete* income—including the most esoteric under-the-table and fringe benefits. To document a mate's income and earning ability may require you to don several hats, but acting as an entertainer, detective, and bounty hunter can prove fun as well as profitable.

To reap benefits as an entertainer, invite your spouse's boss or supervisor to dinner. Set the stereo low, the candlelight on medium, and your curiosity on high. Create a relaxed atmosphere, serve a great meal, and *keep the glasses filled.* Throughout the evening, express an interest in your mate's career and a real desire to learn more about his or her duties, her projects, her future, her pay, and any corporate fringe benefits. Ask the right financially oriented questions, and the answers may well flow like the wine.

As detective, you will want to document the hidden income your partner receives. Gather evidence that shows receipt of lavish gifts, payments (or payoffs) in cash, special bonuses, favors or discounts, and patterns of barter between your mate and others providing products or services. With such proof, you can bargain for higher support and more property in your settlement and perhaps even gain the important advantage — as did Ralph M. — of acquiring some immediate cash. In Ralph's case, Mrs. M. worked as a technician at one of the larger television production studios in California. Easy access to expensive equipment led to sticky fingers for Mrs. M., and Ralph discovered that his wife was regularly exiting the studio with an expensive video-recording camera in tow. After selling the equipment through black market acquaintances, she would store the funds in an empty coffee tin behind the bourbon in the living-room bar. The day that Ralph left home, he packed a few necessities, gathered some clothes, and made his last stop at the bar, but Ralph's one for the road was the several thousand that his mate had squirreled away. Mrs. M. was plenty mad, but to whom could she complain? Though Ralph will have to account for the funds or give his spouse an offset in the final settlement, he gained an immediate advantage in negotiating muscle.

Playing the role of bounty hunter can often add substantially to a support award (and to a property division) by showing that a spouse earned more than the records would reveal. In other words, some high earners receive payments in cash, not declaring much of their income in tax returns or business records. A support order based on only reported income in these cases could fall far short of the amount a spouse can actually afford to pay. If the court is willing to award you sufficient support to recreate — as closely as possible — the quality of your married life-style, help the judge do so by showing him or her a *true* picture of your marriage's financial good health. In addition, hidden cash amounts (or liquid assets like silver, gold, bearer bonds, or negotiable notes) probably belong in part to you, if earned during the marriage years. If you can prove their existence, you can share. The bounty hunter brings back all those cash outlays during marriage that don't show on the books: heavy tips, restaurant accounts and bar bills, trips to the racetrack, and even some business entertaining. A documented pattern of cash payments can mean extra dollars for you, but remember that records, photographs, and even witnesses may be required to establish such transactions to the satisfaction of the court (or your mate, if you wish to negotiate successfully).

Why are we dressing in trench coats and working so hard to establish the full extent of a spouse's earning ability? Because it will figure in the amount of child and/or spousal support that the primary wage earner will be asked to provide. In deciding child support amounts, it is one of only two factors, the other being, usually, the needs to be met. In setting the amount of adequate spousal support, a mate's ability to pay is one factor among many. In California, for example, the court considers this list of factors in setting a monthly figure, as called for in the state's civil code:

1. The earning capacity of each spouse, taking into account the extent to which the supported spouse's present and future earning capacity is impaired by periods of unemployment that were incurred during the marriage to permit the supported spouse to devote time to domestic duties
2. The needs of each party
3. The obligations and assets, including the separate property, of each
4. The duration of the marriage
5. The ability of the supported spouse to engage in employment without interfering with the interests of dependent children in the custody of the spouse
6. The time required for the supported spouse to acquire appropriate education, training, and employment
7. The age and health of the parties
8. The standard of living of the parties
9. Any other factors that the court deems equitable

In addition to the factors previously listed, California judges and family-law commissioners setting spousal support amounts must consider several guidelines. These other considerations are drawn from a prior case in which a California court decided a spousal support issue. In the divorce case of *In re Marriage of Lopez,* the Court of

Appeals enumerated the 11 factors that every California trial court should consider in determining the duration and amount of spousal support it would award. These include:

1. A comparison of the financial position of each of the parties before and after the dissolution of the marriage with due consideration given to property owned and obligations to be met
2. The ability of the wife to work and her potential earnings considered in the context of her age, training, and likelihood of employment
3. The reasonable needs of the wife for sustenance, clothing, shelter, and care due her in the station of life to which she is accustomed, within the ability of the husband to provide, considering her age and mental and physical health
4. The nature of the separate estate of the wife with its actual and reasonable income potential
5. Whether the wife has made adequate effort to find suitable work, consistent with her age, ability, and health, and conscientiously to establish herself as genuinely partially self-supporting, consistent with her maternal obligations
6. The nature and extent of the community property awarded to each of the parties, with its actual and reasonable potential for the production of net income after state and federal taxes
7. Income tax consequences of spousal support to both the paying and receiving spouse
8. The ability of the spouse to pay, based on his financial condition, resources, ability to earn and actual earnings, with due consideration given to income tax and social security deductions, life and health insurance premiums, and retirement contributions, if any
9. Other valid support obligations of the paying spouse to his lawful dependents
10. The duration of the marriage

In fact, as the court noted in *In re Marriage of Fisher*, California courts may consider "practically everything which has a bearing upon the present and prospective matters relating to the lives of both parties."

Clearly, available funds play a major role in setting child and/or spousal support. Hardly surprising, then, that establishing a complete income picture can spell the difference between comfort and stress throughout the many years that such support remains in effect. In many cases, funds run short *before* separation. A 1967 American Bar Association survey of friends of the court, judges, and commissioners of domestic relations revealed that 89 percent of those responding cited money problems as one of the major causes of divorce. Because monetary pressures usually increase after separation, obtaining the maximum possible support can prove crucial to having a profitable divorce.

To ensure that all of a spouse's income is uncovered, consider following one or more of these suggestions:

- Take the office bookkeeper to lunch and ply him/her with requests for information about your spouse's salary scale. If this professional doesn't yet know of your impending marital split, then he/she will probably not bother reporting the incident to your spouse. To ensure silence, you might try a harmless tale, like "I want to surprise Sean with a trip to Europe this coming month, but I'm not sure that our budget can take it, and he may feel that he hasn't done well enough yet this year to get away for two weeks. Could you let me know what his earnings are likely to total at the end of June?"

  If you're just about to announce your plans to leave, do you really care if word of your detective efforts leaks back to your mate?
- Talk to your mate's union representative, if appropriate.
- Ask a friend in the job-placement industry to estimate your partner's earning power in the slot he or she now holds.
- Have a friend with comparable skills apply for a similar career opening.
- Review a copy of your spouse's employment contract, if one has been signed.
- Make friends with a disgruntled former employee of your mate's company or employer.
- Visit the office and skim the books when the company accountant is lunching out (this is recommended only if you have some "right" to do so—have an ownership interest in the business, are married to the company's owner).
- Figure out what personal expenses your spouse is now running through the business. Add back in the total to obtain a true picture of the company's (and its owner's) earning power.
- Add back in to your partner's take-home paycheck total any and all deductions for *voluntary* payments. A contribution to the executive gym is voluntary; assessments by the Internal Revenue Service are not. Support figures are usually based on the after-tax take-home pay of the supporting party, not on what that person has "left over" after financing a newly single life-style.
- Gather bits and pieces of apparently trivial evidence that show your mate's ability to support a certain life-style before the separation date. Sometimes accurate gross and net incomes can be estimated from pur-

> chasing ability during the marriage years. Remember that such evidence can include play or show programs, wine labels, restaurant menus, ticket stubs to sporting and cultural affairs, social calendars, publicity or flyers touting country club events, postcards from fancy hotels, photos of the new car, vacation itineraries, first-class air tickets, and photos of the three-month European tour taken last year. This "scrapbook of memories" will do more than warm your heart on a chilly evening. It can establish a comfortable standard of living *and* show your spouse's ability to maintain you and the children before a divorce.

While you are establishing the earning power of the spouse more likely to furnish support, consider who needs to be brought under the protection of this "financial umbrella." Do you have a dependent adult living with you who will affect your support needs? A child who has reached his physical majority but who is developmentally disabled and forced to live at home? A child from a previous marriage or liaison (with this partner or with another) who has no source of support other than you? In each of these special circumstances, you will want to negotiate sufficient support, or to present to the court evidence of an earning ability powerful enough to provide for the extra burden you will face. You may well do better in negotiating a larger-than-usual support payment for a special dependent, for courts vary in their willingness to impose a support order on the paying spouse for people not related by blood or law. If *your* "special circumstance" is a child by another man, or a child by this partner who has not acknowledged fatherhood, review your state's appropriate civil code sections to see what acts by your mate can convert any youngster into a legally protected support recipient. Such acts range from formal, legal adoption to the mere "holding out" of the child as the parent's offspring. In this latter situation, a man treats the child as his own, and in effect, compiles evidence of paternity with his actions. Acts can consist of telling relatives and friends about "his" daughter, introducing the child as "his son," giving presents "from Daddy" on special occasions, taking the child into his home, and indulging in similar behavior. Check and take action in these remaining months; after separation, any effort may be too little, too late.

By this point, you have begun work in a number of areas that will benefit you later on. But do not overlook the other side of the profit coin: it is crucial that you begin now to avoid obligations based on the marital partnership—new debts created before the separation date.

Your creditors will probably attempt to hold you *both* liable on debts incurred while married, so this is not the time to . . .

- refinance the family home
- enter a partnership or joint venture, or found a new, starting-in-the-red company with your spouse
- cosign a loan arranged by your mate

To provide extra financial protection now and in the months to come, some mates use this period of time to obtain a life insurance policy covering their spouse, and name themselves as beneficiary. Because you will have to get your partner's signature on the application, it is wise to arrange for such coverage well before a separation occurs. Whether you are merely not getting along, or are actually telegraphing divorce messages, your spouse may feel enough tension and stress to overlook normal safety precautions. The subterranean pressures preceeding a divorce often cause anger, frustration, stress, insomnia, fatigue, and a bunch of other problems that invite accidents and injuries.

If this suggestion makes you feel particularly queasy, consider that life will prove difficult on half (or less than half) of your regular income. Also keep in mind that you are counting on the continued existence of a "support bank" for you and/or the children for many years to come . . . a person capable of working and paying that monthly stipend. While some courts will not require the paying spouse to *obtain* life insurance, most would probably endorse an agreement (or order that spouse) to *maintain* a policy for the benefit of a recipient mate and/or minor children. You will help the court, the kids, yourself, and the state (who could otherwise end up supporting you) by arranging for protection *now*.

Next, see what you can do to reduce the community debts before moving out (or helping your spouse to move out). Since the party getting an asset gets the debt attached to it, it makes a lot of sense to pay down outstanding balances before parting company. By bringing down (or paying off) the amount owed on the car, the house, the credit cards, and the furniture, you will benefit both of you after separation and beyond. After all, the higher the net value of common assets, the more to divide and allocate (and the more discretionary income to finance your new life-style and to pay you and your offspring sufficient support).

The second reason to pay off or reduce marital debts at this time is to avoid meeting *all* the community bills if your mate is a poor financial manager. What exactly does that mean? As we have seen, creditors tend to look to both spouses to repay a common or during-marriage debt. If your spouse promises to pay the obligations attached to the assets allocated to him or her by agreement or by trial but fails to do so, guess whose ears will hear the creditors' knock?

Another way to protect your finances lies in turning loans (which require repayment) into gifts (which do not). If you take money from family, friends, or others before the split, try to make the funds a gift rather than a loan to be repaid out of community monies or allocated to one mate alone. Such cash outlays feel, look, and smell more like a gift under these conditions:

- There is no written or oral agreement to repay
- You and the givers have established no custom or habit of repaying such monies in the past
- No actual payments on this amount have been made over a period of time—the longer, the better
- The purpose of the advance was giftlike: a household help, a family outing, a tour or cruise for a special occasion like a birthday, anniversary, or to celebrate the giver's good fortune
- No terms were ever discussed about how the amount was to be repaid
- Best of all: so much time has passed without payment of any interest or principal that the statute of limitations has run out, and no legal effort to enforce payment can be undertaken by your creditor. Different types of debts have different statutes of limitation—the amount of time that must pass before the debt becomes legally uncollectible. Check the civil code in your state to determine which of your obligations may be ripe for forgiveness of this type. While a *moral* obligation to repay may remain, if *you* honestly do not feel it, let your mate repay the funds out of his or her ultimate share of the assets.
- Finally, you can ensure that there will be more funds to finance two lives by upgrading your spouse's physical condition and helping him (or her) to earn a better salary in the remaining time. Doing this for your mate is really helping yourself, for she or he will be better able to earn more money or pay more support. A spouse who is feeling, looking, and earning better will also feel less vindictive about being left behind and more cooperative about working out a good settlement for you.

It is during these months that you will need to determine whether your marriage is salvageable or not. *If there is any chance at all,* decide how much effort you'll give to repairing it, and set an "energy cutoff" deadline. Try hard and sincerely, but when your deadline arrives without measurable improvement, act from that moment forward solely for your own benefit.

Now it may seem contradictory to be working out a social, psychological, financial, and legal timetable for divorce at the same time that you are trying to reknit a failing relationship. It won't be easy, but it *will* put you in a win-win situation: if the marriage grows better, you will prosper; if the marriage ends, you will profit.

One of the ways in which you can benefit either way is to make a commitment to a "career mentality." Even if you decide to stay in your marriage, today's tough economy demands that you seek—and succeed at—more than just a job. Consider these aspects of your life that may need improvement to excel in the working world:

- Put together a *good* career wardrobe (one that makes you look like an executive rather than a secretary or trainee), and include the proper underwear.
- Improve your appearance by obtaining dental care (fillings, caps, orthodontia, bonding) if necessary.
- Improve your appearance by losing weight, getting a new hairstyle, clearing up skin problems, and caring more carefully for your nails.
- Experiment with makeup and perhaps consider plastic surgery.

Job hunting (and dating) in a youth-oriented singles world may require a more polished veneer than you had to maintain at home or in a go-nowhere-but-be-comfortable job. If you incur expenses for such improvements now, remember that they will benefit only you, but probably qualify as a community debt that will have to be repaid by both of you.

You can also prepare yourself for a better life (married or on your own) by finding some potential partners, now, for the work and leisure roles to come. People to share a hobby, help with schooling, trade skills (or advice), and assist in reaching goals can provide crucial aid in the months and years ahead. Remember, though, that these recruits are for *your* benefit—don't draft your team from among your spouse's friends, relatives, or business associates. This is a support network loyal to only you, with whom you will be able to start fresh in a single or single-parent life-style.

In addition to acquiring your own cheering section, begin to build your individual "tool chest" of skills. Watch or aid in making minor plumbing repairs, correcting simple wiring faults, in haggling with tradespeople and repair services, and in doing the small maintenance chores that every home requires. If you remain in the family home, you will do so without someone else to provide these services or act as an interface for you with repair people. Even if you move into another residence, such skills will stand you in good stead and save you funds as well.

Outside your home, check with the state department that registers motor vehicles to determine who has title to the family cars. Wherever vehicles are registered in the name of Sam *or* Nancy B., *either spouse may change the ownership of the car to his or her name alone*. Here is your opportunity to obtain sole ownership of the better (or best) of the transportation choices at hand. Remember that the "best" selection may *not* be the gas-gobbling, block-long sedan; or even the newest vehicle available. To get a valid idea of what each car is really worth, check the *Kelley Blue Book* at your local library for each year, model, and style of car. Find the retail and the wholesale price of each vehicle at the present time and average the two for an accurate picture of fair market worth. Of course, you will want to subtract from the averaged figure any amount still owed on the car. In most cases, people owe more on a car than the vehicle is worth, but occasionally, there is a pleasant surprise. In other cases, a call to a classic car dealer or a little library research can reveal a vintage auto with great value. When you are finalizing your terms of settlement, or during trial, you will have to account for any benefit you received by tootling off in the better car. But a simple offset should suffice, and in the months (and sometimes years) that such proceedings could consume, you can enjoy reliable, low maintenance, ego-satisfying transporation while your spouse struggles with the family clunker.

During these months, you may want to consider starting a business of your own as a means of underwriting your life-style to come. Draw up a simple agreement specifying that your venture's name, equipment, inventory, customers/clients, and all income it earns are to be considered yours alone. Keep careful and *separate* records, and don't let your mate take too active a role in day-to-day business affairs. Remember that conduct is crucial; too much involvement by your spouse may earn him or her an interest in your company's ownership and undercut the best of your carefully spelled-out plans.

This is also a good time to pull any loaned, given away, or "misplaced" personal property back into the marital pot. Such items include loans to relatives and friends, hobby or lawn maintenance tools borrowed by neighbors, furniture or furnishings being stored temporarily at others' homes or offices, and assets that your spouse may have parted with without your permission or for less-than-fair value. If you cannot regain the actual item, make a note of its location and value, so that it can be included in the final asset division "in absentia," and you can receive one-half the value while your spouse receives full but unenforceable (and worthless) ownership rights.

Remember that sometimes the asset transferred or expended is a form of effort or energy. In California, for example, perspiration is community property. Everytime your mate uses his or her efforts and skills to improve or expand his or her separate property, *you* gain an interest in that asset as well. From the court's point of view, since the talents and energies of each spouse remain community property during the marriage a mate who uses this "common asset" to improve or develop his or her own property owes the community some value for diverting this share of the communal energy to benefit only him- or herself. Under this repayment theory, you gain during a divorce when a marital partner has used his/her own efforts to improve his/her separate property.

Upon separation, you are entitled to receive one-half of the value or amount expended, *or* one-half the value your spouse added to his or her property . . . *whichever represents the larger value*. If your mate expends community energies on improving your *joint* assets, then you will automatically benefit from the increased value when you divide the property, allocate it to your mate and take offsetting property in return, or sell it to a third party at its higher price. If your mate's energies flow into improving your common assets, *encourage!* To cover the last possible scenario, let's consider what happens when your spouse expends time, energy, or his/ her separate property improving *your* separate property. In this case, a husband, for example, knowing that his wife received a plot of land as an inheritance and that she alone owns that land, spends his Saturdays grading the property and erecting a mountain cabin. Under California law (and perhaps under your state law), he can expect no reimbursement or share from his efforts because the courts presume that he intended to *give* his mate his skills and time. Under this theory, he can expect no reimbursement or share for his generosity. Such efforts are considered gifts from your spouse to you, and any added value in your separate property need not be shared with your mate.

Because you will bear the burden of showing such expenditures of time, skill, and energy, consider keeping a diary or log that shows hours and funds devoted by the owner spouse to his or her own property. "Before" and "after" pictures may also prove useful in estimating the funds or the value of the "perspiration" added, or the increase in market value. Remember that this theory requires a community property state *and* a situation where one spouse expends after-marriage energies to improve his or her own separate property.

For example:

> When Janice wed Ray, she knew about his stock portfolio, but she hadn't predicted how much time he would devote to research, phone calls, buying, selling, and trading shares. He subscribed to several esoteric books on financial opportunities, pored over the *Wall Street Journal*, and made deals on his car phone on the way to their favorite restaurant. Ray visited his broker almost daily and sometimes spent the hours between sales calls for his regular job just watching the ticker tape reports and comparing prices and trends.
>
> Though Ray's efforts trebled the value of his portfolio, they put a damper on marital bliss. During divorce negotiations, Jan claimed an interest in that portfolio, even though every stock in it was separate property acquired by Ray before the wedding day. The sum was decided by formula: one-half the amount of growth due to Ray's efforts would be allocated to Jan.

As a nonowner spouse, you will profit only if your spouse (the owner) exerts after-marriage energies. Therefore, encourage your owner-mate's expenditures of effort and time. In cases where a separately-owned asset increases in value without a partner's assistance, the character of any gain will remain all separate property. To fully understand this concept, consider how this example differs from Jan's and Ray's:

> Buffy inherited a small apartment building from her mother's estate (separate property) during her marriage to Ken. Not at all interested in real estate, Buffy hired a resident manager to handle repairs and maintenance, deal with tenant problems, collect the rents and pay all the bills. Because the building was always fully occupied and repair and maintenance costs remained low, the manager was always able to meet the bills after collecting the rents. Buffy received a quarterly report, but barely glanced at it before stuffing it in a bureau drawer.
>
> Though the building barely paid its own way on a monthly basis, its equity grew steadily, and its market value continued to rise.

When Ken began receiving less attention than Buffy's quarterly report, he sought a divorce and claimed that some of the apartment building's value belonged to him. "Buffy's efforts in managing that building were community property while we were married," insisted Ken. "Therefore, a part of the current value belongs to me."

"Nothing doing," the court will probably reply. "Buffy's efforts were so minimal that any increase in value appears due only to the real estate market, and that growth of a separate property asset remains separate property."

Ken might have changed the outcome by urging Buffy to take a personal, active interest in managing her building. If those efforts failed, Ken (and you) could always suggest that the original asset be traded for something that would excite a spouse's energies. If the new property is taken in both names, *voilà,* you're already on your way to a hefty profit. If the new asset remains in one name it is still that spouse's separate property, but a property that appears more "attractive" to your mate may well trigger the kind of personal commitment that will gradually earn *you* a share in any gain.

Because your share will depend upon the extent of your mate's personal involvement in his or her separate asset, and memories often differ after separation, document the energies and skills your spouse expends. Mark a calendar, make a tape recording while you ask questions about his or her progress with the asset, or copy books, flow sheets, ledgers, and records that your spouse maintains. All of these can show a pattern of heavy expenditures in the perspiration you're banking on.

Now let's take a few moments to consider ways in which a spouse can gain *more* than half of the jointly owned or community property. Some of these methods require negotiation and an out-of-court settlement, since even equitable-division courts may not decree the particular asset allocation that you have in mind. Most courts, however, will endorse an agreement signed by both parties if each has enjoyed the counsel of an independent attorney and understands the terms.

Let's deal first with those avenues that can work better in "kitchen table" negotiations with your spouse.

1. Gain real assets, but give your mate imaginary property. This approach works well with entrepreneurs and dreamers, who believe that a new business idea is worth limitless profits, though there may be only a battered (empty) file cabinet and a corner of the garage to show for it at the present time. In your talks, offer to give all rights to the new business (its name, its ideas, its inventory, its future earnings) to your mate; in return, you take property worth something in the here and now.

2. Suggest an "equitable" division of assets and debts that leaves more property with you and more obligations with your spouse. Such an allocation is not unfair if, for example, one party will enjoy a much greater earning power than the other. Another reason to take more than half the family assets might be to help with the care, feeding, and education of the children, if you plan to be the parent rendering primary care. A third justification would be if you had worked to help put your spouse through school or aided him/her to obtain a certification, license, or degree. This third scenario might entitle you to an even larger share if you both had agreed that after he or she graduated, you would enroll for the schooling you desired. If divorce interrupts this pact before your first class, shouldn't you receive the means to pursue your educational dreams out of the assets you helped to acquire?
3. Promise to pay most of the common debts, but take most of the assets to offset the financial pain. Such an agreement is fair because it leaves both of you with similar bottom line totals—but is uniquely advantageous to you. Why? Because you can proceed to "redesign" some (and perhaps most) of those outstanding balances. Do this by

- renegotiating the payment terms of existing loans (extend the payment period, reduce the monthly amounts, or both).
- refinancing the original loan.
- paying off the loan with money that is less expensive than the terms of the original obligation.
- working off the balance with a special skill or trade, or bartering a payoff that won't deplete your bank account.
- working with the lender to see if the loan can be converted to interest-only payments for several months or years or converted to a single balloon payment at the end of the term.
- approaching the creditor (if it is a friend or relative) with the idea of forgiving any balance due.

With the following approaches, you may need the court's aid, as they depend upon sufficient evidence or upon particular civil code sections in your state.

1. Persuade the hearing officer that items your spouse insists were purchased for investment only were really gifts to you and are therefore your separate property. Here's the usual scenario when one party raises this issue during negotiations or at trial:

   "Betty always knew those diamonds were to be resold when their value rose," Frank insists. "She understood that she could wear them on special occasions, but when I decided to cash them in, we would do so immediately."

   Betty's version is (not surprisingly) quite different:

   "Frank never said a thing to *me* about 'investing' in these stones," Betty avers. "I only know that he presented them to me one evening as we were getting ready to leave for a dinner party with friends, and suggested that I keep them in my jewelry case when we returned home later that evening."

   Lots of room for doubt about both points of view . . . but the deciding factors will be pieces of additional evidence that either party can (or cannot) produce for consideration by the court. Frank stands firm on his version of the facts. Betty, however, produces the following:

   - Various gift cards suitable for birthdays, anniversaries, and other special occasions, all mentioning the stones.
   - A family album with numerous photos showing a proud Betty displaying the rings and a necklace to admiring family members. The caption reads "Betty's 40th Birthday Sparklers."
   - The third finger of her left hand for the judge's inspection. On it glows a five-carat diamond, carefully set into the generations-old ring that Betty's mother had bequeathed to her. Arranging the setting, says Betty, was an anniversary surprise from her husband, Frank.

Guess which way the court decided? Take a tip from Betty; keep sentimental records that can prove profitable for you.

2. In some states, a partner can recover one-half of family assets squandered or misappropriated during the marriage years. This sum is allocated to the wronged mate without any offset to the "bad" partner. Such repayment for waste requires either ignorance of the act or no agreement to the expenditure at the time it

occurred, and requires that the spending party received nothing in return. Funds paid for liquor have been held to be sufficient consideration; a gift to a friend with no requirement or possibility of repayment may well qualify. Take care, if you are the recouping spouse, that such an award is not made out of common property (which may be half yours anyway), but comes from the separate holdings of the wastrel spouse.

3. Profit from overwhelming debts—a legal concept sometimes created by state law to expedite property matters in low-asset cases, or divorces involving absent spouses. In California, for instance, if the marriage community has overwhelming debts and few or no assets, *all* of the marital obligations can be allocated by the court to the higher-earning spouse. The lower-earning mate may take a share of the assets free of any unrelated debts.

California forums can also award all of the community property to just one of the spouses *if* the net value of such assets totals less than $5,000, and if even diligent efforts cannot locate a missing mate.

Either of these situations, or some other type scenario deserving of special treatment in your state, could give you an asset break that would result in your receiving more than half of the joint property.

These remaining months present an opportunity to assess and characterize all the available assets, so that you can arrange to have the "better" equal asset allocated to you. Although most pieces of property will bear an assessed fair market value, and many will appear to provide material for an equal trade, some assets rank much higher in potential or actual worth than others.

Because the court allocates *net* values (the fair market value of an asset minus any obligations owed for that asset), it is important to consider the *nature* of the debt when you weigh the total worth of the property that you are dividing or allocating between you. You will want to take possession of assets that provide certain advantages, even if on the surface the asset appears equal to property being taken by your spouse. You can lock in such advantages by carefully reviewing the type of asset, or the character of the debt attached to each piece of property.

Some assets may promise brighter futures for you than do others. A car, for instance, is a continuously depreciating asset; a solid, blue-chip stock, however, will tend to rise in value. Consider the future worth of a property before choosing which property you want allocated to you. In other cases, a potential profit may be hidden in the asset itself—some assets are more easily and quickly sold than others, and the sale proceeds could then be invested at a healthy rate of return to help with monthly bills.

A house, for example, represents a large investment and a potentially large profit upon its sale. But selling such a property can take several months and may require you, in current economic circumstances, to help finance the buyer, who cannot afford to pay all cash for your home. Meanwhile, you will have to continue to pay monthly bills and other living costs for yourself and others dependent upon you. On the other hand, shares of stock in a large, solid, publicly held company can be quickly traded for cash.

It is also important to remember that some *debts* have attractive aspects as well. Perhaps the statute of limitations has run out on the obligation involved, barring any court-enforced recovery. Different obligations have different life spans: some debts are legally enforceable for several years, some have a life span of only a year, and others may have expired even before your separation date. To check on the length of time that a particular debt or type of debt is legally enforceable by your creditor, check with the civil code of your state, available in any law or large library. Of course, some debts incur a moral obligation that one or both of you may feel. If *you* do not feel such an obligation, but your mate feels a moral duty to repay, let him or her repay the debt out of his or her share of the marital property.

In some cases, a particular debt will be forgiven because it represents funds extended by a family member or a close friend. Sometimes a debt can be repaid by bartering your skills instead of repaying with cash. One woman executive who possessed great skill with a sewing machine created dresses and sports clothes for neighbors who provided child care during the professional woman's working day.

Other "attractive" debts include those on which the repayment terms can be renegotiated or on which an easier payment plan can be worked out with the creditor.

In other cases, an asset or piece of property may have a high *exchange potential:* it can be traded for other property of a similar nature, and the resulting tax delayed for years to come. For example, an income property like an apartment building can be traded for another income property of a like kind without incurring any tax liability in the exchange. Check with your tax advisor to see if some of the marital property that could be allocated to you would qualify for such treatment.

Because some assets cost more than others to purchase and/or maintain, you will have more invested in them at the time of a future sale. With assets like these, the difference between all the costs (the *basis*) and the selling price is smaller—and the smaller the profit, the lower the tax you will have to pay. Clearly, the lower the tax, the greater the bottom line benefit to you.

A few assets have self-supporting skills. These properties can often be used to pay for or finance themselves (and sometimes you). Assets that can earn their own keep include a house large enough to take in boarders (for a monthly rental or in exchange for gardening, maintenance, or child-care services), land suitable for even a small vegetable patch, a second home in a resort or vacation area that can be leased or rented out, and office equipment that can turn leisure hours into additional income (a high-caliber typewriter, word processor, addressograph). Sometimes supplies and equipment originally acquired to enjoy a hobby can provide the beginning of a money-making venture: woodworking tools, camera and darkroom equipment, automobile repair tools, and even furniture refinishing products and tools. Still other property has great visual appeal—one yacht recipient rented his vessel out for corporate cruises; another, who sought a classic car in the settlement, let advertising agencies rent it for commercials in magazines and on television at a healthy hourly rate.

Occasionally, special knowledge owned by one spouse can pay off for both via a creatively crafted settlement. For instance, the wife in one case was far more experienced than her husband in overseeing real estate developments. She was in the midst of converting a large apartment complex into condominiums when her mate sued for divorce. In negotiations, she offered to complete the project and share the resulting profit with her spouse, if he would agree that a disproportionate share of these funds would be allocated to her. With this incentive in force, the conversion proceeded to a smooth completion, and both parties profited. If he had insisted on an even split, she could have abandoned or sabotaged the undertaking, harming them both. By taking a savvy approach, the husband reaped a healthy windfall, and both parties remained friends. In this case, there *was* no asset to compare with the development project, and the husband did not have a comparable skill to offset that of his wife, but clever bargaining gave both mates a share in a project that became a "better" asset only upon completion and not before.

On other occasions, it will pay to look ahead and consider the tax consequences of taking ownership of a particular asset. For example, it may not matter to you, emotionally, whether you take title to the house and buy out your spouse or take money or property of equal value. But the funds you accept would be taxed; the house can eventually be sold, and the funds can be protected from taxation so long as a new home is bought within two years with the proceeds of that sale. There are other aspects to sheltering this money after a home sale, but in simple terms, keeping the house and giving cash or other property to your mate can prove a savvy choice.

In other instances, two assets of comparable value may both be highly salable, but one may have been owned for several years, and the other owned only a month or two. If you plan to sell the asset as soon as you get it, choose the one you have owned longer, since any increase in value of this property will be taxed at long-term capital rates—a real tax savings for you. Any profit on the newer asset may be taxed as ordinary income, a higher percentage that will leave the seller without full value in the trade.

In general, anticipate the tax bite on each piece of property or each asset that you want allocated to you. If you figure out the *after-tax* totals allocated to each spouse, you can make a fairer (or much better) deal.

Not all of these suggestions will apply to your case or to you. Even if you find numerous good tips here, there may be insufficient time to accomplish them all before you separate. In addition, doing even a few tasks may seem to be too much trouble and effort during this difficult time. Doing *anything* may prove particularly tough if you have always played the more passive role in your relationship.

Each goal you accomplish in these months, however, will help you to see yourself—and your future—in a better light. While we cannot *undo* the past, we can *redo* the present by taking an active, interested role in getting ready for divorce. Few could know this better than George Eliot, an English writer born Marian Evans. In Chapter 29 of her *Adam Bede,* written in 1859, Eliot noted "Our deeds determine us, much as we determine our deeds."

Gathering the necessary information, marshaling facts, compiling evidence, and deciding your priorities—all of these activities will help you through the traumatic months to come *and* bring you dollars later on. Looking out for yourself will also increase your bargaining skills, boost your self-reliance, and enhance your self-esteem.

Taking an active role can save you the frustration of merely *re*acting to a spouse's moods, whims, and threats. By putting yourself in charge, you assume the role of an equal partner capable of bargaining effectively for a fair (or even more-than-fair) divorce settlement. Instead of worrying about your mate's demands, you will instead be channeling energy into your concerns and *you*.

Taking the first steps will be the most difficult. As time goes on and you continue in an "active" stance, these self-help tasks will become easier. When you need encouragement, think of the legal fees, time, and trauma you will save by doing your own legwork and beginning it now, when there's plenty of time to feel your way. If these motivations aren't sufficient, then do the work for a stronger, more capable, more powerful, happier, and more equal *you*.

3

The 90-Day Treasure Trove

ALMOST EVERY marriage accumulates assets that, over the years, lie forgotten and unused or remain hidden to one spouse or to both. As your separation date approaches, take these few weeks or months to uncover the buried treasure that can benefit you both. In these pages, you will learn how to follow *your* treasure maps to the hidden goodies, out-of-sight property, and even the intangible, easy-to-overlook rights that can bring you more property or cash.

During divorce proceedings, the most commonly overlooked assets are those that we don't handle, smell, see, or utilize every day. Easily forgotten, they are left out of the negotiation or trial process, and languish in the hands of strangers or in the possession of the luckier spouse. While any well-drafted marital settlement agreement or judgment will provide for the valuation and division of property discovered after the settlement, it is much easier to deal with all issues at one time. This is because an asset discovered by you may markedly strengthen your bargaining power or your ability to hold out for a good deal. In addition, it will help you to clear up all the details at one time, eliminating the ties to a former spouse that can undo the best intentions to begin a successful life alone.

In considering your situation, note whether any of the following bits of buried treasure should be unearthed before you leave.

Year-end paper rights are those that accrue to an employee and are paid at the close of the calendar year or the company's fiscal year. Such rights to income, assets, or property include profit sharing, bonuses, rewards and prizes, and income distribution in any form. In addition, remember that tax refunds for jointly filed returns are mailed well after the close of each calendar year. If you cannot hang around until your mate actually takes possession of these assets (and, of course, places them in your joint account), suggest *apportioning* the funds when they arrive. You can use a simple formula, shown below, to figure out your fair portion of such an asset; the numerator is the number of months in the calendar or fiscal year that you lived together before the separation day. The denominator is the total number of months in the year. Multiply this fraction by the value of the asset received. This will represent the community's interest in the funds, so you will need to divide this total by half to approximate your share of any benefit earned. As an example, Barry separated from wife Jean at the end of June. As an executive with a large computer firm, Jean received a $10,000 profit-sharing check on December 31 of that year. Barry's computation looked like this:

$$\frac{6 \text{ (months before separation)} \times \$10{,}000}{12 \text{ (months in the year that Jean spent earning the check)}}$$
$$= \$5{,}000 \text{ (the community's total interest in the check)}$$

The maximum amount that Barry, as her spouse, could claim was one-half. Barry's final share, therefore, is one half of $5,000, or $2,500.

In a community property state like California, such a share is practically automatic. In other states, it could be more effective to use such an argument in negotiation sessions, as this concept may prove foreign or unacceptable to the courts in your state.

Contingent fees and erratic income are usually received by realtors, insurance salespeople, literary and dramatic agents, and some doctors and lawyers—anyone who is paid on a contingency arrangement or receives lump-sum payments when the work is done or the deal is completed, and not before.

If the work was performed during your marriage, why shouldn't you share in the money, even if the check is received after you leave? If some of the work was completed while you lived together and the remainder was done after the separation day, you will need to figure out what fraction of the effort took place during the marriage. You can use the formula above to figure out a fair share for yourself.

A spouse who suspects an imminent separation or divorce and who can control his or her income may attempt to squeeze you out of a share in property that belongs to both of you. Having a good grasp of the energy devoted to the account, the case, the client, or the project before you part is your insurance that your claim will have a strong foundation.

Bear in mind that some monies (like incentive pay for reenlistment in the armed services) are considered separate property if received after you leave. Time your exit accordingly.

Suits and claims filed on behalf of your spouse can benefit you, too, if your timing is right. While vague or unfiled, claims or suits against others are not "property" that can be shared, so wait until the suit is filed, or a formal claim procedure is completed. If you leave after that, keep in touch to learn how the case comes out. If the procedure promises to be a long one, estimate the chances of success, and consider settling for a lump sum now and letting your mate have the full proceeds when (and if) they are ever paid. In some states, personal recoveries paid after separation are separate property for the harmed or injured spouse. A business case that garners a win, however, should benefit both mates. A little investigation can show how your mate's claim will be characterized in your state.

Suits, claims, and other rights to payment can include worker's compensation payments, personal-injury recoveries, demands for payment on insurance companies, "commercial" causes of action for trademark infringement or unfair competition and small claims court decisions, veterans' benefits, and administrative hearing awards payable by a union or company.

If your spouse is the injured party, you may want to sue for a loss of consortium, but it is inconsistent to claim loss of consortium rights as you pack your bags. You cannot effectively end cohabitation and still ask to be compensated for a loss of sex, society, and companionship. Therefore, plan your departure date carefully.

Your spouse's work record can often earn profits for you. In preparing for a divorce by gathering all the asset values, include any accrued vacation dollars or sick leave benefits or any "unused" benefits that can be converted to cash. In some companies, employees choose benefits from a large menu of services. Each employee has a total benefit package made up of the various benefits he or she can receive. A worker who does not need (or who chooses not to take) all the benefits available can sometimes ask the employer for credits that can be turned in for cash at a later date. As long as the rights to such benefits were earned during the marriage years, their value when converted to cash may be additional marital property that should be shared with you.

Your mate's work record is also important to you because it forms the foundation for *your* Social Security benefits in years to come. Even if you have never worked, you will qualify for *derivative* Social Security benefits in later years if you have been married to the wage earner for over ten years. Your receiving these funds will take nothing from your former partner's pocket, but your benefits *will* be limited to some fraction (up to 50 percent) of the benefit total that he or she receives. To qualify, remember to let ten years elapse from the wedding day to the entry of final decree.

This second reason raises two additional considerations: the more your spouse earns—even if it takes your help—the more you will eventually reap, and obtaining a divorce before the ten-year mark can prove especially costly in later years.

Sometimes pluses accrue from simply qualifying as a legal spouse, and these advantages could be termed *spousal status bonuses*. As long as you rank as your mate's legal partner, you are covered by medical, dental, car, life, home-owner, and health insurance policies. You enjoy reimbursement for numerous insured expenditures, including possibly special schooling and therapy. You would probably receive all or a large portion of all the assets if your spouse dies without a will, and you reap any wrongful-death, worker's compensation, or other award for your partner's untimely demise. As a legal spouse, you can also often participate in benefits offered by your mate's employer. Such fringe benefits can include financial, psychiatric, and even legal counseling; company transportation, clubs, lodges or resorts; expense accounts and company cars; home-owner coverage; free or discounted meals; day-care services; reductions on company merchandise; subsidized or no-cost parking; low-interest loans, stock-option plans, educational aid, and even access to a company plane.

While no number of financial benefits can compensate for a bad marriage, there is no need to throw all of these assets out with your spouse. It may be possible to bargain with your mate, during divorce proceedings, to keep some of the benefits after the final decree. However, even a sincere promise of cooperation from a former partner cannot ensure a right to receive an insurance payoff or a company benefit if the payor will remit funds only to a legal spouse—in other words, your right to receive insurance awards or many other benefits may end upon the entering of the final decree. Watch out, therefore, that you don't concede important here-and-now benefits for a promise of future coverage or a benefit that is controlled by the rules of the third party and that even a willing spouse cannot possibly guarantee.

A further word on the profits of retaining, or transferring, the benefits of being a legal spouse. If you were never legally married, and your state does not elevate cohabitation to common-law marriage, *but* you belived yourself to be validly wed, consider bargaining for or enforcing your rights as a putative spouse, a concept discussed in an earlier chapter. If there is no common property of your marriage and you qualify as a good-faith putative spouse, you may be able to recover for the reasonable value of the services (housekeeper, cook, chauffeur, hostess, companion, nurse, etc.) that you furnished during the relationship. In many states, you may have to subtract from any claim the value of benefits you received during the "marriage" period. Still, you could recoup a balance in your favor that will help to underwrite a new life for yourself.

If you were validly wed, but lived together for some months or years before marrying, *think about "adding on" that time to the marriage period,* so that you have some bargaining or court-enforced power over property acquired during that period as well. In California, such a concept is called tacking. A separate civil suit is filed in superior court for a hearing on the contractual nature of one party's duty, if any, to share with the cohabitating partner. As a practical matter, however, the living-together period is joined with the divorce issues, and the whole matter heard in the family-law portion of the superior court. In fact, the term "tacking" may have originated from attorneys' practices of stapling (or tacking) the papers from the civil suit to the petition for divorce.

This tactic can effectively stretch the marriage period, so that property acquired during this time is more likely to be characterized as jointly owned. Children born in these years more easily receive court-enforceable support rights. Spousal support awards can be higher and payable for a longer time if this period extends the marital period to a sufficient degree. In short, the "tacking tactic" can pay off handsomely, if your relationship fits this scenario.

Let me here insert a word of caution: many of the suggestions on these pages spring from cases and laws developed in California, a state long recognized as blazing new trails in domestic-relations law. Not all forums display as creative an outlook in resolving divorce disputes, nor one as fair to the nonworking or nonowner spouse. *But if you negotiate with your mate by using these concepts and approaches, instead of depending on the court to do right by you, you can definitely profit from your divorce.* None of the approaches suggested here urges you to do anything but care for and take care of yourself and any youngsters who will be primarily dependent upon you. If the courts in your state do not follow the precepts laid out here, follow them yourself. Most forums are overcrowded, and their personnel overworked, particularly in the family-law field. Every one of them would no doubt welcome a well-drafted agreement, signed by both parties, outlining the resolution of all the property, debt, and support issues in a couple's case. While you should urge your spouse to obtain legal counsel to review and sign any such agreement, you can still often fashion a settlement with a scalpel that is very favorable to you. Because of time pressures and an unavoidable unfamiliarity with every detail of your case, a judge or commissioner can only divide the property put before it with a cleaver. And if that state's law directs that the cleaver slice off many of your property or support rights, you will pay a high price for turning over your expectations to that "stranger" on the bench. On the other hand, by performing your own research on the assets and debts and by bargaining effectively with your spouse, you can carve out a better-financed future for your children and/or yourself.

With that cautionary word in mind, let's return to finding more buried treasure. In many marital estates, overlooked assets really qualify as *hidden loot*. Such hidden loot includes insurance policies' cash or surrender value—the amount of financial equity built up with the company from years of paying premiums on whole life insurance policies. Term insurance, or coverage that is bought year by year, accumulates no cash value—the amounts paid merely take care of the cost of coverage for a specified time. In whole-life policies, however, a portion of the premium is invested and forms a cash fund for the policy owner that can be paid out in an annuity over later years or withdrawn in a lump sum. Because the investments chosen by insurance firms are extremely conservative, they pay little interest and show little growth—even after many years. Decades ago, however, such insurance packages were more attractive to buyers, and many "invested" in their insurance policies. If you or your spouse holds a whole-life policy, it may contain dollars that can be withdrawn at little loss (remember those conservative investment approaches) and divided or allocated between the parties. Even if you choose not to withdraw the accumulated funds, obtain a letter or computer printout from the insurance company showing the cash or surrender value, if any, in all of your insurance policies.

If your mate has insured his, her, or your life through a National Service Life Insurance policy or other military coverage plan, it is important for you to know that such a policy and any cash value it contains has been designated by the federal courts as the separate property of the federally employed spouse. While even a court can therefore not award any portion of such a policy's cash value to a nonowner spouse, you can ask your mate if other property can be allocated to offset this inequity.

As a side note, remember that the power to name the beneficiary of *any* policy remains with the policy owner and with him or her alone. If you obtain a promise that you will remain the irrevocable beneficiary of your mate's policy, be sure to have this term included in the final judgment signed by the court. Send a certified copy of the judgment to all insurance companies involved. Even such a measure, however, may not protect you from losing your beneficiary status if the policy involved is a National Service Life Insurance policy. Federal courts have held that no constraint can effectively bar the NSLI policy holder from changing the designated beneficiary at any time. Your recourse? To accept or bargain for other property (preferably to be transferred immediately) in lieu of being named the beneficiary of such a policy, or perhaps of *any* life insurance policy.

Antiques, collectibles, and junk. According to a recent nationwide survey conducted by the advertising agency Foote, Cone & Belding, 28 percent of all Americans collect something as a hobby. Men tend to gather stamps, coins, and cars; women, books and gemstones. With so many people accumulating items we might have once discarded as junk, there's a good chance that your mate's fetish may add dramatically to the marital wealth in which you can share.

The treasure that your spouse is hoarding may include:

Parking meters
Fountain pens
Hatpins and their holders
Doorknobs
Valentines
Cookie cutters
Golf balls (particularly if old enough to be cowhide stuffed with feathers)
Political buttons (especially if 60 years old or more)
Comic books
Liquor decanters
Ceramics
Matchbox toys
Hummel figurines
Early radios
Antique banknotes
Jukeboxes
Antique games
Slot machines
Oil leases
Christmas seals and charity stamps

Old newspapers
Guns
Knives
Clocks
Playing cards
Sewing machines
Inkwells and quills
Autographs and manuscripts
Diaries
Pocket watches
Antique toys
Camera and photography equipment
Rare or first-edition books
Stamps
Glassware
Bottles
Early pennies
Old mail-order catalogs
Commemorative plates
Beer cans
Picture postcards
Tickets to historic sporting and cultural events
Baseball trading cards
Old movie stills, costume sketches, pen-and-ink drawings of cartoon characters
Movie memorabilia
Photographs
Election memorabilia
Dolls
Antique or foreign rugs
Cash registers
Typewriters
Magazines
Firearms and armaments
War memorabilia
Fishing lures
License plates
Firefighting aids
Smoking paraphernalia
Models and kits
Airline memorabilia
Kites
MacDonald's mementos
Coca-Cola memorabilia
Antique currency
Phonographs
Comforters, linens, and quilts
Travel stickers
and even jigsaw puzzles

Remember to check out any old cereal boxes (a Post Grape Nuts box with a Mickey Mantle photo on the back now retails for $700). Old newspapers can be worth a real bundle, and outdated stock certificates can bring serious dollars if they represent a share in a successful company that has merged or changed its name, if their artwork is valued by decorators and collectors, or if they bear the signature of a now famous financier.

If your spouse has such a collection, and it is easily movable or salable, or if you plan to move out of the apartment or house, take pictures of the assembled goodies in sufficient detail for an appraiser to assess accurately their value. Somyimes such assets "disappear" during divorce negotiations or before the trial.

Secret bank accounts and other cash hideaways require you to "crack the safe" to uncover hidden funds in your marriage. To do this, you might try asking at all the banks and savings and loan associations in your neighborhood and in the area where your spouse works whether there are any accounts in both your names at these locations. At these financial institutions, also ask about any safe-deposit boxes in both your names. You will have no trouble obtaining the balances on such accounts, or gaining access to any jointly held safe-deposit boxes because your name appears as a co-owner. If any accounts are held in just your mate's name, it will be more difficult to learn of their existence. You may try calling the institution and giving your married name. Say that you haven't got the account number with you, but would like to know the balance in that account. If such institutions won't provide the information over the phone, you may find it more effective to visit savings and loans and banks in person, with sufficient identification, and ask about the balances in any accounts.

Before you "take to the streets," check around the house, the garage, the family file cabinet, that bedstand drawer, and anywhere else your spouse tends to keep correspondence, statements, and bills. Opening another's mail is a no-no, but you can certainly make note of printed envelopes and return addresses that can guide you in your financial quest.

If you can obtain access to the safe-deposit boxes, take each one into the private cubicle provided by the institution, empty each box, and photograph the contents spread out next to the box. Make a separate list of the items and date it. Return all the items to the box unless you fear a theft by your spouse. If you do fear a loss, consider secreting the goodies elsewhere for safe keeping during negotiations. When you receive the developed prints, date them on the back and attach them to the corresponding lists. Put your evidence in a safe place.

It is often an effective strategy to treat a soon-to-be-ex as a nice person by giving him or her every chance to voluntarily reveal such assets and include them in the settlement. If the information that you have unearthed is not forthcoming, you've given your spouse an adequate chance to be fair and can now whip out your documented find.

If your mate receives mail that you can legitimately open (or can at least skim when it's left lying around), review bank correspondence for hidden accounts. To do this most efficiently, keep a sharp lookout at year's end and throughout the new months of the year. During these weeks banks send out their statements showing the interest earned on accounts so that the owners can include them in income tax returns. The amount of interest earned will allow you to calculate fairly accurately the size of each account.

For those accounts to which you have access as a co-owner, ask to see the bank's file on you. If the institution has extended a loan or a line of credit to your spouse, a copy of the loan application or a financial statement will probably be in the file. In addition, banks and savings and loans often ask for a previous or concurrent bank reference when someone opens an account, and these leads can reveal hidden accounts.

Many households also keep "informal banks" for access to ready cash. Called grocery funds, mad money, emergency currency, or a mattress bank, these cookie jar funds can escape memory (or disappear with a leaving spouse) during divorce.

Other cash caches are not secretly created by one spouse, but imposed upon both in the form of impound accounts. When people purchase real estate with the help of a financial institution, the lender savings and loan often asks that payments for insurance and taxes, which are due in lump-sum payments twice a year, be deposited in monthly allotments and held by the savings and loan. This procedure protects that lender by ensuring that sufficient funds will be on hand to pay these assessments when due. But most impound accounts earn about 2 percent interest—a real loss for the paying party in these hard economic times. Instead of letting your lender hold your money and pay you a pittance for its use, withdraw these funds and invest them yourself. You will have to withdraw monies to pay the insurance and tax bills, but you'll do much better between payments and probably have something left over to divide or allocate in the property settlement.

Some property occasionally lurks in a spouse's past or in the hands of a mate's *future* partner. In the first instance, property and/or support rights that were hard won in a prior divorce may have been forgotten in later years. A lot of goodies, bitterly fought over during divorce, remain in the garage of the "losing" spouse; never claimed by the "winner" at all. In other cases, support orders that once supplied monthly payments may have been allowed to lapse. These financial arrearages can be recovered via monthly payments or in a lump sum. If *you* are the spouse with rights to past support, wait until leaving to collect from a former mate. If your mate has the right to pursue overdue support, urge him or her do so *now*, then make sure that the funds trickle into the joint account so that you may share. If this seems a bit unfair, remember that if a parent has not been paying support as ordered, it is you—or the household in which you are a financial partner—that has been taking up the financial slack. Some repayment is due.

In the second instance (and this is a painful possibility to face), your spouse may be hiding funds with a new love. People sometimes revert to old behavior patterns when threatened with emotional or financial loss, so looking back may help you prepare for your future. How? The case of Priscilla and Ben provides an example. The two met when Priscilla began working nights at a post office central sorting facility. Because Priscilla's marriage was already shaky, she fibbed to her hubby about her take-home pay and began to funnel a third of her salary into a secret account. As matters worsened at home, Priscilla grew closer to her fellow worker, Ben. When Priscilla's marital partner sought a divorce and started formal discovery proceedings, Priscilla realized that she would have to answer—under oath—questions about any bank accounts held in her name. Taking Ben aside during a coffee break, Priscilla asked him to hold the balance in her account in his name alone. Having successfully avoided sharing her funds, Priscilla wed her friend, Ben, a few months after the final decree. Within two years, Priscilla was yearning for a new life . . . alone. Ben read all the signs and, learning from past experience, made careful note of Priscilla's closest male friends. When Priscilla sought her second legal parting, several of her friends were surprised (and one was mighty nonplussed) to receive a court order to reveal any and all information about any accounts held for the benefit of Priscilla Crafty.

People aids, like cosigners and guarantors, can hold treasure for you. A simple story with a happy ending will illustrate. A young executive, Diane, had recovered well from a rather bitter divorce but was hurt anew when she received mail from a brokerage house indicating that her former spouse had forged her name to stock certificates and sold them during the earlier proceedings, pocketing the funds. Diane thought the money was gone forever, but the stamp and signature of a large downtown firm appeared on the face of the transmittal letters covering the sale. Such companies guarantee, or stand behind, the validity of all signatures necessary to the transfer of ownership. A quick call revealed the extent of recovery: as soon as

Diane signed a waiver of any future claims against this guarantor, the firm would furnish her with one half of the purloined shares (her portion under community property laws). After Diane's shares arrived, a review of the financial pages in her local paper showed that this stock was on the rise. A check of past stock reports showed a much lower price on the date when Mr. Diane sold their shares. In fact, Diane's 50 percent portion brought her more than her spouse had received for selling *all* their shares!

Custody, too can hold some financial pluses, but, to be honest, these rarely outweigh the actual cost of caring for children every day. However, the advantageous aspects of custody include:

- Receiving child support
- Claiming deductions
- Filing as head of a household (which puts you in a lower tax bracket)
- Claiming child-care credits (recently raised to $720 per child, per year)

To realize other benefits of custody, follow these guidelines:

- If you claim a child as a dependent and deduct him or her, you may also deduct all medical and dental costs related to that child.
- The custodial parent of a wage-earning minor is, in some states, the owner of those funds (even if your youngster manages his or her earnings alone, consider charging something for room and board).
- Taking a child who shares some of your interests can allow for exchanging wardrobes, sports equipment, hobby materials, and even cosmetic or health-care products.
- A "partner" child will often help with housekeeping chores or aid in raising smaller children, entertaining guests, etc.

All of these can help, but you might do best of all by avoiding custody of a "costly" child—one whose scrapes with the law cost you bail money and legal fees, one who requires high car or health insurance, one who dates up a storm at your expense, or a child who qualifies as a clothes freak.

Consider what may be the most money-saving aspect of custody—giving it to your spouse. A concept of shared or joint legal custody can help you save face if you fear a soiled reputation for such an act. By allocating the day-to-day care to a responsible, mature person who loves the children, you can pursue schooling, train for a better job, build a new social life, coddle a business of your own, and gain solid emotional footing before taking on a larger share of the physical custody.

Tax returns, particularly when reviewed by an inquisitive CPA or public accountant, can reveal much hidden treasure. Reports of interest earned can lead to the discovery of funds squirreled away. Attached forms can indicate the existence of other businesses, companies, or financial interests. Finally, all "paper depreciation" taken on office equipment, inventory, real estate, and other business assets should be added back in, as none of it represents any "out of pocket" loss.

Asking a friend who is skilled at financial matters to review your joint tax return can uncover a rich harvest in assets or cash. Even if you have to hire someone to provide tips you can later research on your own, the money will be well spent. Keep in mind that any tax return that you sign is your property as well as your mate's. You have an equal right to review it, copy it, question it, and obtain it from the Internal Revenue Service if your spouse has mislaid or hidden your past joint returns.

In some cases property remains out of sight throughout the length of a marriage and, unfortunately, stays invisible during a divorce. The result: out of sight, out of the settlement. Such assets often include *pension and retirement plans,* which one or both spouses tend to forget when parceling out the other, more visible assets.

At the beginning of 1982, pensions and retirement benefit plans were considered marital property in 18 states, to be allocated evenly between parting mates. But in addition to the plan itself (and its accumulated wealth), there are several other details you'll want to keep in mind.

First, there are two kinds of pension plans, *defined-contribution* and *defined-benefit.* In a defined contribution program, the employee or the employer or both allocate a certain sum (a defined amount) to the worker's retirement account. In the other format, both, only one, or neither of the parties involved may provide funds for the plan before its payoff date. In fact, in some companies, an annuity might be purchased shortly before the worker's retirement that will fund the amounts promised in later years. In such a program, it is easy to see that even a detailed computer printout, furnished by the employer, may show that your mate's account is rich only in goose eggs (zeros). Nonetheless, the *right* to receive retirement dollars lurks in that account, and must be shared, in these 18 states, with you.

Second, some pension benefits are "young," unvested, or unmatured at the time of separation, and some are "old," immediately payable—depending on the length of the marriage and the age of the working or pension-earning spouse. *Don't be misled into thinking that a mate with a short working record may have no retirement benefits worth assessing or dividing.* In California, the *time rule* specifies that each working year is as important as any other in the earning of pension or retirement benefits. If your state fosters such a concept, apply it when drawing up your property settlement terms. If your state does not recognize such assets as commonly owed, or will divide only a matured and ready-to-pay pension, apply the time rule in negotiations with your spouse to achieve a fairer, more equitable result than the court would provide.

Here are two additional points about pension and retirement benefits that will stand you in good stead. Before you sit down to allocate or divide the value of either mate's pension rights, *have this asset evaluated by an actuary skilled in appraising the present value of retirement program(s) in your particular case.* If the plan in question is currently paying or is about to pay monthly benefits, you need only apply the formula described earlier in this chapter under suggestion No. 1 for year-end "paper rights." But even if a work record is short, or the plan does not vest for several more years, arrange for an actuary's review; thousands of dollars slip through marital fingers each year because one spouse or both believe the plan valueless at separation time.

The second point is that you may want to follow the lead of some family law attorneys and actuaries who know this field. They believe that in dividing a pension's present value, a fifty-fifty split is *not* equitable, and that *the nonearning spouse should receive more than half of the evaluated sum to provide an equitable split.* How do these professionals come to this conclusion? Because receiving a pension payment is a right owned solely by the working spouse. If the pension payoff rests so far in the future that the nonearning mate opts for an immediate amount in lieu of waiting, there is no danger of losing this asset right. But if the pension payments are already arriving, and the parties arrange to allocate the amount between them, *and* the spouse who actually earned the pension payments dies, then those payments will cease, cutting off all allotments to the other recipient. To compensate for this possible loss of funds, some legal observers advocate giving a heftier share of such monthly receipts to that nonworking mate.

If this is your situation, keep such an unequal-but-fairer division in mind. No court case or legislative ruling has to my knowledge ever officially provided for such an allocation, but negotiation thrives on such "vacuums in justice"—make that "only fair" approach work for you.

In addition, consider insisting on receiving the survivor benefits if your mate's retirement plan includes such protection. Third, obtaining and maintaining insurance on the pension-earning party is a good shield against the costly loss caused by even an *ex*-spouse's death.

Under forum law in your state, you may be entitled to receive monthly payments or a lump sum, *before* your spouse actually retires. This is because, under some state rulings, you may apply for your share of a spouse's pension payment as soon as your mate is eligible to retire, whether he or she actually leaves the firm or not. Of course, your share of such an "early-payment plan" will probably limit your monthly allotment to a portion of the plan's value at that time; a spouse who waits can receive a share of a larger amount payable when a mate actually retires. Immediate payouts are also reduced to a present worth evaluation, so you won't see the same dollars you would later on. Though receiving a pension buy-out may reduce your child or spousal support, in your circumstances a bird in the hand may be worth more than three on the wing.

Here are a few points you'll want to consider in weighing whether to take a lesser sum now as your share in any such pension payments or to wait and receive a portion of the allotments as the employer pays them out.

Pros and cons of settling for a present value amount and receiving monies now

Pros

Avoids prolonging trial or hassles over how this asset should be shared; beneficial to both parties.

Avoids risk that spouse will fall ill, leave firm, or die prior to receipt of future benefits, cutting off your rights to payment.

Eliminates possibility that earning spouse will quit work or instigate a firing to avoid having to share with you at later date. (Not a smart move for the earning spouse, but a spiteful one that sometimes happens.)

Cuts ties between parties, avoids financial control by working mate.

Provides immediate cash or other property for investment at good rates, new business venture, continuing financial independence, other valid reasons.

Gives you a real asset that can be passed on by will or gift.

Immediate receipt simplifies the terms of a judgment, as the court does not have to work out a formula correct for you or retain jurisdiction over this issue for a later decision regarding an accurate split.

Avoids need to *join* the pension plan or seek later court enforcement, and thus lowers legal fees and costs.

Cons

Present-value sums are less than you could otherwise ultimately receive.

If *you* are the paying party, you may end up giving property or cash now to buy your mate out of a benefit that *you* — because of illness or a firing — may never receive.

Pros and cons of waiting until funds are actually payable and receiving later payments

Pros

Ensures that sum in question will be maximum total possible.

Usually ensures receipt, as monies can be paid directly from pension fund to you.

Possibility of receiving more than one-half of each monthly payment to compensate for risk of losing all with death of earning mate.

If you are the nonearning spouse, leaving the funds with a pension fund eliminates money management worries and possible tax problems if you receive too much property in a single year.

Cons

Pension funds, often invested conservatively, may lag behind inflation during waiting years.

No right that can be willed or passed on to others; your right to receive depends upon spouse's continuing to receive payments.

Receipt of immediate cash can reduce sum awarded for spousal support in years following divorce.

Since later participation in a pension payout requires certain legal steps, it is important to understand the term "joinder" when retirement and pension programs pop up in a case. As soon as one of you files for a divorce, any spouse wishing to share in the other's pension plan, whether now or later, may have to serve papers on the plan's administrator. These papers inform the plan of the divorce proceedings, and tells the plan administrator that one spouse may have a share in any accumulated or future funds. What happens if these papers never get served and the couple can't settle the matter in negotiation? Such a retirement program owes its funds only to the employee spouse unless it officially learns of another potential interest or payee. If the pension's benefits have matured, or the employee is ready to retire, *and* the plan has not been notified, it *could* pay all the sums due to your mate, who could dissipate them and reserve nothing for you. If, on the other hand, a plan knows of your potential rights and is ordered (by the court or by your mate) to pay a portion of the monthly allotment directly to you, you can receive payments without depending on your spouse's goodwill and good word month after month after month.

If a joinder procedure is required in your state, have your attorney file and serve the necessary papers on the plan. If the procedure is not followed in your divorce forum, consider other ways to let the retirement program know that it may risk court action if it pays all or any of its accumulated sums to your spouse during divorce proceedings.

Keep in mind that disability payments rank as retirement benefits and are subject to division *if* they are received after an employee reaches retirement age, *and* if they are being paid in lieu of pension income. Remember also that federal civil service retirement benefits are input to the community pot and that state national guard pension plans are also often considered jointly owned property. In other words, the two exceptions noted above bear no such limitation. (Of course, any separate property could be added to the marital "stew" if both parties agree and the owning spouse signs an agreement changing the character of such property.)

Sometimes a concept known as *quasi-community property* can figuratively drag out-of-state real and personal property into your negotiations and, later, into your settlement agreement or trial. In California, for example, this concept means that all real estate and personal property, wherever located, will be considered quasi-community property if it was acquired in a way that would make it community property if it had been acquired in California. This example will help to illustrate this unusual but potentially profitable concept:

> After Arnie and Betty married in Arkansas, they purchased a home together in that state and took title as husband and wife. Arnie paid for the house with his earnings after marriage, and Betty stayed home and cared for their three children.
>
> After the children graduated from college and moved eslewhere, Betty and Arnie visited California and decided to move there permanently. Because they didn't need the cash, they left the house unsold in Arkansas and purchased a small condominium on the coast with some of their savings. The balance of their investments were left in Arkansas.
>
> When they had resided in California about a year, Arnie moved into a nearby apartment and told Betty that he was filing for a divorce. Arnie planned to return to Arkansas when he had obtained the final decree, so imagine Arnie's surprise when Betty's proposed marital settlement agreement suggested sharing the Arkansas real estate and the investments left in Arkansas.

While the Arkansas real estate would probably not be ordered sold by the court, nor could the savings and investments physically be brought to California to be actually divided between the parties, the California court would establish the value of the property in the sister state and arrange a financial offset for the spouse not receiving sole ownership to the Arkansas house and/or the Arkansas funds. How can the California court exercise so much muscle at such a distance? Because everything that Betty and Arnie had acquired in Arkansas would have been community property and subject to allocation or division if it had been acquired while the couple lived in California.

Your state may not endorse such a far-reaching view of the size, form, and location of divisible assets during your divorce. Still, there is no ban on your suggesting that all such property be added in when you are parceling out the assets you have acquired during your marriage years.

Sometimes buried treasure lurks in *"imaginary" rights in real estate.* Such assets can include property that is now being purchased but is still in escrow, an option to buy at a favorable rate or price, a long-term commercial lease that includes below-market terms, and even joint tenancies that you and your spouse may hold with another party. A simple example should suffice to illustrate this concept. Les's parents were growing elderly and wanted Les and Leslie to have sole ownership of their home without delay if they passed on. To establish a conduit through which the title could flow, they placed their home in joint tenancy with their son and his wife. When Les and Leslie decided to end their marriage, Les's parents were alive and well. Still, Leslie had a present interest—her name on the joint tenancy deed—in a piece of real estate that would pass to her in later years. Because neither Les nor his parents now wanted Leslie to share in the home's ownership, Les purchased Leslie's interest in the deed. How much was it worth? Since this is an intangible right that may never arrive (Leslie and/or Les could die before his parents do), the "price" is whatever Les and Leslie can agree upon. Leslie was understandably unwilling to give up a present interest in real estate for nothing; Les was willing to pay her something to get her name off the deed. Together, they agreed upon a value that in effect transferred to Leslie an additional portion of their other jointly owned property in exchange for her agreeing to cooperate in the drawing up of a new joint tenancy deed that would transfer the house only to Les upon his parents' death.

Other buried treasure hides in what can be called *business bonanzas*—the intangible aspects of any commercial concern or company that remain forgotten in many negotiations and resulting settlements. These business bonanzas can include:

- Work completed but not yet billed.
- Accounts receivable.
- Cyclical income or erratic payments on the verge of arriving, or payments whose receipt has been delayed by the person running the enterprise.
- Income tax credits acquired by the company.
- The value of the corporate name, its license fees or rights, its patent holdings, etc.
- Some market value in the corporate structure—some business people shop for "corporate shells"—that may have little worth as a profit-producing enterprise but is valuable because the shell provides a ready form in which to do business.
- Inventory, equipment, and work in progress. Apportioning the profits from such work is usually no more than a "calendar exercise," in which the work performed during marriage (joint effort) is compared to the duties completed after separation (separate property in many states).
- The goodwill implicit in the company, the expectation of future business based on past performance in the industry, profession, or community. Goodwill can attach to a sole proprietorship, a group-owned com-

> pany, a partnership, and even a corporation. Of course, in the last three instances, a spouse-owner/partner/officer will "own" only part of the goodwill value—other people working in the firm will also account for past performance and the expectation of future business.

To give you a good handle on this asset of goodwill, consider the dictionary definition: "Goodwill is the value of a business in patronage, reputation, or established popularity over and beyond its tangible assets."

In other words, the goodwill of a company or professional practice, for the purpose of a divorce, is the worth of that enterprise as a continuing concern. Such goodwill may be appraised by virtually any legitimate method that counts past results but does not take into account any projections or any effort after the separation date. Factors you can consider include the age of the professional, employee, or practitioner, his or her health, any past demonstrated earning power, any special professional standing or reputation in the community, and the length of time that the person has been practicing or operating his or her business.

Various accounting methods, some with esoteric names, can determine the value, including its goodwill, of a business or practice. Some approaches are income multipliers, capitalizing excess earnings, contract formulas, and market values. Any good certified public accountant, business appraiser, or commercial real estate agent can help in setting a valid value for the tangible and other assets in a concern. But here are some warnings to keep in mind when you are trying to assess a business's fair market price.

A recent sale of this or a comparable company or practice is good evidence of an accurate value, but an offer to buy or sell is merely someone's idea of what the asset is worth; it is not binding on either party. Consider contracts between your mate and the employer also only as evidence of your spouse's value to the company—other factors or developments since the signing of that contract may have increased your mate's interest in the firm. Still, such agreements can provide a financial starting point, as they may provide for a sum to be paid your mate if he/she retires or wishes to sell a partnership or ownership interest back to the firm. A tax assessor's guesstimate of the company's worth is merely one piece of evidence and may—because it is based on different factors—exclude the value of goodwill entirely!

Do not automatically believe your spouse's protestations that the business is not doing well, or is losing money, and therefore is valueless. Spouses not active in the business world can be easily misled into thinking that their spousal share of a company's value is one-half the amount that this firm would sell for on the open market. Not at all. *The determining price is the value that your mate places in continuing to operate that firm as his or her separate property after your divorce.* Perhaps it has tremendous value to him as a losing proposition because it provides a tax write off. Maybe a large project is pending that only her firm can handle. Sometimes even a failing enterprise has value because someone else wants to do business under that corporate name, or wishes to buy into an existing corporation without having to process the initial paperwork and face possible delays. In general, then, it is one-half of the amount that your mate would pay for sole ownership that sets the dollar value of your share.

Lastly, if your mate is a professional and claims that the ethics of his or her trade preclude the sale of the practice, remind him or her that this ban applies only to a sale to another practitioner—it does not cut off your right to receive a sum of cash or additional property to "sign off" on a mate's private practice or clientele.

While we're on the topic of values often left out of sight and out of the settlement, don't overlook the profits that certain *bookkeeping strategies* can add. For example, when appraising a spouse's business or company, switch from a cash basis to an accrual basis for evaluation purposes. What's the difference? A cash-basis appraisal takes into consideration only the income physically present at the time an evaluation is done—the funds in the till, as it were. However, evaluating a company, firm, or practice by including all the monies due for work already performed is known as the accrual method, and seems far more accurate a view. This approach is legitimate even if your mate is a "cash-basis" taxpayer—one who does not count income until it arrives. In fact, most of us are cash-basis tax payers. We don't pay income taxes on money until it is received. It's easy to see, however, that a business owner could easily delay a billing, or could ask people who owed him money to pay only after the business had been evaluated. If such an evaluation considered only the dollars "in the till" at the time an appraisal occurred, the fair market value of a firm could run well below "fair." However, by having your appraiser add in the value of all funds due and payable for work performed before the separation date, you can fatten the worth of the business as an asset and dramatically increase your share in it. Of course, if business conditions (or your mate's manipulations) have depressed the company's future earning power, and little income remains unreceived at evaluation date, instruct your appraiser to look to past years for a more accurate evaluation of the firm's true worth.

There are many different ways a bookkeeper can compute a business's value: fair market value, book value, adjusted book value, net book value, replacement value, depreciated value, going-concern liquidation value, salvage value, and even empty corporate shell value. The rule to remember is that any figure arrived at should also reflect a spouse's desire to keep this property and/or operate it alone after your final decree. To get a beginning value of a mate's business or practice, try one or more of these do-it-yourself approaches.

1. Review any contract your mate may have with employees that provides for them to pay a certain sum to the owner/operator's estate.
2. See if your spouse's employer carries "key man insurance" on your spouse. If your mate plays a major role in his or her firm, that employer will often maintain an insurance policy to provide the company with funds to "buy you out" if your spouse dies and his/her ownership interest in the firm passes to you. Because the other partners in the firm don't want to deal with a grieving "outsider" in the event of such a death, they purchase coverage sufficient to buy back any business interest that passes after death, insuring their ability to run the firm without considering you. Remember that their actions aren't personal—they're simply making a good business decision. But in doing so, they've provided you with an "instant assessment" (via the amount of insurance coverage) of the value that "those in the know" have placed on your spouse's ownership share.
3. Ask a businesslike friend to call your mate, saying that a client of the caller's has expressed an interest in purchasing the firm. Your friend insists that the client's identity cannot be disclosed but that he would consider buying the commercial concern if the price were right. How much is your spouse asking for all ownership rights (or for his or her share, if such a divided sale is feasible)?
4. Some publications (try the reference librarian or a friend in the insurance industry) estimate the value of certain types of busi-

nesses or practices in certain fields, taking into account the clientele, inventory, type of firm, length of time in business, capitalization and other factors.

5. Some Internal Revenue personnel are skilled at estimating a taxpayer's net worth or income by working backward from a specific life-style. Sometimes a multiple of a company's earnings can provide an accurate indication of its worth.

Other publications and services make a habit of estimating a company's value within certain categories. These include *Dun & Bradstreet*, the *Manufacturer's Register*, and some insurance industry guides. To do effective research, learn what the business grosses, how long it has been operating, the number of employees, the type of service(s) that it provides, the geographic area it serves, and any other factors that could affect this asset's value.

Other hidden wealth that is frequently forgotten includes *rights in real and personal property*. Sometimes these treasures lurk in cupboards and drawers and emerge only for special occasions. Such everyday loot includes silverware, china, crystal, and antique or rare or valuable serving trays. If you're unsure of the true value of your serving pieces or silverware and if some time has passed since you received or purchased the items, call a local department or specialty store, ask to speak to a salesperson who's been in that field for some time, and ask what your pattern or setting is selling for these days. If you feel that there will be trouble convincing your spouse of this value, ask for a letter from the salesperson, or take a quick photograph of a display of your pattern with the current price prominently displayed. If you're lost when it comes to estimating the value of furnishings and think that a piece might be worth something, buy or borrow Emyl Jenkins's *Why You're Richer Than You Think*, (Rawson, Wade, $15.95 in hardcover). Does this price seem high? A walnut corner cupboard that cost about $250 in 1966 may today sell for more than $1,300! The book contains, according to one review, "step-by-step instructions for compiling written and photographic inventories of your household items and valuables, along with advice on how to determine the replacement value of possessions." Other property you might forget in the trauma of preparing for a divorce includes:

a. Stocks, debentures, and bonds.
b. Loans extended to others and now owed to your mate or you.

c. Investments with no interim payments to you (trust deeds, limited-partnership payoffs, personal loans with balloon payments, etc.).

d. "Office gold," like artworks, sculpture, antiques, furnishings that belong to you or your mate, special lamps, Oriental or other valuable carpeting, tapestries, weavings or wall decorations; drawings, graphics, and multiples (prints) of all kinds; rare or expensive reference books, a personal library, office equipment, if owned by the company, and even a small refrigerator; crystal, liquor, china, or other serving implements, if your mate or you often entertained during business hours. Office gold can also include any business papers of interest to a museum, library, or institution (such a recipient might not purchase such items, but if they are donated the institution can document the items' value, which can dramatically reduce a tax overload), stock options (exercised or not), deferred salary that your spouse has not yet received, trade names and copyrights, tailored fringe benefits (and any cash value for such benefits not used by your spouse), and even tax-loss carry-forwards that a mate may use to offset earnings in years to come.

e. Financial treasure can exist in foreign accounts (other countries and other states), in a person's status as the beneficiary of a trust, in being part or full owner of an account ostensibly held in the name of another, in bonds that show investment in your home or other states (often held in the broker's office, or in that other state), in safe-deposit box(es), and in the right to withdraw from a bank or savings account on which another name or names appear. Include any unreceived stock dividends, any credit balances on charge accounts, and deposits with utility companies if you intend to move out of the apartment or family home. Don't overlook children's savings accounts, uncashed U.S. Savings Bonds, any tax refunds due but unpaid, government bonds or income from federal agencies, gift certificates and even unused airline tickets. If you're sure that such bonanzas couldn't happen to you, keep in mind that according to a recent issue of *Changing Times* magazine, about 10 percent of all Americans may be entitled to some unclaimed property. A good number will never connect with their stored loot because many asset holders regularly disregard the search statutes, which define an asset holder's obligation to locate beneficiaries, and others exert little effort to find the true owners of forgotten assets.

To find potential assets, write to the unclaimed property or treasurer's office in your state or any other relevant state. Be ready to offer proof of ownership, any maiden or former names, and the names of people from whom you inherited.

If you think that an ancester who's gone on before may have left some insurance funds for your here and now, write to the American Council of Life Insurance, 1850 K St., N.W. Washington, D.C. 20006 and ask for a free policy search.

Sometimes, *title companies* will help you uncover assets that could fund a post divorce life. These local title companies will often punch up computer searches under your spouse's name and provide a rundown on all real estate held by your mate. Include calls to the title company's other branches in adjacent counties to extend your search to all reasonable boundaries. With this call you also may be able to learn the names of any other owner(s), the current market value of the property, and the size and number of any mortgages or trust deeds recorded against the asset.

Every state's *record-keeping offices* include one that maintains creditors' security agreements. These documents outline how much a borrower has received and what asset the borrower has pledged as security for the loan. It is entirely possible that you may discover assets pledged as security that you didn't know your spouse possessed. You may also uncover records that indicate your mate is a creditor— someone who owns a right to foreclose on another's property if the borrower lapses in servicing the debt. This right to take ownership of another's goods to ensure repayment of a debt is an asset that may benefit you during an allocation or division as a result of divorce. Of course, you may also receive disturbing news: an asset that you always regarded as belonging to both of you may have been pledged by your mate to float a loan that is benefiting him or her alone. This obligation may drastically reduce the net value of a mutual asset. But even bad news like this can serve a good purpose: imagine agreeing to take an asset that you assumed was owned free and clear and finding that a good deal of its value was pledged to a stranger until your ex-teammate paid off the balance on a debt. If your ex-spouse does not make payments, that stranger could levy on the asset tokenly in your possession. How hard will your former helpmeet work to pay off a debt that, if ignored, will cost him or her not a jot? You know the answer to that.

Bankers and friends in *the financial community* can help you obtain a credit report, a Dun & Bradstreet overview, or provide other insights into the true asset picture of the marital community you share.

The *local record-keeping authority* showing the true ownership of businesses operating under cover names can reveal other assets. As you may know, a person doing business through a firm that does not bear his or her own name must register with the county to assist anyone seeking the true owner(s). Your mate may own, in whole or part, profitable business ventures that remain unknown to you. Another good source for information on secret business interests is your city or county's licensing bureau.

Court records in the county where your spouse previously won his or her marital freedom can contain assets for you. Papers of a prior divorce can reveal assets that your mate fought for during a hearing or trial but never transferred to his or her new home. The file may also reveal an allocation or confirmation of separate property that your mate never shared with you—which you might yet transmute to joint ownership before divorce proceedings begin. Court files—which, unless sealed, remain open to public review—may show that your mate is entitled to child and/or spousal support that he or she has allowed to lapse or has never pursued. If you have been helping to meet monthly obligations without the aid of this support, urge your mate to enforce these rights and collect any arrearages so that you can share in any acquisition before separation day.

The department of motor vehicles (or other agency that registers vehicle ownership in your state) may show you records listing automobiles, trucks, campers, vans, trailers, dune buggies, motorcycles or other wheeled vehicles that you did not know he, she, or the both of you owned.

For a quick idea of the family vehicles' worth, visit your local library and peruse the *Kelley Blue Book*. It will provide both retail and wholesale values for almost all makes, models, and years. After averaging the retail and wholesale values quoted for each car or vehicle, subtract from each any debt remaining. The result is the net value of each vehicle, but don't be disappointed if you find that you owe more than a car is worth. Because of cars' rapid depreciation and the high interest rates on car loans, it is customary to discover that you owe more than you own. Sometimes, however, you can uncover a classic or near-classic vehicle that is worth more than you could have guessed. Remember that the *Kelley Blue Book* may treat such a treasure merely as an old car, so check with some local classic auto dealers to avoid overlooking a four-wheeled find.

Title companies and real estate brokers remain good sources for determining exactly how much your home (or other real estate) would bring on the open market. Why should this asset and its worth appear as a form of hidden treasure? Because most people assessing the market value of their own homes set the figure too low. If you don't have a current, well-informed idea of your residence's fair price, call a local title company, or contact several local and ethical real estate dealers and ask each to send a salesperson to walk through the premises and make an informed estimate of value. If this would prove too awkward, see if a local realtor will provide you with an estimate based on reviewing, by computer or by personal study, comparable homes that have been sold recently in your area. If he or she is still available, call the realtor who sold the house to you, describe any changes or improvements, and the home's current condition, then ask for an updated estimate via telephone alone. Be careful not to limit your estimate to the figure quoted on your last tax assessor's bill, neighborhood gossip, or your own common sense after a quick review of your local paper's real estate pages.

A home ranks as one of the major assets (and sometimes, the only large asset) in most divorces—don't cheat yourself by undervaluing this property.

In some cases, *intangible goodies* fall between the cracks when a couple (and their lawyers) sit down to negotiate a fair settlement. Among these are diplomas, graduate degrees, certifications, and special training; because of recent legal developments, these may now be includable in the wealth of a marital partnership. Until now, such assets, even if gained during the marriage years, accompanied the student into his or her new life. Little if any offset ever compensated the supportive (and supporting) mate who helped the other obtain additional schooling or skills. After sometimes years of deprivation and hard work, a nonstudent spouse faced postdivorce bills with often limited resources and little earning power. In recent months, a California court joined others in Iowa, Oklahoma, Kentucky, New Jersey and elsewhere in declaring that a husband whose wife had helped put him through medical school now owed her some sort of compensation for the sacrifices involved. Though the California decision is now on appeal, you can ask for a share in the value of such a decree. If you succeed, you may avoid the unfairness of one spouse's enjoying a much greater earning power that was gained, in part, through the efforts of a mate.

If your marriage contains one or more special degrees, consider the case of California's Janet and Mark Sullivan to see if their example can benefit you. Janet helped her young husband through medical school by doing office work, but shortly after Mark's residency, he filed for divorce and opened his urology office in Orange County. Blessed with some secondhand furniture and two elderly cars (neither of which was paid for at the filing), Janet was awarded $500 as her share of the community property by the judge who presided over the divorce. On appeal, Mrs. Sullivan argued that Mark's medical education and the future earning potential his degree gave him represented a community asset in which she should share in some way. The appellate court agreed and accepted an estimate of the degree's worth of $660,000. A final hearing by the California Supreme Court should determine whether such an asset is indeed an asset of the community or whether some offset should be decreed before such property is awarded to the learning spouse. As a consequence, the form and extent of payment remain unspecified at this time. Avenues of possible sharing include a larger share of the community property, a more generous child and/or spousal support allotment, an outright gift or allocation, or a schedule of equalization payments, perhaps based on the proportion of effort that Janet provided, or a reimbursement of the monies she expended to support Mark's educational goals. As the doctor's wife-turned-financial-analyst explains it, "I made an investment," and she now seeks to be repaid as a continuing partner in the doctor-operated going concern.

In a New Jersey case, Superior Court Judge Conrad W. Krafte set a value of $306,000 on Dr. Robert Lynn's medical degree after a three-week trial. In addition to awarding Mrs. Lynn alimony, he allocated $60,000 as her share of her husband's M.D. As Judge Krafte phrased it in an Associated Press story, Bonnie Lynn's "contribution, both financially and emotionally, to the furtherance of plaintiff's educational goals and attainment of his dream—a license to practice medicine and surgery—was crucial, substantial and incontrovertible."

In both these cases the degree was newly obtained and the supporting partner would never recoup any benefits (save a higher support payment) from the extra education. In other cases, where one spouse has been operating as a surgeon, a therapist, a veterinarian, or other advanced-degree specialist for some time and both mates have prospered from the education obtained, recovery may well remain limited or even be disallowed. Should this discourage you? If you negotiate a settlement, not at all! Keep in mind that one of you will be carrying away more earning muscle and will soon enjoy a better life-style with a rosier future. If you're not that lucky spouse, try to bargain for some repayment if you helped your mate through school. To negotiate is to profit without legal precedents if the goals strike you as fair and the principles apply to your case, your spouse, and you.

Sometimes, we're not sure that treasure lies hidden, but we're pretty certain that the *treasure maps* in our relationship may lead to buried loot. Treasure maps consist of those clues sprinkled throughout any marriage that indicate hidden wealth. Little emotional flags, nagging instincts, overheard conversations, mysterious-looking mail, changes in behavior—all of these and more form the "directions" to your personal treasure chests.

The first avenue to secret assets lies in an approach called "candlelight and questions." If you really need an explanation of this strategy, you've lost the sense of romance that led you down the aisle. Even if you no longer feel tender toward your mate, muster some instinctive skills and add fresh flowers to the table setting. Next, light some candles, ask pertinent questions about your spouse's business day, learning everything you can, and praise, praise, *praise*. No human being ever told more than one secret to a critical audience, so bite your tongue and play it smart. Information about business interests, investments, other companies, joint ventures, and even swollen savings accounts could provide your something sweet for dessert.

While you will want to employ a more straightforward approach in dealing with others, you can still gain valuable asset insights from a mate's business associates, from mutual friends, from people calling for your spouse, and by driving by or visting the names and addresses appearing on business correspondence that comes to your home.

Another map may lie in your professional relationship with an insurance agent. If your spouse has dealt with a single agent for years, ask about any cash or surrender value in all life insurance policies (don't mention, at this stage that a divorce may occur . . . simply voice an interest in adequate coverage and find out whether any accumulated monies are earning top dollar where they are). In addition, ask the agent or company for a copy of any home-owner's policy and any coverage for home furnishings or personal property in your spouse's name. An unusually high coverage level should provide a hint that buried treasure may lie concealed with that junk in the garage. Other documents, called inland marine policies, or personal floater policies, often insure investments, antiques, special jewelry, and valuable collections that your spouse may be keeping at the house. Some of these policies list the items covered in such detail, including the estimated values of each piece of property, that they provide excellent evidence of actual worth and form a valid start for outlining asset division and allocation. Such policies are particularly helpful if the value estimates have been recently updated and if the items covered would be difficult to appraise accurately or impossible to remove from the home for evaluation by an expert.

If you apply yourself to applications, you may reap rich rewards. Every time your mate fills out a form to gain a line of credit, a loan, a charge account, or a credit card, he or she will paint the most positive possible financial picture. Such forms can therefore reveal hidden assets, hidden income, additional business interests, and collateral you may know nothing about. Financial "boasting" is natural. High earning ability and net worth make most of us feel good about ourselves, and your mate is probably no exception. If he or she insists on bragging on paper, you may as well profit from it.

Some people keep copies of such forms and applications at home or at the office. Others leave the original with the institution they're pitching for that credit card or loan. If you have a joint account at any institution, ask to see the company's file on you and/or your spouse. If you share a credit card, seek out the store's credit file and request a viewing. If all else fails, obtain a credit report from one of the major credit-checking services and use their list of creditors to track down other parties to whom your spouse has made applications for credit; they might allow you to verify your information by looking at their files.

A Treasure Map may also lurk in your spouse's office. By reviewing and copying your mate's appointment book, you can substantiate the volume of business, the existence of creditors or borrowers (people who owe money or goods to your mate), the pace and flow of income-generating appointments, and other possible business or investment ventures. In one case, a wife who knew she was unfamiliar with her husband's law practice visited his office one day while he was absent, and copied just one telling sheet from each of his client files. Her amount of copying was virtually undetectable, she completed her mission within an hour, it cost her no funds, and she built a solid case for a high appraisal of this practice's value. If you take this route, make sure that the sheet you choose to copy has a current date, contains the name of the client or patient, and shows the case number and the court where filed (and perhaps the nature of the matter for which your spouse was retained). If your mate asks clients or patients to sign a retainer agreement outlining payment terms, such copies could prove helpful as well.

If you uncover these maps after separation or during legal proceedings, have your attorney subpoena all financial information from any financial institution from which you are seeking information about checking or savings accounts. You may react with delight to the fund of potential treasure this approach can unearth.

While pursuing that bank or savings statement, look for service charges that could mean the institution is collecting payments on a promisory note or trust deed for the benefit of your spouse. Check the form for any indication of a regular charge for a safe-deposit box. View regular withdrawals as potential payments on a hidden asset or business interest. Heavy withdrawals—regular or erratic, recent or not—could suggest waste or misappropriation during the marriage that should be repaid, in part, to you, without any balancing of assets to your spouse.

Systematic deposits of similar amounts could mean an income property, a dividend-paying stock, a money market account, or some other asset that is generating funds and in which you should share.

Pirates for hire can provide excellent professional tracking aid, frequently for a reasonable cost. By utilizing records, instituting searches, making telephone calls, and furnishing "finder's fees" to key people within certain large corporations, these "asset bloodhounds" can often uncover a spouse's real estate, life insurance policies, cars and other vehicles, bank accounts, investments, business interests, and other property. These professionals advertise in law newspapers (check your local law library or a large news vendor, or visit a nearby law school), in legal journals (try the reference librarian at your local branch or central outlet), a general newspaper's classified advertisement section, and via mailings to attorneys and legal personnel (ask a friend in the law community to watch for such mail and save one or two pieces for you). Also, check the Yellow Pages under detectives, search firms, and related services.

The way your spouse acts—his or her behavior patterns—may

also lead you to a treasure. Habits, interest, hobbies, and activities can point to buried gold. For example, a mate unusually close to neighbors, business associates, or other members of a hobby group may also join them in investments or lend them joint property that both of you may have by now forgotten you owned. In a different view, unexplained absences and sweaty returns may signal your spouse is having an affair, but more likely indicates an expenditure of marital effort to add value to an asset that your mate may hold in his or her name alone. Under many states' theories, perspiration is a community asset; any rise in a separate property's value due to your mate's efforts may belong in part to you.

Sometimes, a wallet or purse can offer clues to more wealth. In California, for example, wallet cards showing membership in the Screen Actors Guild, Screen Extras Guild, or the Writers or Directors Guild indicate current or past memberships that often entitle the holder to residuals for work in past movies and films. Residuals are payments made to the major participants in a filmed or videotaped production when that movie, special, or series is rerun. Such payments decrease with each subsequent showing, but can total a generous sum if the series, for example, is syndicated for reruns to numerous television stations across the country. If you can find no such cards but know that your spouse worked in one of these industries, notify the relevant organization to see if some accumulated residual payments or other rights have been languishing because office workers lost track of your mate. Though monies payable now for work done prior to the wedding remain separate property, income after separation is still community property if the work was performed during your marital partnership. In states less involved with film production, look for wallet-size cards from unions, guilds, clubs, or other organizations that may provide financial and other benefits for their members.

Occasionally, the key ring in a person's wallet or purse will provide a valuable clue. Unusual keys can mean items secreted in a safe-deposit box, a professional storage area, in an office safe, or with a friend. In one case, a young executive woman who failed to tell her husband about her most recent raise used the extra funds to purchase furniture in preparation for separation day. She stored each coffee table, chair, and pillow in her mother's garage, which she outfitted with a padlock, slipping its key onto the metal ring she always carried with her. One evening, while Ms. Exec showered, husband sorted through her purse to borrow car keys. Imagine his curiosity—and later surprise—at finding the unusual key and tracking down its location and use!

A regular check of your mate's reading habits may pay off as well. if you've married an engineer but your coffee table now bears periodicals on stamp collecting, stock market investments, antique gun ownership, or real estate news, your partner could be acquiring assets or profit rights in which you could—and should—share.

Unusual household activity may mean new business associates, a new asset, or a new investment venture. Tune in to unusual telephone calls and correspondence bearing return addresses from brokerage houses, law, or realty firms; stroll slowly by when your mate holds Saturday confabs with structured agendas in the living room, and note any gifts that could be a finder's fee or a welcome to an investment scheme.

Correspondence containing club membership dues or privileges, bar bills, or golf-green fees all indicate an interest in "property"—the right to utilize and enjoy a recreational facility of some kind. Even if your mate received the membership as a corporate perk or from a grateful employer, this asset probably belongs partly to you (perspiration is community property), and you can ask for funds or other property if your spouse intends to own alone such a membership after you part.

Treasure maps may even lurk in your imagination: simply think where *you* would hide extra assets, funds, or property. Have you checked the garage, the attic and basement, all car trunks and glove compartments, closets, storage areas, second homes, tool sheds, and any other areas you might use to keep an asset out of sight or simply out of the way.

While you're searching some of the mustier, memory-laden areas of your home, drag out the family Bible and scan its first pages for recorded marriages, births, and deaths among your relatives and those of your spouse. Besides a pleasant stroll down yesteryear lanes, this exercise can . . .

—reveal strong ties to other states or countries where additional assets, belonging in whole or part to your mate, should be "remembered" when you negotiate a marital settlement pact.

—show the possibility of an inheritance due in the near future from the other side of the family or from yours.

—remind you of a forgotten debt owed to you.

Consider all aspects of your spouse's occupation to see if wealth may hover there. One husband, for example, discovered that his wife, a successful dentist, routinely ordered Kruggerand coins under the guise of purchasing gold supplies for her practice. Because the medallions stayed in the office safe, a less aware mate could have overlooked this asset in settling the property issues.

Other people carry a treasure in their face or name because they sell (or could sell) endorsements or testimonials for products, or they work (or have worked) successfully in promoting products via radio, newspapers, or television ads. If you qualified as this party's teammate in life while that reputation, name, expertise, or whatever grew to full flower, then why not suggest that you share in an asset's value that soon only your successor will be able to claim and enjoy.

If one of your mate's while-married-to-you past occupations includes a stint in the armed services, a benefit of some kind may be due. See if that benefit can be turned into cash that you can direct to a mutually beneficial purchase or into a joint account.

In some states, legal presumptions can aid you in gaining additional property during a divorce. In California, for example, the court presumes that any real estate received by a woman prior to January 1, 1975, is her separate property if the deed rests in her name alone—even if the woman was married at the time. To overcome that presumption, her husband would have to show a separate agreement, a later deed that included his name, his financial contribution to the purchase, or some other evidence justifying an ownership share.

If you're a husband whose wife enjoys sole title to real estate received before the start of 1975 (including any leasehold of one year or more), and you would prefer to collect on an ownership share, try to get title changed to include your moniker before any marital breach can occur.

Even if you don't live in California, you may prove able to profit from such presumptions, which the courts regard as "legal conclusions." You can often uncover these presumptions because they are clearly stated in the portion of your state's code that governs marriage, separation, divorce, and other aspects of family law. Such statutes usually appear in a state's civil code as in The California Civil Code. If library card catalogs only confuse you, visit your nearest law library and ask the research or reference librarian for his or her help. You may even find such a code at your local library, if sufficiently large. If the applicable code sections appear lengthy, copy them for later reading, and for reference or proof if your spouse disagrees.

Keep in mind that even if you cannot convert a mate's separate property to a jointly owned asset, your spouse's separate wealth, once uncovered, can provide extra income for larger child and/or spousal support. Therefore, use the tips and treasure maps throughout this 90-day treasure search to increse commonly owned wealth, to discover forgotten property of your own (which you certainly know how to protect by now), and to maximize your spouse's holdings so that you can profit from them even after the final decree.

Now that you've got your mitts (or at least your eye) on some of the previously hidden assets of your marital partnership, study these suggestions to determine—easily, accurately, cheaply, and without leaving home—what some of this property is really worth.

All you need is a telephone, camera, envelopes, and postage stamps. You may occasionally invite an appraiser or expert to keep you company. If you *want* to make an outing, a trip to the local library may prove as far as you need go. The following series of experts and appraisal possibilities can bring treasure to your door, but make careful note at this section's close of some common pitfalls.

First, good sources for informal but accurate appraisals are people who sell, repair, or restore the item you wish evaluated. Check the Yellow Pages and local news ads, or ask friends who own similar property whom they call for these services.

Second, consult publications offering insights, news, and views. These include the *Kelley Blue Book* for automobile valuations, books appraising collectibles, tomes listing the worth of antiques, and advice columns written by local experts, many of which may appear in your local paper or special newspaper section. Columnists specializing in financial and property areas write for *Money* and *Changing Times* magazines and for nationwide supplements that accompany your Sunday newspaper. Most solicit questions from readers and may answer questions privately as well as in their column copy.

Third, telephone sources include people whom you can call to have certain property appraised over the phone. These include auctioneers, antique dealers, art gallery owners, pension plan administrators (but don't forgo an estimate by a trained actuary in this field), insurance agents, car salespeople, and realtors. Other telephone sources are stockbrokers, accountants, and bankers. You may even find it helpful to call an officer of the company that makes the asset or product you wish to evaluate.

Fourth, try some good appraisal specialists like owners of similar property, salespeople in specialty or department stores, and dealers in classic cars and used furniture.

Fifth, "neighborhood experts" can play a valuable role in assessing a property's value. For example, people involved in a hobby or industry that has a bearing on the asset, can include land and home owners in your vicinity—even fellow cocktail party guests, if they are familiar with your neighborhood and are inclined to gossip about local development and recent property sales. In fact, these easily approachable friends can prove unique sources of esoteric information.

For instance, when Harvey moved his years-old electric train set into the garage and began an almost nightly worship of tiny switches and cars, Helen evaluated their fading relationship and decided that divorce seemed inevitable. Reasoning that others who enjoyed train sets could do so only in the garages of this neighborhood's no-recreation-room tract homes, Helen waited for evening one summer weekday and started a slow tour of adjacent streets. Within three blocks, Helen found another train enthusiast. One half hour of conversation later, she had a comprehensive and accurate idea of what Harvey's hobby was worth. In negotiations, Helen offered to let Harvey keep every flatcar, bridge, and bush . . . if she could have sole ownership of a jointly owned antique she had always loved. When Harvey protested that the chiffonier's value outweighed his ancient Lionels, Helen directed him to the helpful neighbor, who quickly apprised Harvey of the true (and hefty) market price his set could bring.

Of course, if Helen's initial search had proved fruitless, she could have contacted a local hobby club or written or called a nearby hobby shop . . . perhaps the one whose name appeared on those sales slips that Harvey carried home.

In another case, a husband's drive through the outskirts of town revealed a neighbor whose chassis-packed yard showed a car-restoration business in full swing. Stopping for a few minutes, this man asked the craftsman to zip by his residence within the next week and eyeball-evaluate a 1952 Hudson parked on the street outside his front door. Receiving a "windshield quote" enabled this couple to put a value on the car, and helped them reach an agreement about other property they wanted to sell, allocate, or divide.

Six, you may want to call upon court personnel if your case has gone to hearings or to trial. These experts, named on lists kept by the court, offer appraisals of houses, household furnishings, corporations, partnership rights, other business interests, patent rights, equipment, currency, stamps, securities, and a wide range of other assets. Asking help from these professionals has several advantages: fees remain reasonable, and usually the report can be introduced into evidence without having to bring in the expert to testify to the finding's accuracy or its admissibility into evidence, thus saving costs for both parties. Deciding on a single such expert, who remains beyond the control of either spouse, also eliminates a war of words when "his" and "her" appraisers take the stand to argue over value.

The seventh category of appraiser includes eggheads—people knowledgeable in a select and often narrow area. Museum curators, artists, sculptors, art dealers, department heads at local colleges and universities, and other heads of specialized-learning, cultural, or service centers form an intellectually muscular group that can offer the definitive words on an unusual piece of property.

Eighth, remember that *you* may qualify as an accurate appraiser of an asset's value. Special knowledge is important (are you the East Coast expert on rubber widgets?), and the court may well allow you to testify about the value of your home. To make sure you have a good grasp of this asset's current value, scan real estate pages, tune in to local gossip, visit open houses of similar residences in your neighborhood, and stay informed.

Make sure that you keep the following in mind: finding and evaluating assets sometimes takes you only two-thirds of the way home. You may need some objective evidence of a property's worth to convince a doubting spouse. Such hard proof of an asset's value can take the form of computer printouts of comparable, recent home sales, a written appraisal by a coin or gem expert, or a copy of any insurance policy obtained to cover specific items (furs, jewelry, a collection, art, or antiques) that you keep at home. Other hard evidence includes proof of recent sales of comparable assets, a newspaper report of an auction sale of an item just like yours, or a brochure from a show or exhibition listing prices on work that is very similar to something you own. Make sure that any comparison is of a *recent* sale or trade and that the item involved is very close in size, age, style, etc. to one that you own. You can still find more relatively objective evidence in any agreement fixing the value of a partnership or other ownership interest if the party falls ill, dies, or decides to retire or withdraw. If *you* are the employee in this case, however, take a lesson from one attorney who, in the throes of a bitter divorce, persuaded his partners to value his interest in the law firm at a single dollar. Some years later, and long after the final decree, this legal eagle sought to withdraw from the firm and set up a practice of his own. Imagine his surprise when his peers offered him a dollar bill and told him "goodbuy"! Now that you've enjoyed a good chuckle, note the moral of this tale: attempts to hide or devalue property in which your spouse deserves a share can often backfire. It is not unusual for a good Marital Settlement Agreement or Final Judgment to include a term which allows a cheated spouse to share in any later-discovered asset—at an often-increased value on or near the date of discovery. In addition, divorce cases reopened on charges of fraud can prove costly to a mate who once thought him- or herself a clever manipulator.

When gathering information on assets to prepare for negotiation or trial, try to avoid falling into these common (and costly) traps. None of the following estimations of value is accurate or binding. Each may represent *evidence* of an object's worth, but none, taken alone, should serve as evidence of an asset's value. These frequent problem causers are:

1. Offers to buy
2. Offers to sell
3. Any tax assessor's estimate of valuation

Now that you have followed all your treasure maps and other suggestions and gathered your 90-day treasure trove, add any lately discovered items to the asset list outlined in Chapter One. Wouldn't it be a shame to use creativity, imagination, and guts to gather all this information and proof, and then forget to include extra assets in the overall list of assets that will form the basis of your negotiations with your spouse?

Even assets we cannot see, smell, touch, or weigh often have enormous financial value. Don't discount them as "imaginary" gains or leave them out of the bargaining process or out of your final terms.

In addition to including *all* the assets in Chapter One's list, consider arranging now—during property, asset, and debt negotiations—for financial support for you and/or any children in the years to come. You can ensure your rights to collect *derivative* Social Security benefits if your marriage lasts at least 10 years from the wedding day to the final decree. You may also succeed in bargaining now for a share of your spouse's Railroad Retirement Act benefits, payable in later years. Though RRA benefits remain separate property (under federal law, which is binding on all states), your mate can agree to share such monthly allotments with you as they arrive. Of course, if such income lies too far in the future, you may want to negotiate for an offset based on a fairness approach. Even if your spouse receives payments now or will in the next few months, have your mate sign certain forms ordering the paying institution to pay you directly, so that you can wriggle out from under an ex-mate's financial thumb, thus avoiding plead-and-threaten sessions to collect your support.

Let's explore how you can hold on to more of the assets, before and after allocation, by taking advantage of the tax laws. First, if your share of the goodies includes an item purchased only shortly before the separation and you intend to sell that asset and reap a profit from the sale, hold it for a year or more, to enjoy a lower tax assessment. Second, consider income averaging in the year following receipt of any lump sum that is *not* a division of community property. Third, if you get the house, and you wish to put it on the market, but you haven't yet occupied it for a total of 2 years, hold off completing the sale until 2 years have passed. If you have already sold the family home, invest an amount equal to your half of any profit in another principal residence within 24 months of finalizing that sale. You do not have to use the same dollars, nor must you purchase a residence that sells for as much or more than your old pad. The Internal Revenue Service merely wants you to commit to buying a new place that equals *your share* of the profit realized on the previous sale.

Fourth, if you receive alimony (sometimes called spousal support or spousal maintenance), consider opening an Individual Retirement Account. Such accounts are available to all individuals now, whether or not you're covered by a pension or retirement plan at your place of employment. These IRA's provide a government-endorsed means of directing present income into a savings or investment plan without paying taxes on it until you retire at the age of 59½. At that later time, it is presumed that you will be in a lower tax bracket because of retirement or lower earning ability. Although you can withdraw your funds before reaching this age, you will pay a penalty for sums taken out too soon. For that reason, you should entrust to an Individual Retirement Account only those funds that you don't foresee needing for some years to come.

In choosing the right type of IRA for you, note that some of these accounts are run by banks or savings and loans, who invest your funds conservatively but in insured opportunities. Other IRA's are self-directed, so that you can purchase stocks, real estate, or limited partnerships with your funds, and move your monies around to take advantage of promising investment possibilities. The latter course requires more financial knowledge, and involves more risk; choose the path that better suits your personality. Remember that your IRA houses your retirement fund; it may prove better to end up safe than sorry.

Because your spousal support counts as income (remember you must pay taxes if you're the receiving party), you can avoid paying income tax now on these sums by directing the monthly or lump-sum payments directly into your IRA. Ask your banker or a friend knowledgeable in finances about opening such an account and determining which investment vehicle will best suit your current tax bracket, age, health, and retirement plans.

While considering IRA's: any beneficiary of a work-related pension plan who receives cash in a lump sum upon retirement can put the liquid assets into an Individual Retirement Account without paying taxes on the sum paid out.

Fifth, so long as you rate as a signatory on any mortgage or trust deed agreement relating to real estate, you can write off for income tax purposes your portion of any taxes and interest paid. Often, a marital settlement agreement will spell out what fraction of such deductions will be claimed by which paying party. Time your final decree so that you can take full advantage of declared losses and gains in jointly owned property. Both are affected by the date the court records your final decree, so plan now, with the help of an experienced family-law attorney or certified public accountant, to adhere to a savvy schedule in transferring title between yourselves.

Your state (like California) may expressly bar any tax reassessment of a family residence if title changes hands between *married* people. However, the residence is fair game for a higher tax bite if one "legal stranger" takes title from the other. So transfer the property title before your divorce becomes final. Don't find yourself the divorced, proud, sole owner of a home that costs you more—in suddenly higher taxes—than you bargained for.

If you remember only one thing from reviewing the 90-day treasure trove, make it this: relying solely on your mate for information about the assets in your marriage or their accurate value can prove a costly—and sometimes uncorrectable—mistake. Why?

- Because your spouse may not harbor tender feelings for you any more nor think of you as a teammate; or he or she may want to advertise what he or she has earned alone.
- Because even the court in your state (if you've proceeded that far in your case) may not compel a spouse to reveal all, reasoning that no "fiduciary duty" or care is owed the other half of a now-parted couple.
- Because even a friendly or unsuspecting spouse may not *know* the full extent of marital assets, may overlook or fail to mention an out-of-sight-out-of-discussion piece of property, and may have no concept of an asset's current fair market value.
- Because relying on another for crucial information that you can obtain for yourself is taking a passive role in one of the biggest undertakings of your life.
- Because you will gain self-esteem, financial knowledge, bargaining savvy, and problem-solving skills that will prove powerful allies throughout the rest of your life.
- Because of dozens of reasons you will think of for yourself if you're honest in accepting divorce and in accepting sole responsibility for YOU.

4

Final-Weeks' Insurance for a Profitable Divorce

IN THESE final weeks before separation, even though it will seem that time is growing short, you will want to take careful steps to ensure that the court will have jurisdiction over your mate, will have sufficient evidence to award you adequate child and/or spousal support, and will know enough about your assets to give you, if at all possible, a sure-to-pay support source that can remain beyond your partner's control.

Chapter Four will lead you through the steps to obtaining good legal advice (available free of charge) and to choosing the right attorney for you.

This chapter also includes an "insurance checklist" that will cover far more than policy coverage; you will learn of ways to obtain credit and to protect yourself from a spouse's bad-pay record or habits; get a quick look at some of the tax laws affecting divorcing parties, and read some tips on avoiding expensive tax traps. It provides you with avenues to some powerful skills and awakens you to the importance of choosing priorities and making careful—but imaginative—plans for a happier, smoother, more profitable divorce.

You may have noted several references to the court and to "giving the court power" to help you. Does this mean that you should abandon the idea of negotiating with your spouse for an out-of-court settlement? Never! From the day you decide that divorce seems inevitable until the last moment of trial (if you *must* go to court), try to make a deal that is fair—or a little more than fair—for you without resorting to the courts.

Why? Because court procedures tend to be traumatic, time-consuming (you may wait for hours or even days until a judge or other hearing officer is available for your case), and ultimately unsatisfying. Tensions run high in court, and there is little pleasure in hashing out the details of your case for the court recorder and an audience of strangers. To add to your discomfort, your legal fees will mount whether you are in trial or merely warming a bench in the courthouse hall over several hours or even days while you wait, with your spouse and two attorneys, for a forum or hearing officer to adjudicate your case. Today, such fees can total $1,000 or more per attorney, per day. Even after all this, you may find even a fair decision unsatisfying because *you* had no opportunity to tailor a judgment to the needs of your particular case. Even a skilled judge remains a stranger to the details in your divorce. He or she can only divide with a cleaver what you and your mate can carve up with a scalpel. Only you really know what you want from this parting, and in the most ultimate and personal sense, you and your mate have the solutions within you to orchestrate the kind of settlement that will suit the two of you. You do need an attorney to guide you through the legal jargon, to take advantage of local laws, to save you tax funds, and to draft and review any documents before you sign them or file them with the court. But, knowing your mate, your needs, and your goals as you do, you can sculpt the basics of an agreement better than anyone else!

For these reasons, negotiate however, wherever, and whenever you can. The only time *not* to attempt or continue negotiations directly with your spouse is when he or she will no longer communicate with you in writing, by telephone, or face to face; or when it becomes obvious that your spouse will negotiate only so long as you keep giving in. You do not negotiate to lose . . . but to win. Even if you can no longer talk with your mate, or his/her demands remain unreasonable, try to keep negotiating through your legal counselors. Keep in mind that your attorney is your employee, and your wishes should prevail. If you have a counselor who seems unwilling to bargain, or who expresses the belief that everything should be decided in court, find another gladiator—one whose muscular power lies in bargaining skills and making creative suggestions helpful to your spouse and you.

Now, let's get on with this chapter's special topics, including our first: obtaining "jurisdictional muscle" over your spouse. Whether you end up in court or not, your mate must be validly served with papers formally notifying him or her that a divorce action is pending. Unless you fulfill this notice requirement, you will be unable to obtain a divorce and you will limit the court's power over your spouse; if this happens you will never be able to impose certain obligations, even if the court awards rights to you. To spell out exactly what we mean, consider this: a court can control all real and personal property located within its state's boundaries—but it cannot make an order for personal performance, or for the payment of child or spousal support, for custody, or to protect your property from waste or you from a spouse's physical violence unless it has personal jurisdiction over the other party. Personal jurisdiction can often be obtained by having the marshal or a registered process server, present the necessary papers to your spouse. Different states have different requirements for establishing the necessary personal jurisdiction. Check your state's civil code for alternate methods of service that may suffice, and for the facts or circumstances you have to prove before your court will order an out-of-state mate to pay, for example, child or spousal support.

To help the process server, and therefore the court, stay in touch with your spouse, with his/her employer, with mutual friends, or with business associates so that you can tell the person serving papers for you where to go. If your mate threatens to leave or disappear, let your attorney know so that you can complete the filing papers and complete service as quickly as possible. Do your part by avoiding fights or hassles that would speed your mate's flight.

Personally serving an itchy-footed spouse before she or he moves away may be especially important if you live in a community-property state. In California, for example, you may use the concept of quasi-community property to fatten your asset list only if you both reside in a community property state at the time that you file for divorce.

Once you have given the court power to assess spousal support (sometimes called alimony or maintenance) against your mate, bring into the negotiations all the reasons you deserve support, based on the factors affecting support in your state. (Review those laid out in Chapter Two if you need help in approaching your mate.) In addition, however, you can increase your chance of gaining spousal support via negotiations or by court order if you rank as the lower-earning spouse and show that it would be unfair to remove your partner's income and "cast you adrift." Though the following reasoning can apply to either sex, here's how a court justified a continuing award of spousal support in the case of *In re Marriage of Brantner*. As one justice phrased it:

> A woman is not a breeding cow to be nurtured during her years of fecundity, then conveniently and economically converted to cheap steaks when past her prime.

Perhaps a bit harsh in the wording, but the theory is a valid one; several state legislatures have passed so-called "homemaker laws," which provide consideration for the years that one mate has devoted to raising a family and/or making a home for the primary breadwinner, to the detriment of her career, justifying her seeking monthly support. In fact, California's civil code places the following factor first when it enumerates the evidence in fixing spousal support:

> The earning capacity of each spouse, taking into account the extent to which the supported spouse's present and future earning capacity is impaired by periods of unemployment that were incurred during the marriage to permit the supported spouse to devote time to domestic duties.

In dealing with gaining child support, it may prove helpful to review the bases for awarding such dollars, outlined in Chapter Two. Keep in mind that a growing trend toward joint custody can mean that the parents will share more equally in the physical care of the child than used to be the norm. Clearly, while some expenses (extra bedroom, toys, utilities, pool maintenance) continue whether a child lives in one home all the time or not, an equitable sharing of day-to-day care can affect the payment and amount of child support. If you need money more than time, you may offer to care for offspring most of the time. If you need time more than money, propose a liberal visitation schedule that in fact allocates most of the physical custody to your spouse, and ask for a lower monthly amount.

Though it often proves difficult for mothers to consider an extra generous (or even total) allocation of custody to a male mate, my personal view is that such an arrangement can benefit all concerned. Several mothers who insisted on almost total physical custody later discovered that their daily care sapped too much energy to pursue a career effectively, to seek additional schooling, or to enjoy a social life. As a result, many find themselves commuting to the same "just-helping-out-the-family, entry-level job" years after their final decree. Free of daily child-care duties, their spouses have invested time and energy in a career that has substantially boosted both earnings and life-style in the intervening years. For these reasons, you may wish to hang on to legal custody but allocate far more than half of the physical presence of your kids to your former parenting partner. Another alternative is to *temporarily* allocate day-to-day care to an ex-spouse so that *you* can finish college, obtain a better job, land that MBA degree, or perhaps meet someone special without calling home on the hour.

If you feel that you couldn't *possibly* "give up" your children, perhaps an objective look at this course of action in another will widen your view:

> A beautiful redhead, new psychologist Renee had just celebrated her 36th birthday, but her private practice had attracted only a few clients when she decided on divorce. Never having worked outside her home, Renee had spent her 15 years of marriage helping her mate with his career and raising their two boys, now 12 and 14. The house was too expensive for Renee to maintain alone, even with her new teaching and part-time counseling job at a local university. Building her practice and getting on her professional feet would take at least two years of full-time energy.
>
> Meanwhile, her spouse's successful career meant that he often returned home no later than 5:00. She was the first to say that Stan loved their sons deeply, helped with their homework, took them on outings, listened to their problems, and patiently ferried them to and from ball games, friends' homes, and back and forth on an occasional date. In commuting one morning, Renee spotted a vacancy sign on a small apartment building near their home. A check of the paper revealed a rent within her budget, if her practice continued to grow.
>
> Renee desperately needed to escape a relationship that she consistently described as "poisonous," but she couldn't see any way out. When an attorney suggested that she move into that apartment and let her husband pay for the house and continue to care for the boys, she regarded him with horror. He might just as well have suggested that she turn the boys over to an ax murderer. Dr. Renee couldn't bring herself to put even her temporary needs before her only-I-can-raise-my-children-right concept.

However you allocate the physical care of any children, consider some of the following suggestions to put a payment source beyond your spouse's control if you will need child or spousal support and if you fear that regular payments may prove only a dream.

1. If you agree with your mate that it will not affect the amount of support, consider asking a boarder or two to share your residence for extra cash. If you fear that any additional income would compromise your support allocation, ask the boarders to furnish home maintenance, child care, gardening, or housecleaning services so that you realize a gain, but not in the dollar category.

2. Arrange to have some real estate put into or kept in joint tenancy, with the provision that neither spouse will sell a portion or borrow against any equity and that title can revert to your mate when the youngest child reaches majority, or when your spousal support terminates. Because joint tenancies include the right of survivorship, if your mate dies before these obligations are paid in full, you will immediately gain full ownership of the property involved.
3. If your spouse receives (or can receive) payments from a third party, arrange to have that party or company pay to you directly all or a portion of the funds due as and for support. Such third-entity sources can include insurance annuities, deferred salary from an employer, stock or bond dividends, income property payments, disability from a prior injury, a pension plan or retirement benefit program, the defendant or losing party in a claim or suit who now owes your spouse, or even the borrower on a personal loan.
4. Have your mate start and fund a trust. She or he can use an income property or other source of income-producing asset for the body of the trust; any income—or a designated portion of the earnings—can flow directly to you.

If your spouse and you now own such income-earning or other property but your mate seems in a hurry to dispose of it, watch out! There are several reasons for such behavior, but none spells good news for you. First, your partner may be disposing of income-earning assets to depress income and reduce any support assessments. Second, he or she may be converting hard assets to cash to secrete them during property division and allocation negotiations. Third, a spouse sometimes converts visible, immovable assets to cash in order to place the proceeds into secret accounts and then declare bankruptcy. Fourth, a savvy spouse may anticipate converting easily salable assets to pocketable cash, so that a division or allocation of property may leave you with equal-value items that remain costly to maintain, cumbersome to enjoy, and difficult to sell. If the reverse occurs (your spouse keeps converting cash and savings or other liquid assets), he or she may plan to reduce the fund from which support can flow, eliminate ready cash to force a better settlement at an earlier stage, or merely convert easily evaluated assets (money) into other, more esoteric property whose value he or she can hide during negotiations, hearing, or trial.

How can you protect yourself if you see this scenario developing? Refuse to sign any documents necessary to list such property or to transfer ownership to a third party. Insist that you disagree with the wisdom of a sale, and ask that the particular assets (if possible) be divided down the middle. If your partner wishes to then convey his or her share, fine—such a sale represents less danger to you.

Now that you've learned how to keep an open eye at home, try to fit into your schedule some regular time to learn some of the law, procedure, and strategies relating to the field of family law. This won't be difficult, and it can even prove pleasant. Following up some (or all) of these ideas can provide you with valuable knowledge, with a feeling of power, with priceless negotiating information, and with familiarity with this field of law and the way it works—or doesn't work—in your state. Any one of these suggestions will help, but doing all of them can help put you and keep you in the driver's seat while dealing with your spouse and/or legal counselor.

1. About once a week, visit your largest local library and skim through the biggest legal newspaper in your area. Some of the cases will be designated as "domestic law" or "family law holdings." There may be a condensed version of the legal holding in the body of the paper and then a full, printed account in an insert, so leaf through every page. Whenever you find a fact situation like yours, you can use the court's ruling in negotiations with your mate and to help your attorney, if he or she has not yet studied this case.

   If your library doesn't subscribe to a good legal newspaper, find out the name of the publication and subscribe to it yourself for the months or year it takes you to finalize your parting. If you fear that your mate may learn of your intentions if he/she spots this publication in the house, or you suspect that he/she may glean something that can be used against you, have the periodical sent to a friend's address, rent a Post Office box, or pay a few month's charges for a private mail drop address in your area.

Marie put down the money for her and Tim's "marital hide-away," but the two took title as "Husband and Wife, in Joint Tenancy." They parted two weeks after the wedding day. In California at that time, two cases outlined rights to the family home. One depended on title; the other on the source of purchase funds. The two rulings directly opposed each other. In one case, a joint tenancy held by a California husband and wife meant that the asset should be considered community property. The other case ruled that a spouse who could trace the source of any payment to a separate property source could claim that portion of the home as his or her own. Because the down payment came from Marie's earnings prior to the wedding, she argued that a large segment of the home's value belonged to her alone and that the bulk of the monies from the sale of the house should flow to her. Tim, of course, took the other view, insisting that title controlled, and that all sales funds had to be split in half.

The disagreement raged on, with Marie (a well-established executive) offering Tim (a newly graduated master's student) only $3,000 as his "fair share" of their common property. Tim, a subscriber to the local legal newspaper, that morning opened his "Bible" and read, splashed across the front page, "California Supreme Court Says *Lucas* Prevails!" or words to that effect. Tim let out a yell—this case supported his title argument! Within hours, Marie's and Tim's attorneys worked out a settlement that put $30,000 (instead of $3,000) into the previously impoverished student's pocket.

Need we say more?

2. Next, if you know—or can obtain access to—a family-law judge or commissioner outside of your jurisdiction, quiz him or her about the likely outcome of the major issues in your case. Steer clear of judicial officers who serve in the district where your case will be heard.) Don't bother the jurist with "who-gets-the-pots-and-pans" questions.
3. Last, and most fun, visit your local courthouse and view some family-law proceedings in action. If you call ahead or approach the court clerk when the judge is in chambers or when court is not in session, you can learn when the next hearing will take place that will resemble your action Are you scheduled to appear for temporary support, or for an interim custody determination? Will you and your mate appear later for a hearing on a particular issue, or for a full-fledged trial because you can't agree on *anything*? Your local forum will feature them all—and each can help you.

When you show up, sit where you can see as much of the parties and their counsel as possible, while getting a straight shot at the judge. Take in a hearing for temporary relief (sometimes called an order-to-show-cause matter), a custody battle (if you feel that this could turn into your Waterloo), and even a protracted dissolution of marriage trial (and they can stretch over four or five days, sometimes more). Listen to the questions being asked and to the answers that *count*, or rank as relevant, and to those that don't. Study the body language of the witnesses, the parties, and the judge. Which postures convey truthful testimony and which scream *false!?* Do any tactics seem particularly effective in introducing crucial evidence, while others seem a waste of time? What evidence weighs most heavily in which issues, and which is a waste of time? If you don't understand something, consider approaching the clerk, one or both of the lawyers involved, or even the judge, if she or he is not working or on the bench. Since courts schedule most matters in the morning and fewer matters continue until afternoon, the later working hours make good opportunities to quiz court personnel and judges.

You may happen to see a lawyer in court whom you wish to retain as counsel, but your decision on legal counsel is a crucial one and requires a good deal of research and thought. Do not act on impulse. Hiring correct counsel for your needs may take as much energy (perhaps more) as choosing your spouse. If you follow these guidelines, however, you should find a good guide through your divorce.

First, consider the recommendations of a friend, but make sure that your acquaintance's problem matches yours. A lawyer may prove a whiz at settling personal injury claims, or draw a business contract that more than earns his fee, but only an attorney handling a lot of divorce work will have the experience, the library, the sources, and the legal knowledge to really help you through. While a counselor need not restrict his or her practice to family law to prove adequate, changes occur rapidly in this field; keeping up requires time and dedication to this limited area. Though there is no need to hire a real heavyweight in the field if your assets rank as modest, *do* steer wide of attorneys who take *no* family matters (but will do your divorce "as a favor for a friend"). In particular, avoid lawyers who do a lot of civil litigation (presenting arguments to juries), and lawyers who take criminal matters. Why? Because the first may feel inclined to "slug everything out in court," or to produce a "show" for the jury, which will do you little good, since family-law matters require only a judge. The criminal lawyer attorney must—according to the U.S. and various state constitutions—help in providing clients with a "speedy trial." Because criminal matters come up for hearing within relatively short periods of time and criminal law work can demand unusual hours, you and your divorce case can end up taking a backseat to the attorney's other cases.

If you haven't found an attorney through a friend, call one or several lawyer-referral services (listed in the Yellow Pages of your telephone book, under "Attorneys"). Spell out your needs, the nature of your case, any geographical limitations, and especially any budget constraints. The service should provide you with at least three names. Call each and pay attention to how the phone is answered, how pleasant or competent the office help sounds, how much difficulty you encounter in asking for an introductory meeting, and how long you will have to wait to interview that counselor. Many attorneys will see a prospective client for free for a brief first interview. The promise of new fees almost always raises this businessperson's interest, but remember that you will be interviewing each other. You need not retain a lawyer you dislike or whose philosophy runs counter to yours; and the attorney may choose to decline your case. If the lawyer wants a minimal fee for an initial meeting, consider paying it—you will pick up lots of worthwhile information if you arrive well organized. If you cannot afford even a nominal fee, or find that none of your callees will see you at less than their regular hourly rates, call your referral service for another set of names.

When you arrive for your meeting, avoid launching into the particulars of your case. There will be plenty of time for this with your chosen legal partner. Right now, you need to find that partner, so ask the lawyer these questions, and add some of your own:

1. How long have you practiced law?
2. What portion of your practice relates to family law (domestic relations) work?
3. Will you be the attorney working on my case, or will you assign it to another person on your staff?
4. What options do I have for resolving the issues in this case? (This question in particular should smoke out the "court's-the-only-answer" practitioner. An up-to-date counselor in this field will mention several or all of the following: therapy; trained divorce mediators; arbitration;

consultation with a religious leader, disinterested third party, or mutual friend of you and your spouse; direct negotiation with legal guidance; lawyer-to-lawyer negotiation; or even a legal separation or "friendly parting" until tempers cool and property issues loom less large.)

5. How much do you charge, and how do you bill? Hour by hour? Retainer and hourly? Flat fee? Or a combination of these?
6. Do you have a personal philosophy of divorce? (I believe that a dissolution of marriage can constitute a growing, maturing experience when clients take an active role in a divorce and join in the negotiation and work; other lawyers hold different views. Your conselor's attitudes can prove as important as his or her legal skills.)

In choosing a legal guide, you may want to call your local bar association (listed in the white pages), and ask if one or more of the attorneys you're considering has ever been disciplined. The American Bar Association now operates a national computer-based information system called the National Discipline Data Bank. State and federal courts and administrative agencies voluntarily supply facts on lawyers who have been publicly disciplined. The information is available to the general public. To obtain a free brochure, write the National Center for Professional Responsibility, American Bar Association, 77 South Wacker Drive, Chicago, Ill., 60606.

In these final weeks, obtaining "insurance" for a better (single) future can actually mean checking the types of policies and the personal and property coverage now in effect in your life. In fact, this might represent a perfect time to undertake measures like the following:

1. Take out insurance on your spouse's life. Obtaining his or her signature on the application should prove no problem at this stage. If this seems particularly cold, remember that a deceased party cannot pay child or spousal support. Arrange for generous coverage on the party likely to pay such monthly allotments, and base the policy's face value on the total amount to be paid on all the years to come.
2. Check your home-owner's insurance coverage amounts. Is the policy up to date? Will it pay for damages due to vandalism, fire, windstorm, hail, flood, theft, and even those caused by a berserk or angry spouse?
3. Make sure there is sufficient insurance on the cars and other vehicles and on any personal collections, jewels, furs, etc. kept in

your home. Are policy limits adequate? Are they paid well into the future with present funds? If you aim to keep the house and its contents during negotiations or for some years in the future, the cost of protecting many jointly owned assets will fall to you. So why not obtain extended coverage now on such items with jointly owned funds instead of paying for this solely from your separate income or your share of the property?

Take out (or update) any health policies protecting your children and you. Stressful times exact physical tolls, and it's wise to ensure low-cost or free medical, dental, and even therapeutic care for the coming months.

Review your policies to see who ranks as the owner of each policy and to make sure you are the beneficiary on policies covering your spouse's life. If you are not the policy owner, suggest that ownership be transferred to you right away. If you can convince your spouse to make the policy and any value in it an outright gift to you, so much the better. You should not then have to share any of the cash value residing in the policy. Only a policy owner can determine or change the beneficiary, only an owner receives notice of any lapse in premium payments or changes in coverage, and only the owner will be able to float a loan against the policy's face value or withdraw any cash or surrender value.

You can also retain adequate coverage under a whole-life policy—without paying any more premiums—if your policy is sufficiently mature (if you've built up enough cash value to pay your future premiums as they fall due). Call your insurance agent to see if any policy insuring your spouse has accrued enough cash value to be declared "paid up." In such a case, you need pay no more premiums out of pocket, but you may have to choose whether you want the policy to remain in force for only a limited period, or whether you want a long period of coverage but a lower potential payout if your mate dies.

Keep in mind that if your mate injures another party while doing something that does *not* benefit your marriage, don't let your commonly owned property be used in paying any assessment or claim. For example, if your mate, absorbed in whispering sweet somethings in another's ear, slams the family Chevrolet into a corner fruit stand, any damages should be paid *first* from separate property of your spouse, and from mutually funded insurance only if absolutely necessary.

Second, a warning is in order that illustrates a good general approach to assume while negotiating your marital settlement agreement as it relates to insurance: don't give up here-and-now assets for the promise of being named a beneficiary of a future insurance policy if the power to name (and change) that beneficiary status rests completely with your spouse. In other words, wouldn't you feel foolish if you allocated some of your share of present assets in return for a promise that only *you* would remain the beneficiary of an insurance policy, and then discovered that your spouse had dissipated those assets and promptly designated a new love to receive any insurance proceeds? Treat potential benefits as *expectations*, but don't forgo a bird in the hand.

These "final insurance" weeks also provide an occasion to check your own credit and any attacks on that credit by parties you may not even know. Check with the central credit reporting service in your area to learn about your current credit rating, to find out about any balances due for purchases that you may not know about, and to discover any problem in your credit file that might haunt you long after divorce. In California, for example, TRW (named for founders Thompson, Ramo, and Woolridge) is a widely used credit-information-gathering service. TRW gathers information about thousands of consumer's spending and credit habits, and keeps them on file for the benefit of shopkeepers, businesses, and corporations wishing to ensure the creditworthiness of a prospective buyer before completing a sale that will require payments over time. You can request a copy of your credit file by sending your full name, your address(es) for the past five years, your Social Security number, the year of your birth, and your signature to TRW, Box 5450, Orange, California 92667.

You may also want to consider applying for credit in a new name that you plan to take after separation or in your present name as a single wage earner. If you encounter problems in obtaining such credit, you should have sufficient time before the parting to iron out any wrinkles and start a new life with adequate access to extra money and a fresh credit slate.

But it is not enough to check your credit rating or to arrange for "plastic wealth" for your new life. You may also want to check whether anyone has filed a lien against your commonly owned property or your family home. Once recorded in the County Recorder's office, a lien "tells the world" that the property involved stands as security for a debt owed to a creditor of the owner of that property. A lien holder can foreclose on this debt, forcing a sale of the real estate involved. Usually, though, lien holders wait for a voluntary sale of the property to a third party, then receive payment from the buyer or the seller before allowing title to pass. (The protection of lien holders provides an excellent example of how an escrow holder serves both buyer and seller. If the buyer acquired title before such lien holders had been satisfied, he would have paid full price for a property encumbered by debts. If the seller had passed title without paying off any liens, the property would remain liable for these debts, and the seller might have to pay the buyer a sum for the buyer's expenses or inconvenience in defending against the seller's creditors.) A lien may be placed on the house if, for example, someone, like your mate, arranges for work to be done around the business or home, then fails to pay the bill. Firms selling home improvements or additions file a lien or a charge against a residence when the owner cannot or will not pay the debt in full. Occasionally the Internal Revenue Service, a state, federal, or administrative agency, or a home-owners' association will obtain a lien against a home for an occupant's refusal, failure, or inability to pay a tax payment that falls due.

Checking with the recorder of the county in which any real property is located can uncover these liens. Some title companies will also, for a small fee, send you a copy of every lien recorded under that property address or owner's name. Such checks often turn up no such charges, but if they *do* exist, and you remain unaware of them, you could transfer valuable assets to obtain full ownership of the family home, then find its value dramatically reduced by liens and judgments that your mate did not pay. These could trigger a foreclosure, causing you to lose your home.

Because you will want protection from other potentially nasty surprises after you have parted from your spouse, take these weeks to consider some of the possible advantages that lie in federal income tax laws. If you've always tuned out when tax views and news crept into a conversation, for just this once, *tune in!* It is not too early to decide the following questions:

1. Do you want any or all monthly payments to consist of spousal or child support? Would some combination of the two be better?

Keep in mind that child support is neither deductible for the paying party nor taxable for the receiving party. The payer of spousal support dollars does, however, get to deduct them if the payment schedule meets certain rather simple standards set out by the IRS. The payee receiving spousal support funds, though, must declare the amount and pay taxes on it. If you will be the party caring for the children most of the time, and your tax bracket promises to be much lower than your mate's, you may want to receive "spousal" or "family" support, but ask for additional dollars to help pay any taxes assessed. A high-earning mate, eager for tax write-offs, may readily agree to this because he or she may retain a bigger share of earnings, despite a higher monthly payment. Such an outcome depends upon actual earnings and personal tax brackets, but labeling all monies "spousal support" or "family support" may provide a win-win opportunity for both of you.

2. What facts will enable you to file as head of household when your taxes next fall due? You may well feel a smaller tax bite if you file as Head of Household, rather than as a married person filing separately, or as a spouse filing jointly with your mate. You may want to have a financial expert work out the actual tax burden in each circumstance to see which form of filing best benefits you. Since you will need to meet a short list of requirements to file as Head of Household, check with a CPA, or ask a reference librarian to steer you to the proper section of the Internal Revenue Code. To make IRS brains work for you, consider asking for a "letter ruling" (advance opinion) based on your facts. Check with a local IRS office for procedural details.
3. How much of your future tax burden should your mate help you to bear? Does even a small portion sound too profitable to be true? If the tax bears certain characteristics, a California spouse must bear half the weight! Even in your state, the court may apply (or follow the theory of) the *Jean Carrieres Co.* case, decided in 1975. The case affirming this decision held that the spouse receiving a taxable gain deserves financial aid from a mate to help pay state and federal taxes when assessed. To fully understand this concept, consider Marcia and Milt, a California couple with only one major asset to divide—Marsha's pension rights with a large manufacturing firm.

An actuary assessed the separation-date value of Marsha's retirement benefit rights at $60,000. Because all Marsha's working years occurred while she was wed to Milt, the state regarded that asset as community property and set Milt's present-value share at $30,000. The two had remained apartment dwellers, and though they had no real debts, they could claim no assets of any size.

To retain full and sole rights to her pension plan, Marsha borrowed $30,000 from her sister and conveyed it to Milt. Because these funds sprang from a source outside of their marriage, Milt's sale of his pension rights was not accomplished via a nontaxable division of community property. Instead, this sale resulted in a taxable $30,000 gain to husband Milt.

By figuring out his tax bracket as a single man, Milt was able to determine his probable tax. Because of the *Carrieres* holding, Marsha had to ante up one-half of Milt's tax charges.

Your state's laws may differ from this, of course, but if you negotiate such terms out of court, you may achieve an inherently fairer outcome. After all, the *Carrieres* case only points out that *every* allocation of property between spouses needs to be considered in after-tax dollars to provide approximately equal totals for each mate. If you qualify as a "Marsha," let your conscience dictate whether you will help bear your former partner's tax burden or not. If you are a "Milt," you'll surely want to raise this tax-sharing approach as being "only fair."

4. Will you or your spouse stay in the house? Before you bravely offer to depart, remember that in an ultimate sale of that residence, only the *occupant* will be able to avoid taxes on any gain—by purchasing a new home that costs more than one-half the profit from the previous house. A mate who moves out, however, and who therefore sets up housekeeping at another address, will not be able to avoid taxes on this often hefty gain because he or she has not sold a "principal residence." To master this concept, study the tale of Quenton and Paula.

When they decided to divorce, Paula moved out and took a small apartment nearby. Over the next three years, while they worked out the details of dividing their property, Paula filed a married-but-living-separately tax return from her new address. Quenton remained in their home, filing *his* tax return from their old address.

After those three years, both agreed to sell the former family home.

They conveyed the house for an even $100,000, paid off their mortgage, and pocketed a profit of $28,000 each. Quenton then purchased a small condominium for $50,000, and Paula acquired a home on the outskirts of town for $62,500. Quenton was not taxed on his gains because he bought a replacement principal residence at a cost that exceeded one-half of his gain from the previous sale.

Paula's new home also cost enough to shelter her gain from the sale of her former home, but she could not avoid taxes because she had not sold her "principal residence," but merely a structure where she *used* to live.

If you are a Quenton, you may want to help your mate pack and move out of the family home on separation day. If you are a Paula, reconsider any first instincts to exit and obtain a new place of your own. Whichever you plan to be, bear in mind that to avoid taxes you must purchase a new principal residence of sufficient cost *within 24 months of a sale,* though you have slightly longer if you plan to build a new home.

There's another reason to stay in the family home: at 55 you may qualify for the once-in-a-lifetime tax forgiveness of $125,000 on the profit from a sale of your principal residence. To shelter this sum from taxes, however, you must be 55 and have lived in that home for at three of the five previous years. If you've remained the "house spouse," there's no problem. But if you've moved away and now rank as the "out-house spouse," you will have to fulfill those live-in requirements in your new principal residence before you can reduce any tax bite by claiming the forgiveness rule.

This one-time-only tax forgiveness when you sell that principal residence and scoop up the profits belongs to either a couple or a single person. If one of you qualifies for this tax break and takes it while you are still legally wed (before the filing of your final decree), then *both* of you will be forever barred from seeking this favorable IRS treatment again. Far better if you agree that the eligible spouse will apply for this forgiveness only *after* the final decree, thus effectively preserving the maximum tax protection for the other spouse.

If you want to learn more tax tips (and think of the dollars you may save if you do), write to the Internal Revenue Service and ask for pamphlets No. 504 and No. 555. Both are free of charge.

In concluding this chapter, I would like to pass on some philosophies and advice from clever clients undergoing divorce. First, decide what you really want—custody? the house? generous support? a special asset or piece of property? funds for additional schooling or a business of your own?—and what you really can live without. Once you have "prioritized," work hard and bargain effectively to obtain the items or rights on the top of your list, and taper your energies as you move down through the less-important numbers.

If you're blocked on that big need or dream, or if *everything* seems equally important right now, try imagining your ideal life-style or greatest desire. If you're like the woman who moaned "I've *got* to get out of my marriage, but all I have are fantasies," remember that a fantasy is the first step to a plan. Tap into your emotions to find out what's really important to you.

Second, polish your "option outlook." Most of us feel most panicked when we feel helpless or trapped—when we can see only one way of accomplishing a goal. If you can't come up with several ways to solve each potential problem, gather a group of close, creative, and *discreet* friends and ask for help in reaching the goals you've set, or in overcoming obstacles you can foresee cropping up during and after your divorce. You'll be surprised—and relieved—at the creative options that fertile minds and group energy can produce.

Third, try to build your problem-solving skills as added insurance for a better future. While you are commuting to work, tuning out during television commercials, or standing in line at the bank, imagine how you would overcome a sudden setback in your life after your divorce. What if you suffered a broken leg? a foreclosure on your home? the loss of your savings? discovery of a socially awkward disease? Not only will you rapidly build "coping muscles" through your imagined solutions, but also, by comparison, surviving a divorce will also soon appear well within your expanded capabilities.

Fourth, remember that you need not plot, plan, or cope alone. You have already seen that divorce at best is a team effort—a joining of appraisers, actuaries, realtors, bankers, brokers, personal-property dealers, therapists, search experts, attorneys, etc. Your team needn't be limited to these "traditional" divorce associates; you can put together your own team of friends, advisors, career mentors, listeners, business advisors, trained or naturally skilled psychological aides, and others who can help you through. In the months before and during her divorce, Barbara S. even formed an informal "board of directors" to help her make important decisions at times when she didn't feel capable of doing so alone.

As you enter these last weeks before separation day, you will probably feel ambivalent about ending your marriage, and you may possibly suffer some severe attacks of feeling selfish or guilty about preparing so carefully to profit from your divorce. Keep in mind that if you feel knowledgeable about the law and your assets and if you feel that you are working a plan instead of being worked over, then you can have a positive effect on your legal counselor, your spouse, the children, the proceedings and the outcome of your case. It is also helpful to remember that this process of parting will end, but that you are building the assets, self-esteem, self-confidence, and problem-solving skills that can last the rest of your life. Try to view divorce as a sort of beginner's class or training ground for other challenges sure to come your way. In this context, think of orchestrating a positive departure as "Lesson Plan No. 1: Learning to Protect Yourself and to Part Profitably." Consider too that you may never find another marriage partner. You may well spend your coming years alone, relying only on yourself. If, in addition to coping alone, you will probably have the daily care of any children, their welfare will depend on yours. The better you equip yourself to survive, the more they will thrive. Finally, you will probably hear plenty of What-took-you-so-long's. Recruit the best of these supporters to carry you through, and you will build a network of friends who can make your new life far richer than the old.

5

A Few Days Before . . .

NOW that only a few days remain before you depart or announce your intention to seek a divorce, you'll want to follow especially carefully the suggestions in this chapter. Although you may feel very tense during this time, and you may suffer many ambivalent feelings, it will pay you to remain a stern task master in completing those "assignments" that apply to your case. For instance, you'll want to study some aspects of custody that will help you to make a final decision on this topic, ways of protecting your interest in the family home, and methods of locking up your future rights in other assets. You'll also learn how to use your own "little black book" in a very unromantic but profitable way and how to cancel out your spouse's chances with the best legal competition in town.

But first, a little philosophy to help ease this perhaps most difficult time. During these days (and nights) you may find yourself playing that old game, What If. What if I'd been more patient, you think. What if I hadn't devoted so much energy to my career (the kids, the house, my friends)? When all of the what-if possibilities fade, you may enter this game's second phase: I *Should* Have . . . this and that and everything else. You get the idea. As California "media minister" Terry Cole Whittaker likes to warn, "Don't 'should' on yourself"—especially now. You will need a cool head, a capacity for rational analysis, and the unemotional conviction to stick by your plans. This may prove difficult. Another natural reaction is to start storing up petty grievances and angers to work up the courage to leave. Parting successfully with sufficient assets is your goal. Feelings of guilt or a desire for revenge can only be obstacles.

No one would ever undertake a difficult endeavor if he or she didn't foresee a reward, a benefit, or a something better at the end of the trail. If, in reviewing the ideas in this chapter, you keep imagining awful terrors along that trail, try a trick that therapists and risk counselors advise: Consider the worst that could happen and figure out how you would deal with it. This process should help to keep even large fears under control and build your confidence to deal with almost *anything* effectively.

Now to deal with a potentially fiery issue with some degree of cool: you must determine whether you really want full-time, part-time, or very-little-time care of any minor children. As a man, don't think that you have no chance at gaining custody or a major share of your children's custodial care. But don't think, if you're a woman, that you *must* take custody or take on a larger share of caring for your offspring than your spouse. Your kids may thrive under your mate's care or under a combination of activities that both adults divide and undertake. The one basic tenet to remember in deciding who should take the children is *what is best for them.* Even state superior court justices base their custody decisions on the best interests of the child. Does this mean the parent with the most bucks, or who can coach Little League, or who keeps the house spotlessly clean will be the children's best caretaker? No. Custodial factors include emotional benefits as well as material comforts or relative wealth. If you can negotiate or—better still—share custody, do! But if you remain convinced that the children would be better off with you, consider the following steps in setting the stage for a custody award in your favor:

1. Show the court—or the other side during negotiations—that you will work to foster a close and continuing relationship between the children and their other parent. Suggesting broad visitation rights, with extended periods of visiting during holidays and school vacations, can go a long way toward showing that you can share.
2. Draw up a detailed plan that shows how well you can care for the children and their needs on a daily basis. Have you researched or interviewed housekeepers or babysitters for child-care services when you cannot remain at home? Arranged for potential problems or special travel needs? Investigated local schools, youth groups, and other activities? Drawn up a detailed plan that shows

how you intend to provide for the children's needs every day as well as on special occasions? The more time you invest in fine-tuning your plans, the better your chances of prevailing in court and in convincing your spouse during negotiations to allot custody to you.

3. Figure out what, if anything, you will need to change in your schedule *or* environment to provide safe, wholesome, nourishing, and stable surroundings for your offspring. Will you need to change your personal life-style? Keep different friends? Limit your indulgences? Move to another neighborhood or part of town? Give up or curtail career plans or business travel to spend time at home? Allocate a good deal of your leisure time to the repetitive and sometimes thankless tasks of raising children? Perhaps custody is losing some of its appeal . . . or perhaps a more equitable sharing of cares and joys is appearing a bit more feasible.
4. Arrange the circumstances so that you have, for all practical purposes, physical custody of the children from the separation day onward, while negotiations or hearings drag on. If you choose to leave the family residence, then try to make arrangements for shelter that will allow you to keep the children with you. Of course, you must ensure that this new location will allow them to attend a good school, receive adequate supervision, and will provide a healthy, safe environment. If taking the children with you will imperil their health, welfare, or safety, then you face a difficult choice: If your move endangers your offspring, you may lose custody at a later hearing; if you must leave them behind with your mate, then he or she can begin accumulating evidence of how well he/she can care for the kids on a daily basis. A "track record" showing the ability to care for any offspring is crucial, for a court hearing on your custody issue could remain months away, and the parent in possession will have ample time to create a strong argument that the children are doing well and should not be disturbed. In short, the with-kids spouse can present a strong status quo argument that your children have become accustomed to living with him or her, in their present environment, and that any change now would prove more detrimental than beneficial. Children thriving in a caring, stable environment will rarely be moved if some time has passed and if a shift would prove disruptive without providing any benefit for the youngsters. You can

show that you have created such a result if the kids appear happy, healthy, clean, well cared for, and well dressed; if they are doing well in school; and if they are enjoying local friends, sports, and other neighborhood activities. In addition, you can strengthen your role in their lives and increase your chances for custody by involving yourself deeply in their daily lives. Do you help with homework? Participate on the paper route? Serve as a scout leader? Cheer the local team, band, and cheerleader squad?

5. You will dramatically enhance your chances to get sole or major custody if you have cooperated in arranging visits, so that all the kids have been seeing their other parent on a frequent basis and feel on their way to establishing a good balance between two loving, responsible adults and two different households.
6. In many courts, if a child is of sufficient age and capacity to reason, the presiding officer may ask each child where he would like to spend most of his time. Such conferences usually take place in the judge's chambers and involve both parents as well as a session in which the judge may want to see the child alone. Some judges will refuse to question a child, feeling that such a conference puts an unconscionable burden on the youngster and makes him or her the lynchpin of the custody award. Most judges who do listen to the children's desires have gained skill in hearing spoken requests, and will discount a choice triggered by parental promises of a fun schedule or material goods.

If, despite all your efforts, your spouse gains physical custody of the kids, ask the court to supply you with written reasons for its decision. Such bases may change, and you can later apply for a change in custody if there has been a sufficient change in circumstances since the previous order or agreement. If you reach a custody allocation by negotiation but it is not in your favor, spell out the facts surrounding your decision in a written agreement, so that you can later use it to prove changes in your circumstances that could support a change in custody.

If you will be the primary custodial parent, the following information should help you reap all the benefits possible from custody:

- The earnings of a minor child usually belong to the custodial spouse. Even if you want your child to learn to manage his or her own earnings, you may assess a small amount for room and board, or ask that a teenager pick up some expenses relating directly to him or her.

- The Internal Revenue Service has recently raised the allowable income-tax credit for child-care costs you expended during the previous year. To determine the amount of your credit, check with a CPA, or review the correct portion of the Internal Revenue Code, available in any large library. If the Code appears overwhelmingly complex, refer to the Index at the end of the Code to guide you to the right page, or ask the reference librarian for aid.
- You get a deduction on your income tax return for each dependent child.
- You will need to claim at least one child as a dependent in order to file as a head of household when completing your tax return. This will place you in a lower tax bracket and save you dollars each year that you qualify.

Custody negotiations can be uplifting or messy, and in custody negotiations, as well as in other matters that you discuss, the party who thinks ahead will usually obtain a better, more profitable result. In this "chess" theory, you always consider what will happen a few moves down the road. By predicting or guesstimating a mate's actions, you can gain a negotiating advantage and prevail on important points.

If your spouse wants custody but hasn't played a major role in the children's upbringing, discipline, leisure, or daily care, you may want to agree to a temporary transfer of care that need not be legal, binding, or even in writing. When your mate realizes what's involved in caring for children of any age and wants out, agree to take over only if you can receive another concession, right, asset, or other advantage that is important to you. If this custody arrangement works out on an informal basis, consider leaving it that way. You should prove a winner either way.

The following points relate to less inflammatory topics, but they deserve careful thought during these last few days before separation.

1. Should you file a *lis pendens* against any real property belonging to you and/or your spouse? This document merely informs any potential buyers that there may be an adverse claim to the title and should protect your ownership interest in any property that you fear your mate could or would transfer alone.
2. Do you want to arrange for a new will? The filing of a divorce action, the signing of a marital settlement agreement, and/or the

divorce itself *may* destroy any joint tenancies you share. In any joint tenancy, the surviving partners take full title. No will can interrupt an automatic transfer of title. Once action by one or all parties destroys a joint tenancy, however, the parties hold that asset as tenants in common—a different legal status—and any owner can borrow against or sell his or her share. This means that one or another step in your divorce action may automatically convert your joint tenancy to a tenancy in common, which does not provide for an automatic inheritance by the surviving spouse. Once you individually own one-half of the house, apartment building, or raw land, it would be wise to draw up a simple will or alter your existing will so that your chosen heirs will inherit your interest in the event of your untimely death, instead of your almost-former mate. Of course, if you've carefully retained a joint-tenancy form of ownership in certain property throughout your divorce proceedings, and your spouse suffers from poor health or is elderly, you may want to consider specifically retaining any joint tenancy holdings, so that you may profit from a partner's possible demise during divorce proceedings.

3. Decide whether you want to apply for new credit cards in your name alone or arrange with your spouse which of you will use which "plastic authority" and who will remain responsible for all debts on the different cards after you part. If you feel that you may need help in establishing your own credit record or rights or have already encountered difficulty in this realm, try one or all of the following sources for aid:

Credit Handbook for Women and *Establishing Credit 101*
Public Affairs Department
American Express Company
Sixth Floor
American Express Plaza
New York, New York 10004

Fair Credit Reporting Act Consumer Information Center
Department 608J
Pueblo, Colorado 81009
Send $1 for this government booklet discussing your legal right, including guidelines on how to deal with an agency that carries unfavorable credit information about you.

The Credit Game—How Women Can Win It
Women's Legal Defense Fund
2000 P Street, N.W.
Suite 400
Washington, D.C. 20036
Send $3 for this book explaining the mysteries of good credit and how to get it, earning a good credit rating, or establishing one after a new start or under a new name. Includes self-help information and sample letters to credit agencies.

Women's Credit and Finance Project
PO Box 10849
Marina del Rey, California 90201
Send $1 and a stamped, self-addressed envelope.

Women's Credit Rights Project
(213) 461-3622
Manual and help lines for women with credit questions and concerns.

4. Decide whether you want to write or call all companies and agents with which you and/or your mate carry life insurance, in order to determine whether any cash or surrender value lurks in any of the policies. As a still-married partner, it *may* prove possible for you to withdraw any such funds before leaving. Frankly, however, such a right is probably reserved for the owner of the policy alone. If you can reap such monies now, however, you may use them for paying community debts (those incurred before the separation), for support after leaving, or for career training or necessaries like food, shelter, clothing and medical care. You may never have to pay these funds back if they constitute a form of involuntary but informal support for any children, or for you if you would normally receive spousal support. If you do have to refund a portion of these funds later on, you may be able to offset this credit against another amount that your mate owes you, or perhaps agree that the amount owed can be paid to your spouse from the future sale proceeds of another asset. The important concern—which we will cover in some detail in the next chapter—is that you obtain sufficient liquid assets to survive possibly protracted negotiations, hearings, or even a lengthy trial. Clearly, if your spouse and your insurance agent see each other frequently and enjoy numerous social or friendly exchanges, you probably will not want to query this agent about the possibility of any cash or surrender value in a policy. Your mate's friend, not knowing about your plans, may innocently tip your hand, triggering the same action in your mate that *you* sought to take. In such cases, avoid communicating with that agent; bypass him or her and contact the company directly by letter or phone.

Here are two quick tips that you can begin on now and that will prove beneficial for you for months to come. First, start to fill in your "little black book." In this case, we don't mean a listing of potential lovers but a collection of questions and concerns that you will want to ask your legal counselor. At the hourly rates charged for legal fees today, don't waste your lawyer's time by fumbling for points you need to discuss, don't leave his or her office chastising yourself for a forgotten question that you meant to bring up, and don't pester the law office with phone calls about matters that could and should have been covered in a cohesive, comprehensive way during your last conference. All of these represent costly catch-up information-seeking methods that can leave you feeling out of control and confused about legal procedure, strategy, and the progress of negotiations and perhaps torn as to whether the next step will be catastrophic or correct.

Second, consider taking this time to cancel out the best legal competition in town. This is a technique utilized by a Beverly Hills businessman who correctly predicted his wife's divorce plans. He feared that a clever, accomplished attorney might part him from many of the assets that he considered his alone. This husband carefully telephoned the top family-law attorneys in that affluent community, made appointments, and personally visited each legal eagle to discuss the possible outcome of his case. He revealed information about the community property, his earnings, his feelings about a potential settlement. He then paid each practitioner before leaving the office. After three days of this, he returned to his daily schedule with a spring in his step and a Cheshire-cat smile. Why? Because when his wife finally gathered her courage and visited these same counselors, each had to inform her that he or she could not take the case. Nor could this wife hire anyone in that lawyer's firm to represent her while she divorced her wealthy spouse. The reason is that each divorce—

no matter how friendly—is regarded as an adversarial procedure. For each piece of property awarded to one spouse, the other suffers a loss. For every favorable ruling for husband, wife loses an asset or a right. Every dollar ordered paid to wife for spousal support must come from husband's checking account. It is clear that each mate deserves an advocate dedicated to obtaining a favorable result for him or her alone. Even if you've shared one attorney for past business ventures, and both of you like him or her, neither of you should retain that professional to represent you for your divorce. Why? For two reasons. First, because that counselor has enjoyed an intimate knowledge of your mutual business affairs. Using that inside knowledge to benefit one spouse at even a potential loss to the other is regarded as a serious ethical breach. Second, an attorney once retained by you as a couple (even if you weren't active in the decisions reached) should not appear against you (as a former client) in a later case.

In other words, once you've hired a lawyer, he or she cannot take a case against you, unless:

The present adversary matter is completely different from previous work, or

Sufficient time has elapsed to materially alter the facts, property, relationship, and/or rights existing during the prior work, or

The attorney who formerly served both spouses obtains the written permission of the mate who must retain a new legal counselor, or

The present case involves a fee dispute between your prior lawyer and you. So, even though Mr. Wealthy might never see any of those counselors again or actually retain any of them to represent him during his divorce, each lawyer remained ethically banned from advising—or even seeing—Mrs. W. regarding her case.

In the next chapter you'll learn ways to get immediate cash for bargaining power and breathing room, make money on your mate's "guilts" or "independence highs," and read about other tips you'll want to use to carry you through. In addition, you'll get a healthy helping of information and insights to make you feel better about this situation and yourself.

6

Ways to Gain Assets During the Split

THOUGH Emily Dickinson never married, she noted in the late 1800's, "Parting is . . . all we need of hell." When those partings involve children, debts, and assets, they seem particularly hellish, because emotional issues remain interwoven with legal precepts and practical concerns.

Surviving and continuing to function during this traumatic period may be easier if you realize that you've got plenty of company. About 40 percent of today's marriages are troubled relationships, and almost half of the marriages of people now in their late twenties will end—or are ending—in divorce. In fact, one in four American households consist of one single person, and one-parent families (mostly headed by lone mothers with children) now account for one in 10 family units. According to a recent report by the Bureau of Labor Statistics, the traditional family portrait composed of a wage-earning husband, homemaker wife, and two cherry-cheeked children now represents a mere 5 percent of households nationwide.

But it's understandable if learning all this still doesn't help. Each parting pair faces unique facts and circumstances, and no situation is exactly like any other. For this reason, the tips and practical suggestions included in this chapter qualify as savvy but flexible. Bend, color, twist, and build on the ideas that follow to continue increasing your assets—along with your self-esteem, self-confidence, and healthily selfish new skills.

While this emphasis on "selfishness" may make you feel petty, picky, hostile, or worse, remember that after divorce you can depend only on you. If this sounds a bit harsh, and you're thinking that child and/or spousal support will provide you with ample funds, this is a good time to study the following odds on your financial happiness.

First, even court-ordered child support may be paid late, erratically, in part, or not at all. An article in a Los Angeles legal newspaper recently noted that only about 60 percent of those mothers living with their children but not with a spouse could claim a court order allocating funds directly to them. Of these, about one-half were receiving all the money they were entitled to. As for the other half, the average amount owed by an uncooperative father totaled about $2,000 a year—a lot of macaroni.

This article went on to say that nine of every ten single parents are women and that women traditionally work in jobs that pay barely enough to support one person, let alone a family. Within days of this article's appearance the April 30, 1982 edition of the *Daily News* announced that the U.S. commissioner of labor statistics, Janet Norwood, said, "More than half the women who run families on their own [live] in poverty." Commissioner Norwood went on to say that "women who maintain families without husbands have a median annual income of $6,179."

If you think that such financial hardships couldn't befall you, consider how one reader responded when Ann Landers suggested that divorced women caring for families were only recently feeling the result of less generous judgments. In her letter, Nina Rothchild, a member of the Council on the Economic Status of Women in St. Paul, Minnesota, quoted the following figures from the U.S. Department of Commerce, Bureau of the Census (Divorce, Child Custody and Child Support, June 1979): "More than 90 percent of single-parent families are maintained by a woman, [and] more than three-fourths of the 4.9 million mothers who are divorced, separated, remarried or never married do not receive child support. Either support was not ordered, or the fathers ignore the court order. Three-fifths of the women who do receive child support get less than $125 per month."

It is no accident that most of these statistical scenarios star females. While divorced male heads of households also face financial limitations, it is former wives who find that divorce—and life after divorce—costs far more than their available resources. In fact, a June 6, 1983, *Los Angeles Times* article stated baldly, "Divorce is financially profitable to men and an economic disaster for women and children. The Los Angeles County portion of [our] research found that men enjoy a 42 percent improvement in their standard of living in the first year after they divorce, while their former wives and children experience a 73 percent decline." Yes, men often move out of the family home and pay support each month, but according to this "comprehensive ten-year study of the impact of divorce in California," . . . "more than half of California's state's divorced fathers could comply fully with court orders for support and still live above what the federal government defines as the 'high standard budget.' " Not only is the median child support allotment about half the actual cost of raising a child, but "only 13 percent [of mothers] are awarded any spousal support while rearing young children." In fact, in *all* states, so far only jail seems to rank as an effective "collection motivation." Michigan, the only forum with a practice of locking up nonpaying parents, claims the best support payment record in America.

Are these statistical horrors included to cause you sleepless nights, or to chain you to an unhappy marriage? No. They're highlighted to show the importance of following Step No. 1 in preparing for a profitable divorce. *No other single suggestion in this book will provide you with a better chance for a profitable divorce.* For no matter how much treasure you've uncovered, how carefully you've planned a new life, or how well you've prepared for life alone, you may lose all you have gained if you cannot hold out, during possibly long negotiations or a delayed trial, to solidify your asset and support possibilities. To hold out, nothing will serve you as well as a generous sum of *ready cash.* Therefore do follow . . .

Step No. 1: Get your mitts on enough liquid assets to carry you for several months, and preferably for at least one year. Even if you work, or plan to work, and can earn an adequate salary after separation, you may end up paying for expert appraisals, business assessments, cash-flow projections, asset evaluations, court appearances, unusual medical, dental, or therapeutic expenses, and other costs that only imagination could foresee. Immediate, ready funds can give you breathing room as well as bargaining power. There are a few major decisions—and you'll be making plenty during the first year or so after separation—that should not be made during divorce proceedings. Having sufficient cash in the bank, available only to you, can forestall financial pressures, provide for cool assessments of situations, and prevent costly mistakes. Cash will "insure" your ability to negotiate comfortably, calmly, and from a position of strength. Ready cash will also enable you to wait as long as necessary to obtain the property deal, the support commitments, or the assets that you want.

If you're not sure that taking one-half or all of the funds in any joint account appears warranted in your case, consider this common scenario:

> Janet felt bitterly unhappy in her marriage. Divorce seemed inevitable. Concerned for the children, Janet had maintained the facade of a good relationship for many years. Then one spring Saturday afternoon, Janet gulped four martinis at the local golf course bar. Fueled with booze and the "support" of her foursome, Janet swayed home. Announcing that she intended to file for divorce, she asked Jake to move out.
>
> While Janet wove boozily up to bed, Jake hopped into their better car, dashed to the nearest 24-hour mechanical teller, and withdrew all the funds from their joint accounts.
>
> The following Monday, while Janet readied their three children for school, Jake called his employer and explained that he'd be in a bit late. From 8 till 10 a.m., Jake emptied their safe-deposit boxes of the Kruggerands, the coin collection, and their unset diamonds. He also wrote to their insurance agents and made arrangements to withdraw any cash value in their policies and have the funds sent to him.
>
> Lastly, he opened a new checking account in his name alone, at a bank near his job where Janet had no contacts and did not do business. There he deposited all his acquired funds and made arrangements to bank all his future paychecks.
>
> Later that week, Janet was surprised to learn that her check bounced with a local merchant. Upon checking, she found zero balances. With no ready funds to buy groceries, clothing, doctor bills, pay the mortgage, or have the assets appraised, Janet fell further and further behind in meeting the bills. Though she landed a part-time job, it did little to meet the family's monthly financial needs. Within weeks, Janet realized that she could not even hire legal counsel to negotiate with Jake, who refused to answer her letters or calls. Soon, Janet's nerves reflected the pressures of living on a fraying financial tightrope.
>
> When Janet received Jake's eventual settlement offer, she accepted its terms with gratitude, though she could see that most were patently unfair.

As Jane Welsh Carlyle wrote to Thomas Carlyle in 1855, "When one has been threatened with a great injustice, one accepts a smaller as a favor."

In short, the spouse with "money muscle" often refuses to negotiate and orchestrates court delays to grind down the resistance and even fair demands of the cash-poor spouse. By the time a mate who can afford to wait offers a sum for support and a property share, even inadequate terms look awfully good. To avoid being a Janet (whether you're male or female), use some or all of Jake's sources and these others to gain ready cash early in the game:

1. Sell, pawn, or borrow against your jewelry. Indian women wear anklets, bracelets, and numerous silver doodads as a sort of "portable bank account" that can provide economic independence during (and after) marriage.
2. Borrow on your life insurance policies. Some policies allow you to borrow cash at a low interest rate of 5, 6, or 7 percent. Check with your local financial institution; many now offer to help clients withdraw these funds and invest them in a vehicle providing a higher return. The right kind of vehicle can also provide you with liquidity—the ability to withdraw the funds as needed. To facilitate such borrowings, some institutions will arrange for additional insurance coverage for the amount borrowed, so that you need lose no coverage. Such loans diminish only the face value of the policy, and the borrowed amount will not adversely affect you unless the insured dies and you collect the policy amount. If the loan is of reasonable size, it should not diminish the amount received to any damaging degree.
3. Cash in any savings bonds, unused travelers' checks, or other negotiable instruments.
4. Use your credit cards to obtain stocks of groceries, needed house repairs, other basics, legal advice, and even cash. Yes, this debt will be assessed against you and interest will be charged on it, but if your purchases constitute support for you and/or the children, your expenses may be considered "support in advance," and the obligation may be allocated entirely or in some part to your spouse. Be sensible in your charges, and keep careful records. This is an expensive means of gaining ready cash, so use it with discretion and only if absolutely necessary.
5. Utilize the check overdraft protection on your account. The same warning given in No. 4 above applies to this source, so use it carefully.
6. Seek help from your employer by asking that bonuses, commissions, or proft-sharing pay-outs be held and paid to you after you separate; by asking for a low-interest loan or salary advance; and by asking if your employer knows of any union benefits that could help you through.
7. Arrange to be the second spouse to endorse any joint tax return

refund check, then deposit the check in your account. Remember to keep records showing that you utilized these jointly owned funds for the kids or to preserve common assets (paying the mortgage, for example), so that you may avoid having to reimburse your mate.

8. Cash in any stocks, bonds, or other sources of ready cash, but follow the record-keeping warnings given in No. 7.
9. Sell your share in the family home to a third party for cash. You may have to break a joint tenancy to do this, but a quick meeting with a skilled real estate attorney or a review of the relevant state code section at the local law library should show you how to do this. Be sure that a recent, professional appraisal has provided you with an accurate idea of the house's value and that no children or other dependents will be harmed by your action. Some possible buyers include your mate's new lover, a relative of your spouse who wants to help him or her, or even a friend of yours who wants to invest in a solid asset but does not need or want to actually inhabit the house. In fact, your "buyer" may well be your spouse.
10. Transfer your interest in other jointly owned or community property to your spouse for its fair market value. Such assets can include campers, hobby supplies and power tools, other real estate, furniture, and extra vans, trailers, or cars. To ensure that you receive a fair amount, do not rely on your mate for an assessment of value, but check out the asset's fair market price via another, impartial, source.
11. Borrow from relatives, business associates, or friends. These are not ideal sources, but your ability to repay them will depend upon your ability to hold out for a fair or even generous share of assets and allocations of support.

In addition, consider *all* other alternatives to paying cash for needed supplies or services. You may be able to charge adult children who are living at home healthy rates for room and board. You may prefer to take in boarders who can maintain the garden, care for the children while you work, keep your home in good repair, or fix a troublesome car. Even if others do not live with you, you may be able to barter a special service or skill for paying an expert for something you need. One woman made dresses in return for some handmade furniture. Another painted a house while its owner prepared the painter's income tax return. Totaling up all the wealth in your "barter bank" can help keep the wolf *and* depression from your door.

If you do dip into your barter bank, however, by performing services in exchange for others, keep in mind that acquiring income may affect your success in obtaining support from an absent spouse. On the other hand, services performed by others may not diminish your support rights, even though they save you cash. If you find this concept confusing because you've learned earlier that one mate may share in the fruits of the other's perspiration, consider the following. If your efforts acquire a service that benefits both of you while still together, no harm is done your spouse. If your efforts net you an asset or service that your mate would otherwise be obligated to provide for you (food, clothing, medical care, etc.), your perspiration has saved your spouse cash. If the item or service obtained benefits only you, but your spouse knows that you're expending communal energy and does not object, then he/she can be deemed to have made you a gift of his/her share of your perspiration. Finally, if you have already parted, note that your energy becomes your separate property after the separation date, and therefore, anything you acquire with that effort also belongs to you alone. If your circumstances don't match any of these scenarios, and your mate *should* share in something you acquire, then allow him/her an offset or credit for one-half of the value that you receive. The important thing is that you don't deprive yourself during this period, or fall behind in handling creditors, for either situation can begin to undermine your self-esteem.

Along with the above suggestions, consider getting a job. If it will not harm any small children, and if you face receiving a small amount for spousal support (or a struggle in collecting it), the extra income should prove more a benefit than a boomerang. Earnings after separation constitute separate property, so you need not share them with your mate. In addition, a job will use your skills, enhance your self-esteem, take your mind off your worries, and free you (at least in part) from being controlled by a financially powerful spouse.

If you obtain support dollars from your spouse — whether voluntary, negotiated, or court-ordered — be sure that the funds you receive do not come from a commonly owned source. You have gained little if the monthly allotment comes from a jointly owned account or other asset which you may own half of anyway. Try to have all support come from your spouse's earnings after separation. Otherwise, these payments use up assets in which you should share. A court cannot order support payments to cover any time period in the past, so arrange for support quickly after the parting, and make sure that no community-property source remains available for your spouse's payment of these obligations.

Now let's consider another suggestion for gaining assets after the split. This strategy deals with staying in the family home and helping your spouse to move out. As more and more states adopt a no-fault attitude toward divorce, individual behavior before and during divorce becomes less important. Courts are indicating that they are more concerned with treating each partner fairly in terms of dividing the property, allocating any debts, and providing minor children or dependent spouses with adequate support. Therefore, it may be possible for you to move out of the family home without suffering any punishment or property loss resulting from outdated concepts like abandonment. Because state divorce laws do differ, however, check with an attorney or the applicable civil code section before packing your bags. Once you're sure that an "out-house spouse" will still receive fair treatment under your state laws, you can consider leaving the house, but as a practical matter, remember that unique benefits can accrue to the spouse who stays at home.

In fact, gaining a sort of informal exclusive use and possession of the family home at this time can be one of the smartest actions you'll take in the course of your divorce. The rewards of remaining a homebody include the following:

1. You can personally maintain your real estate, the furnishings, and all personal property located in your home or on your lot.
2. Your eyes will be the first to see the daily mail—a good way to keep track of assets, business deals, additional income, and to trace any hidden property.
3. You will receive—at least for a time—all telephone calls relating to you *and* your spouse, your holdings, your joint property, and any pending acquisitions or deals.
4. You may save money, as your mortgage may total less than rents for comparable housing in your area. Remember that an out-house spouse with youngsters of different sexes may have to obtain a three-bedroom apartment to facilitate overnight visitations and may have to live in an unsafe or undesirable neighborhood to stay within budget limitations. As an in-house spouse, you will also find that familiar surroundings can help reduce stress and

give comfort during divorce proceedings that can continue for months and sometimes stretch into years.

5. You may well receive a heftier support payment, since part of your expenses include maintaining and paying for a "communal" asset (the home) that will benefit both parties at a later trade or sale.
6. You should find custody of minor children easier to obtain, as they will doubtless remain with you in the home, and most courts remain reluctant to upset the status quo at any later custody hearing if the children appear to be happy and healthy where they are.
7. You may be able to use the house as a resource to help support yourself and any children during these financially trying months. Divorcing mates who continue to occupy the family home can raise vegetables in the backyard, rent their homes out to boarders, collect fees for movie or commercial filming on their premises, begin a business or work during leisure time in a study, den, or extra bedroom; exchange the use of the house to vacation in another country or in another part of the United States at tremendous savings, run a small catering service from the kitchen, or even start a day-care center for the children of working mothers.
8. You should find it easier to demonstrate your standard of living and obtain funds to preserve it if your life-style and expenses remain more or less the same.
9. You may find that your spouse, after initial complaints, grows more accustomed to living alone in other quarters, begins to adapt and enjoy his/her freedom, and seems gradually less interested in forcing a sale of the house or in promoting an immediate division of other assets.
10. Your home constitutes your principal residence. A later sale to a third party will generate funds that can be "rolled over" or invested in another principal residence. By purchasing another primary residence of sufficient value within a two-year period of time, you will be able to shelter from taxes any gain you realize on the sale of this home. The out-house spouse, however, will not be able to claim that the family home still ranks as his or her principal residence, since that mate has been living elsewhere before the sale. Result? Your mate must pay capital gains taxes on his or her portion of the sale proceeds; *you* can defer those

taxes until a later date. In fact, it's entirely possible that you may not pay taxes on your gains until years from now, when you ultimately decide to sell a residence and never purchase another. Even when considering an ultimate sale, study the next suggestion to see how staying in your home now can save you tax funds in years to come.

11. You may be able to claim the once-in-a-lifetime tax forgiveness of $125,000 *if* you resided in the primary residence (the one you're selling now) for at least three of the past five years and if you have reached the age of 55 at the time of sale. The out-house spouse, even if he or she is already 55, most establish a three-year residence stay in that new location to qualify for this special tax treatment. You do not have to wait.

So much for your motivation — but what about your technique? If your spouse has shown a violent nature and has threatened to strike you (or has actually assaulted you) in the past, you can probably obtain a restraining order (sometimes called a kick-out order) to exclude her or him from the family residence. If you have a law-abiding or gentle-natured spouse, try suggesting some of the following reasons why it would benefit everyone if he or she moved out:

a. The children would do better in school and feel less stress in the home environment.

b. Everyone could think more clearly, sleep better, and generally enjoy life more if you spent some time apart.

c. If you part before tearing each other apart (physically or emotionally) there remains a better chance of preserving a relationship between you, of reaching a cooler, calmer assessment of your situation, of effecting a possible reconciliation, or of resolving the property, debt, and support issues in an amicable way.

d. The spouse moving out will escape mortgage, maintenance, and home-care costs and perhaps commuting hassles, but will retain all rights to profit equally in any net proceeds of that home's ultimate sale. This argument should appeal strongly to an investment-oriented spouse because it can pay off well in future years.

e. The mate on his or her own can enjoy a freer, livelier, unmarried life-style, work long hours, party frequently, attend night school, read till three in the morning, and in short, fulfill all those secret dreams.

f. You will share the home furnishings, supply an adequate "home starter kit" (towels and sheets, bathroom and kitchen necessities, etc.), and even help with the move. Why would you want to appear so generous? Because this way, you can dispense with duplications in kitchen ware and get out of the house all of that stuff you never liked anyway. By keeping a careful list, and perhaps asking your spouse to sign it, you will obtain a credit that can pay off when you finally divide the other common property. As an extra plus, remember that you earn this credit with items you've wanted to dispose of for a long time. Further, you'll feel quite noble, the kids will think you're great, the judge (if you cannot negotiate a settlement) will like your attitude, and your mate—not having to purchase everything anew—should have more available funds to pay you for support.

If a through f appeal to you more than Nos. 1 through 11, and *you* opt to become the out-house spouse, make sure that you take with you any items of separate property that you fear may suffer damage or disappear in your absence, and enough furnishings or supplies to start your new life as comfortably as possible. To the inevitable stress of parting you need not add the experience of eating spaghetti cold from the can with a plastic spoon.

Whether you stay home or move out, make sure that the in-house spouse keeps careful records of any maintenance costs or mutually-agreed-to home improvements. In addition to utilizing the rollover-of-any-gain provision and perhaps the lifetime forgiveness provision, you will both want to save tax dollars by showing less profit on your home's sale. You can do this in part by adding to your original cost of the house all additional expenses for improvements. This provides a higher basis, meaning that you now have invested more funds in the home before sale. A higher basis means a lower profit margin. Maintenance and regular repair bills will probably not qualify to raise your basis figure, but adding a new roof, a new room, or remodeling a kitchen or bath can increase your base figure and reduce the net profits on which you will be taxed.

To gain assets even during parting, try to negotiate as much as you can as soon as you can. Once parties live apart for a time and lose daily contact, communication often lags or seems less clear. You will probably both remain happier and find that you have more energy to tackle sticky issues if you can decide now who will occupy the house, who will pay how much support and for how long, who will take certain personal or easily movable property, and how you will handle standing bank balances, existing credit cards, and family debts.

If you have intrusive neighbors, nosy friends, or children who don't need to hear you settle such issues, consider dining out with each other and a short agenda. Public places serve as excellent forums if you have a mate with a short fuse or who has tried to win previous "discussions" with intimidation or threats. Few people, no matter how volatile, want to appear an idiot before the maitre d' and two dozen strangers. When Farrah Fawcett and Lee Majors hit a roadblock in their celebrated and well-lawyered trial, they dined at a posh Los Angeles eatery, and amid the white latticework, ferns, and soft lighting, agreed on the disposition of their $2.5 million mansion in the Hollywood Hills.

While an offer to negotiate always appears attractive and can save legal fees, eliminate courtroom trauma, produce creative settlements, and encourage continuing compliance because both parties worked out the terms, negotiating *can* have pitfalls.

First, you may not succeed in negotiating effectively if your spouse knows more about the assets, the debts, the family income, and the tax repercussions than you do.

Second, you may emerge tattered from negotiations if your mate revels in playing psychological games and typically uses emotions, personal attacks, or underhanded methods to break down your self-esteem and your resolve.

Third, if you don't have a comprehensive plan you can find that negotiating issues as they arise (in a piecemeal fashion), can result in leftover demands for which you have no ammunition. As an example, let's say that you know your spouse wants control of her business, full rights to her pension plan, and certain furnishings of your home. That is your bargaining arsenal. If each of these issues is negotiated separately, however, you may well find that you overlooked property important to you, but that you've traded all of your concessions in previous talks. As a safeguard, make a complete list of the property, the debts, support requests, and other issues. By viewing every area of concern at one time, you should be able to utilize offsets, credits, trades, and compromises in a way that won't leave you bargainless too soon.

Fourth, if you begin negotiations too early, you may find that your feelings of guilt or your "independence highs" skew your logic and undercut your bargaining ability. The mate who first speaks of divorce can suffer enormous guilt about breaking up the marriage and "deserting" the children or a mate. In this mood, he or she may convey "guilt-edged securities" to compensate for such a wrong. A person on an independence high is one who is so carried away by a sense of freedom and escape that he or she neglects to bargain realistically to satisfy present rights and future needs. If you have announced that you're eager to fly, don't fail to bargain for necessary support or a fair share of (especially liquid) assets. If you're entitled to alimony, don't turn it down. Consider its Latin source, *alimonia*, meaning nourishment or sustenance. Flowers bloom best when nourished well. If you're thinking that's so much nonsense, and you'll make it without help, just shovel that monthly allotment into a savings account for winter's chill. If you feel the guilties coming on, delay making important decisions about asset allocation or support commitments until your sense of self-preservation returns.

On the other hand, you can often make money on a spouse who's feeling guilty or overly independent. If you suspect that your mate's suffering an attack of the guilties, close in on support and property allocation requests. You may also succeed in orchestrating an uneven allocation of the family obligations if the primary wage earner wants to pay as a means of feeling better inside.

If you can't wait to start a new life, don't let your euphoria obscure practical considerations. Many previously dependent spouses feel high when approaching sudden freedom. Some get so excited that they envision a life without that burdensome mate but in which nevertheless a steady income is somehow "mailed in." They forget that in the real world, the mate comes with the cash. Don't bargain for important, long-range support or asset rights in such a euphoric state of mind.

In fact, if you will need support funds after separation, turn this need into a strength by mapping out a "reentry program" that can set you financially free. In your negotiations, lay out a plan—including costs and a time estimate—of how you plan to become self-supporting. Set your goal, then investigate what resources, funds, and time it will require. Write it all down in a way that will make sense to the "banker," your spouse. Will you need a degree, a certification, practical experience, an apprenticeship? How much money will you require? How long will it take? Will you be able to provide some of your own support during this time? Can you offer your mate a sliding scale of expenses, so that as you become more accomplished in your chosen field, you will need fewer dollars for support? Planning toward this goal will make you feel better about your possibilities and yourself and can dramatically increase the amount of funds that your mate (or the court) may grant you in support.

However, if you anticipate playing the role of the $upporting spouse, you have the right, under California law at least, to ask that the mate seeking funds undergo an examination by a vocational training consultant. Such experts determine a spouse's present marketable skills, training potential, and ultimate earning ability in a given field. Clearly, such a review can discourage your mate's unrealistic earnings expectations, offer guidance in training, and ensure that support dollars underwrite a practical program leading to self-reliance and an end to support.

Within this period of time, you may also want to protect your rights to common assets that have yet to be divided. For example, you may feel that you need to ask the court for a restraining order to prevent your spouse from wasting or spending assets over which you have no control. If you and your mate can work out the wording of such constraints on spending or on transferring earnings or property, you can draw up an agreement at the kitchen table. Remember to file your agreement with the court to make its terms enforceable. Once obtained (by informal talks or by court hearing), you will need to have such orders served on the banks, money market funds, or other parties holding common assets. Depending on the codes in your state, you may be able to effect this service by certified mail, or deliver the papers yourself to third parties to save funds. No order is effective against asset waste if the third party or your spouse never receives notification.

Such crders or agreements aim to preserve the status quo until assets can be appraised and final allocations or divisions can occur. As a practical matter, they work well with basically law-abiding spouses—the kind who probably don't need such an order anyway. A party determined to make off with the goodies, waste earnings, splurge away the joint accounts (at least half of which should already rest in your possession), and conceal profits or overestimate operating costs, may well do so despite an order from the court.

Still, restraining orders can prove helpful in some situations, and these include controlling the actions of other people somehow related to your divorce proceedings. For example, your state may provide for a joinder procedure, which means a joining of parties and plaintiffs or defendants in a suit. It would enable you to restrain *any* third party who holds or controls some asset of which you may deserve a share. Serving such a party with the proper papers effectively bars any transfers or waste and can recapture for division or allocation assets that have left your (and perhaps your spouse's) day-to-day control. Such parties can include a debtor who owes funds to your spouse, an insurance firm that remains obligated to pay a sum to your mate, or even a neighbor or friend who holds property owned by you or your mate but who might prove susceptible to entreaties by your spouse to exclude you from sharing in the asset or the proceeds of selling it.

In fact, at this juncture let me call your attention to possibly the most crucial use of a joinder—to notify your mate's pension or retirement plan administrator that a divorce is pending and that the value in the plan may have to be divided between the parties. By serving the necessary papers on a retirement plan, you give the court power to decide your share in such an asset, and the power to order the plan to pay a portion of that monthly allotment directly to you. In fact, serving the plan administrator with notice of the pending action can prove most important if your spouse could withdraw funds from the plan and spend or hide them before you could obtain your share. In other situations, your mate's plan may be years from the withdrawal stage, but if the administrator does not know of your right to share, he may—with impunity—pay the funds eventually to only your mate. Wouldn't you rather receive a check directly from the Riveters Union of America than nag an unwilling spouse for monthly payments? (When considering a mate's pension plan value, remember that even an unvested or young retirement program contains value. You'll want to consider hiring an actuary or trained CPA to appraise the present value in any such plan. Keep in mind also that in figuring the communal share of such valuations, the early years rank as highly as the last months in which vesting or a pay-out occurs. Just because you've shared only the early working years, you need not feel that your contribution rates as less crucial than later, higher-earning time periods. Although your state law may not call for sharing such an asset, terms reached in *negotiations* need not follow state law to qualify as enforceable or fair.)

Even if you've uncovered a pension or other assets under a third party's control, it may prove more practical to establish that asset's value and, in essence, to kiss it good-bye. Does this mean that you'll never see your share? Not at all, only that there's more profit in gaining an additional share of an easily protected, here-and-now asset than in chasing property, via expensive legal maneuvers, that may forever remain beyond your control. In other words, establish all the assets in which you can legally share, then arrange an offset by taking more of the readily available items and trading off your rights in the more peripheral property. Let your spouse get headaches trying to collect that insurance payment or attempting to regain funds loaned to her business friend. You'll need to take such actions as joinders and restraining orders early in the proceedings, or the transfer or sale you fear may already have been orchestrated by the third party or by your fast-acting spouse.

If your "communal estate" contains real property (land, house, apartment building, etc.), you may want to file a *lis pendens* with the recorder for the county containing each real property asset. The lis pendens form, when filed, gives notice to all that a suit is pending that concerns the ownership of the asset in question. Since any title search conducted before the sale of the real property will show the lis pendens filing, it can effectively halt your mate's efforts to sell such property or to put it up for collateral when seeking a loan. A new buyer who *does* purchase (or lend against) the property after learning of your pending claim would take title subject to this cloud on the title, and would remain obligated to pay you for any share that you could show belonged to you. Clearly, a lis pendens can prove a powerful protective tool if your marriage community contains property in which you feel you own a share but which stands in your mate's name alone.

To protect your rights to a family business that you formerly operated as a team, consider arranging (through negotiation or court order) for terms that will enable you to keep in touch with the business. Such terms can include:

- Full or shared authority to run the business until divorce proceedings conclude and the final ownership is decided.
- A schedule for regular written reports showing the business completed, pending, and contemplated. If you can still communicate, oral reports in a public or friendly setting seem much preferable — and on the business premises, even better, so that you can pick up the atmosphere, employee signals, and a "feel" for how the firm is doing.
- An opportunity, at given periods of time or at "any reasonable business hour" to review the company's ledgers, books, customer service notes, sales results, or even telephone logs.

- Access to the accountant or bookkeeper for the company (often more valuable if such a person remains beyond your spouse's control; the safest such professionals are those who remain independent and require certification, to whom hiding or obscuring records for the benefit of a single client is not worth the potential loss of a license).

You may start to hear many people urging you to begin formal proceedings by filing for divorce. You may feel uncomfortable taking such a step at this time, and if you feel you need to wait, do so. Filing is an important step that requires weighing several factors. The more discovery and negotiation you can do informally, the more money, time, and hassle you can save. In addition, you can probably emerge with a more creative settlement that both of you feel more willing to obey because you tailored it to fit your practical, financial, and emotional needs. While the court in your state will need to join eventually in your action in order to legitimitize your divorce and approve your plan for support, for custody, for allocating debts, and for dividing assets, many couples prefer to put off filing for divorce until they have worked out most or all of their settlement terms.

There are some dangers in delaying: your spouse may waste or convey property, may continue beating or berating you, or may refuse to leave the family home or pay support until ordered to do so by the court. But if none of these factors apply to you, work at informal talks until you can resolve all or most of your differences. The service of formal divorce proceedings, even via the mail, places a distinct gulf between parties and can incite emotion, cloud judgment, and compromise cooperation because it introduces a "stranger" into this very personal negotiation stage.

On the other hand, if you have a spouse unwilling to negotiate or communicate or who refuses to recognize the probability of divorce, you may as well file and ask the attorneys to begin negotiations or the court to order compliance from your spouse.

Whenever you *do* decide to begin formal proceedings, try to be the first to file. The advantages are described below:

1. In many cases, only one spouse ever files, the case being decided in negotiations or by default, when the second party fails to respond or make an appearance in court. If you are the only filing party, only your papers will appear on the judge's bench, and he or she may see only your listing of the assets, the support needs, the custody suggestions, and only your requests regarding the payment of joint obligations. Even if you tell the court nothing but the truth, whose version of the facts, needs, and considerations in your case would you prefer to place on your judge's bench?

2. The information appearing on the filing papers may be accepted by the courts in your state as true unless controverted by divorce papers filed by your spouse. Such papers can include a listing of all the property you claim is communal, requests to confirm certain property as separately owned, requests for attorneys fees and court costs, appraisal and experts fees, and an outline of the funds needed to operate the household and care for all the kids. In California courts, for example, "Rule 1238 provides that unless controvened in the response or unless a motion to quash is made, every material statement of fact in the petition shall be taken as true for the purpose of the proceeding. . . . If all [community property is] properly set forth in the petition, and if there is no denial, no additional proof is needed as to the extent of the community property." To obtain more information on state laws governing divorce, consider asking a lawyer friend what books he/she uses in doing research on family law issues. The information about California Rule 1238 given above, for example, is quoted from *The Handbook of Family Law 4th* by Stuart J. Faber, published in 1982 by Lega-Books, "California's Largest Publisher of Legal Texts in Paperback." For a list of this publisher's works, write or call: Lega-Books, 658 South Bonnie Brae Street, Los Angeles, California 90057 (213) 483-5832.
3. Because your state courts may not award more than what was prayed for (requested) in the petition, you can be assured of receiving your full share of any assets or support only by being the party completing and filing the petition in your case.
4. As the filing party, you will involve either the central court system or the branch court that holds jurisdiction over your residential location. In other words, your home address determines the courtroom in which your matter will be heard. Clearly, jurisdictional limits can prove convenient for you and possibly extremely *inconvenient* for your mate. (Few factors can spur settlement on your terms better than several cumbersome, time-consuming, expensive trips to a distant forum by your spouse.)
5. By serving as the filing party and therefore determining the hearing forum, you can give the court

- Jurisdiction over your spouse by making personal service more convenient.
- Easy access to crucial evidence or a convenient forum for neccessary witnesses.
- The power to apply local or state law that favors you instead of your spouse.
- Enforcement advantages, since a court can more easily enforce orders that affect people and property within its immediate jurisdiction.
- Access to an asset or property that may have to be viewed before allocation or division can occur. (In the Farrah Fawcett-Lee Majors divorce, for example, Judge Harry Shafer visited their Hollywood mansion to determine the value and the "sex" of the creative touch responsible for the extensive improvements to the home that stood in Lee's name alone.)

A central court (which holds jurisdiction over the whole county and so is always a possibility) may prove a better choice for you than a branch court or more local forum. It depends. If you seek immediate support or the immediate sharing or allocation of an asset (like the family home), you may do better in a less crowded branch court where your case may come up for hearing much more quickly. If you face an assessment for support or anticipate losing an important advantage when the gavel descends, as the first to file you may choose to set the issues in a more crowded, metropolitan, central forum with a crammed calendar to delay an inevitable loss, or to increase, over time, the financial pressures on your more-burdened spouse.

During the actual parting, time may seem to move too quickly for you to organize your assets, your needs, your emotions *and* your thoughts. In some states you may be able to call for a procedural "time-out" at this stage by seeking help from especially trained court personnel. In California, a county-by-county "conciliation court system" provides such assistance to couples experiencing marital difficulties. In cases containing disagreements over custody or visitation rights, divorcing couples *must* visit "conciliation court" personnel, who will see the parties and children together and individually in trying to resolve the parties' differences in an amicable way. Though this system bears the word "court" in its name, its procedures, staff, and setting little resemble a judicial forum. No judge, for example, decides when conciliation court sessions will occur because this "court" operates from separate quarters within (and sometimes outside) the courthouse itself. Such a system can offer you definite advantages. For instance, even when a child's feelings run high, and that child wants to let a judge know where he/she wishes to live, many judges will not see the child—even in chambers—because they fear that such an interview places too much pressure on any youngster. In conciliation court sessions, however, the children and even third parties can speak freely about their wishes, wants, and fears. Conciliation counselors see the divorcing couple and their children in comfortably furnished offices where they employ professional therapeutic approaches in attempting to reach compromises on custody allocations and visitation schedules. In fact, the qualifications required in California for these court-directed mediators include a master's degree in psychology, social work, or other behavioral science, two years' experience in counseling or psychotherapy, and a knowledge of the court system.

Parting or troubled California couples can petition (apply) for a conference date, whether or not either has filed for a separation or divorce and whether or not children are involved. Either party can obtain the petition from court offices, fill in the information requested, and submit the short form (no filing or service fee is required). A conciliation court staffer then contacts both parties to set a mutually convenient time for the first session and, in one or more meetings, works to help the couple reconcile, deal effectively with custody or visitation disagreements, or part with more understanding and less animosity.

The conciliation court's jurisdiction extends over troubled spouses living in its county, and, if children are concerned, the parties need not be wed to call on conciliation court services. A party can also seek such counseling help in situations of domestic violence, whether or not the family circle contains any children, and regardless of the kids' parentage. In fact, conciliation court material states that this service's purpose is "to protect the rights of children and promote the public welfare by preserving, promoting, and protecting family life in the institution of matrimony, and to provide means for the reconciliation of spouses and amicable settlement of domestic and family controversies."

California's conciliation courts have the power to undertake the following:

- Issue a citation to any party to appear.
- Require the attendance of necessary witnesses.

- Convene the "hearing" at any time and place within the county.
- Hold the sessions in chambers or otherwise.
- Recommend (with the consent of both parties) the aid of medical or other specialists or scientific experts, or the participation of a pastor or director of any religious denomination to which the parties may belong.

If either party seeks conciliation court assistance, California law bars the taking of any other legal action for divorce or separation for 30 days while the couple meets with the trained counselor on an informal basis.

There is no charge for conciliation court services, and all exchanges remain confidential. If the parties cannot reach an agreement with the help of the conciliator, then a hearing or trial is scheduled so that a judge can hear testimony, weigh evidence, and provide a ruling on the visitation or custody issues that remain (along with decisions on issues not falling within the purview of the conciliation court). During such a formal hearing or trial, neither party can introduce any discussion or offers of compromise that occurred during any conciliation court session. Such protections encourage each person to disclose information and offer settlement terms in a safe environment, since the other party cannot later use such evidence against them in open court. Wherever these courts or their equivalent operate, however, they have the power to bind parties who agree to terms after one or more conciliation sessions. Once the agreement is drawn up by the conciliator and signed by the parties in the case, the document is sent to the judge presiding over the case (sometimes located just down the hall). If this judicial officer gives his/her approval to the agreement as drafted, his/her signature converts the agreement to a court order with the stroke of a pen. As an order, these terms bear the same weight as if the judge had pronounced the same provisions from the bench after a trial lasting hours, days, or weeks. If either party breaches any part of the order, the other can seek a judgment of contempt, levy on a bank account, have the marshal or sheriff attach personal property, garnish wages, or arrange for enforcement via some other authorized, court-endorsed means.

If your state offers similar services, do take advantage of them.

Our next topic concerns "emotional adaptation" and negotiation during the period when parting feels especially painful.

Mourning for a lost marriage is like grieving over a death. Your relationship's demise is, after all, the death of an ideal, a creation, an entity that existed apart from both of you. Few griefs cut more deeply than a regret for what might, could, or *should* have been; few efforts encompass more goals or dreams than a marriage does. Therefore, when you part, allow yourself time to mourn. Expect to hurt at odd times, or over suddenly remembered events. Find an understanding but objective friend who will accept hearing about your pain, but who will tell you when you're lapsing into excess sentimentality or maudlin meanderings. Choose a friend who will let you know when enough becomes too much, and who will help you redirect that energy—before too long—into something positive for you.

Try to use any anger you may feel to fuel the discovery of assets, obtaining a job or getting a better one, coping with the children's concerns at this time, or even sorting out your feelings and hurts in therapy. It's important that you channel your fury into projects good for you, that you take active steps to improve your situation instead of letting those feelings destroy your self-esteem and undercut your efforts to care for yourself. It's also crucial to direct these destructive feelings outward (so that you don't blame yourself), and away from your spouse (so that you can preserve the best possible relationship for present negotiations, for future psychological or financial support, and for any children, who will need frequent visitation in the friendliest possible atmosphere).

Expect good and bad days. Use the good days to forge ahead by negotiating with your mate, by researching points of law, by helping in discovering assets that you have not yet explored, by looking for employment or moving ahead in your career, by devoting special attention to any children, and by improving your appearance, your résumé, or your social life. When you have bad days (and you must expect a few, even if you've planned this parting and grieved for your marriage for a long time), keep that bubbling stew of emotions to yourself. Unplug your telephone, curl up with an entertaining book, go to the zoo, lunch with a friend, cuddle up with a classic film on TV, *but try to avoid talking to your lawyer or your spouse*. A confused, angry, and revenge-seeking state of mind can prove extremely costly because you risk setting unreasonable settlement terms that you later find difficult to retract. People suffering from such feelings often mix emotional debts in with property and support demands, open old wounds that skew logical thinking, and alienate even mates determined to cooperate. Julie's actions during her first weeks of parting illustrate this point:

Though Julie and Joe had frequently and calmly discussed the possibility of divorce, Julie found herself shattered when Joe finally moved out. Though Joe's catering business was suffering a slump, he sent Julie fairly generous monthly checks without an agreement or any order from the court. In her better moments, Julie revealed, "I know that Joe wants the best for me and the children, and I know that he's sending us money even when he has to do without to send us those checks." Despite this knowledge, Julie one day called Joe and chewed him out for several minor oversights that Joe had not had time to handle yet. While furious, Julie visited a well-known divorce attorney and demanded that Joe be hauled into court and ordered to pay three times the support that he had voluntarily (and regularly) been sending to her. Confused, angry, and hurt, Joe stopped mailing home the checks and notified several of their creditors that he would no longer pay Julie's bills.

What result? Julie soon felt a severe money crunch. Joe stopped visiting the children, paying any of the bills, or giving Julie funds for daily expenses. Julie's attorneys duly filed the required papers and had the marshal serve Joe at his office (during a client conference, as it turned out). Within the week, both parties felt miserable, but neither felt a retraction was due. In talking with a mutual friend and in reviewing her knowledge of Joe's business, Julie concluded that she'd enjoyed support dollars that Joe could ill afford. Now she felt even worse.

Meanwhile, Joe had retained counsel to oppose Julie's exorbitant support demands and felt that he, as the "wronged party," should not have to suggest a before-court figure. Besides, he didn't see how he *could* pay more.

Each party felt that he or she would lose face if either made the first move to compromise, so they limped ever closer to their hearing date.

Finally, recognizing her error, Julie called Joe and apologized for blowing her stack. She promised to call off the court hearing on support if Joe would reinstate the payments and resume visiting the kids, Julie then phoned her attorney and explained that she knew Joe was paying all that he could, and that she felt capable of asking him for more when his business grew more profitable. In return, Joe called his lawyer, called the children to make plans for an outing, and mailed Julie a check for the amount he had reserved for his lawyer's time in court.

A full month and many sleepless nights after that angry phone call, Julie swore that she'd keep her next tantrum to herself and make "requests" of Joe only when she was in a good mood.

Don't (like Julie) inflate small pains into large angers as a means of obscuring the enormous agonies contained in parting. Working your way into a fury over minor matters can provide energy to cope, and a sense of power. But ranting and raving can boomerang, and does little toward building a new foundation for your better (single) life. Besides, there's a good chance that this rage really masks destructive emotions that you'll need to deal with more honestly if you ever want to feel free. As George Eliot put it in *The Mill on the Floss*, "Anger and jealousy can no more bear to lose sight of their objects than love."

Involve yourself in new people and new enthusiasms. You may have devoted years of energy to friends, leisure pursuits, and favorite friends of your spouse. This is your chance to spend your time and energy where you want to. Concentrate on building a new life with the potential to satisfy and please only yourself.

Beware any reconciliation offer from a spouse that doesn't ring true. One wife welcomed back her wayward mate a few weeks after parting, then discovered too late that he really sought access to her credit cards. His second (and final) leaving barely preceded the receipt of monthly charges addressed only to her and totaling sixteen thousand bucks.

Forget about counting on another love interest to throw you an emotional or financial lifeline. You'll feel vulnerable for some time, but don't let this natural neediness masquerade as infatuation or love. Affiliating to a lover at this time to the exclusion of other people or possibilities can prove unfair to you and your potential. You may well find that your new sail increasingly feels like an anchor. Too much dependency on another person can negate all the efforts you've made to end your marriage and can cripple your chances to forge a new life.

Deal immediately and effectively with false deadlines that a spouse advertises to speed along his or her own goals. "I've got to catch a plane to Europe tonight," "I promised to drive to Seattle on Wednesday," and "The house will have to be listed by next week because I'm leaving the state" all represent ploys to make you commit yourself, without thinking, to a course of action that might not prove wise for you. Insist on holding your ground. Make the other person change his or her plans, or wait until taking such action seems good for you. At the very least, stand firm for some thinking time, so that you can weigh without pressure the options and courses open to you.

Don't fall for a demand for an all-or-nothing settlement. Such proposals often bear an unrealistic time limit (see above), your ex-mate demanding that you sign or accept an offer that claims to wrap up all the issues in one neat bow. In one case, a man married 26 years couldn't (or wouldn't) understand why the interrelated issues of child support, spousal support, division of the house, appraisal and allocation of a pension plan stretching over several states, custody of the kids, and the evaluation and disbursement of several unusual pieces of personal property shouldn't be "all worked out before I leave for Ohio this Monday." When his wife refused to submit to these bulldozing tactics, he filed papers, served her by mail, and left for Ohio anyway.

In the months that followed, this man's California spouse thoroughly investigated all the personal and real property and determined (with the help of an actuary) the exact present value of the absent mate's pension plan. With such information in hand, she consulted with her lawyer and proposed a fair property settlement agreement by mail. The Ohio transplant accepted the terms, and the California contingent entered the final judgment some seven months after the husband's departure. No harm came to hubby while waiting, and the wife in this case utilized those months to realize the full value of her share in *all* the property.

Resist hoping for permanent solutions on a "right now" basis. You may want to heft, smell, and get used to a suggested solution for a time before deciding if it suits you. Both of you will find that your attitudes will change as time goes by, and more creative solutions will pop into your minds as you grow increasingly familiar with the law and with all the factors relating to each particular decision. Let's say, for example, that you have no children but a large home. Initially, you both want to live in the house, but you find that it doesn't contain enough rooms to allow you each the necessary solitude. You may suggest each spouse's taking the house for a few months to determine who copes best with the hassles of maintenance, repairs, improvements, security, and with the mortage and other charges. Who deals best with support services like the pool person and cleaning crew? When all is said, felt, and spent, which of you really feels inseparable from that home?

Making major decisions in an atmosphere of tension and on the basis of ambiguous facts doesn't make much sense. Even though you may want to end all your hassles and escape further negotiations or courtroom procedures, steel yourself to take time and live in confusion for a while to ensure a good deal.

Perhaps most important, try to make major decisions—about custody, property, support, and who will pay the debts—after checking your emotional baggage and pocketing the key. Working to open your mate's old wounds (or responding when he or she cuts into a nerve) will only undercut your reasoning abilities and confuse your sense of logic. You'll need all your energy to make plans, discover assets, negotiate effectively, and build a foundation for life on your own. You didn't marry a dummy; your spouse may prove extremely helpful in suggesting creative solutions to your mutual problems during divorce. Why not use your partner's smarts to help you finance your future? Besides, keeping all communications on a higher plane will let both of you concentrate on the issues and will free up *all* your capabilities for your joint benefit. Even if you must play referee, do it to save both of you the energy you could otherwise waste thrusting and parrying with old hurts and memories. While you both should profit from this approach, if you are the orchestrator and moderator, you will probably profit even more.

7

Ideas for Postseparation Asset Boosting

WHEN it comes to asset-boosting ideas, *nothing beats negotiation*—especially after separation. Despite the fact that you may be growing tired of hearing this advice, consider the expense of litigation, the trauma of court, the possibility that you may not prevail on unsettled issues, and the probability that you will lose important assets or rights where your state law does not favor your claim. In other words, negotiation frees you from constraints set down by legal precedents in your state. Through negotiation, you remain free to seek—and perhaps acquire—assets and rights that *should* be yours under the dictates of fairness.

In addition to these pluses, negotiation offers two major advantages in gaining profits from your divorce. First, it allows you to bargain without revealing all that you know. While you should share the value of assets for which you have obtained appraisals, you have no duty to share information that will affect the future value of an antique, shares of stock, or your earning ability. Second, private negotiation removes from those strangers in the court system the ability to probe, pry, and divvy up your property. As one California court guide puts it, "It is the court's obligation to determine the extent and value of the community property unless a prior written agreement has been reached by the parties." Even a well-worded, completely enforceable marital settlement agreement can remain discreet about the parties' personal worth; a court-ordered judgment may reveal all *and* tell it to everyone, since almost every divorce file remains open for public viewing for years to come.

Additional negotiation pluses can include sessions that:

Can be scheduled at your convenience.

Start on time. To compare negotiation with the purely adversary procedure, visit your county's main superior court. Pretend that you're one of the parties listed on the court's calendar for that day. Await your turn, and follow the parties around the courthouse, if necessary. Note what time their matter concludes on that day.

Cover an agreed-upon agenda, so that you move at your own pace and spend extra time, if necessary, on those issues most meaningful to you.

Reduce discovery costs and time, since parties often allocate the work in uncovering values and share necessary information during conferences.

Diminish or eliminate witness fees, because the parties ordinarily agree upon a single expert or appraiser for each major asset.

Eliminate hard-to-get-to hearing locations, since the parties can set negotiation sessions at any convenient, quiet spot that is reasonably discreet.

Cut down on anxiety-building "waiting time." The average delay between readiness and trial still totals some 14 months in some California courts.

Limit the price rise of appreciating assets, so that a value arrived at now will cost you less than buying your spouse's share after an appraisal close to trial, many months from now.

Dramatically slash your legal fees. A day in court with one well-known family law practitioner located in Beverly Hills costs a client $1,250; his in-office charges run $200 per hour. The tab for even a relatively simple (but court-fought) divorce can range from $5,000 to five times that amount. Even with a good income, you may have trouble attracting a skilled, experienced counselor. One family-law attorney in private practice less than ten years screens out cases unless the community includes "at least one million dollars in assets, and a minimum of one spouse earning $100,000 or more annually." While thousands of capable family-law attorneys charge less, your costs will mount at the rate of at least $75 per hour and can total thousands in a remarkably short time. Most attorneys are caring, sympathetic people who enjoy helping others, but with law office overhead eating up 50 percent or more of their gross income, these business people must consider financial concerns along with the facts of your case. Finally, you might weigh the fact that when cash runs short, some attorneys suggest taking a lien against the family home. Such a right includes foreclosure powers, so that you *could* find yourself facing your attorney in court.

Involve third parties who can speed up resolutions. Consider hiring a retired family-law commissioner or judge to hear and decide your case, arrange sessions with a therapist trained in mediated divorce, retain an arbitrator knowledgeable in family law, ask your local court system if it includes personnel skilled in helping couples work out divorce-related issues, or turn to a person you both admire and consider fair, like a family friend or an elder in your church or synagogue. See legal counsel as needed during negotiations, and remember to review all documents or agreements with your lawyer before signing your name.

Encourage agreement on a separation date advantageous to you. You may choose to evaluate some or all of the assets as of the separation date, the date of filing, the date of negotiation, or some other time. No matter which date your state law dictates, you can *agree* on any other date you please. Play it smart by evaluating assets that you wish to buy from your spouse at an early date if they are rising in value. Use a later date if the property you want promises to lose value over time. Determine whether the assets that you intend to sell or trade to your mate are rising or falling in worth. Utilize the correct approach to buy low and sell high, thus maximizing your gains. Since you don't have to use the same appraisal date for every asset, put your noggin into overdrive to assure the greatest profits for you.

For all these reasons (and because it clears overcrowded court calendars), family-law judges and commissioners often urge couples to settle out of court. Even Chief Justice Warren Burger noted in the March 1982 issue of *U.S. News and World Report*, "Courts should resolve only those issues that cannot be resolved in any other way."

Negotiation wins converts because participating couples often feel that they have crafted an agreement especially suited to each one's needs, and the parties therefore tend to comply with those personally tailored agreements.

Another reason to negotiate is that a temperamental spouse often reveals—in anger, frustration, or disgust—news that can mean dollars for you. In Dorothy M.'s case, a marriage of 27 years approached its close with loud and furious arguments during attempts to reach settlement terms. Losing his temper one evening, Dr. M. yelled, "I don't care what else you get, but keep your hands off my ski lodge." An alert Dotty pretended that she hadn't heard, but soon made a note to find out more about this asset that "I didn't even know he had!" Such profitable blurt-outs can sweeten substantially your share in the business of divorce.

If you must hash it out in court because your mate refused to negotiate, tell the judge. The bench tends to award attorneys fees to creative counselors who try to negotiate out-of-court settlements. Encourage your judge to charge some or all of your legal fees and case costs to your spouse—that unreasonably stubborn party.

Even if you cannot agree on all points out of court, you may settle some terms and thus dramatically reduce the number of issues to be decided by lawyer conferences or by a judge. Every difference resolved reduces the scope of argument, fosters a climate of compromise that can pay off later on, and means a healthy saving in trauma, money, and time.

What can you do if you want to negotiate, but your mate doesn't? Offer some attractive rewards if your spouse will agree to start talking, and to ensure results, don your "economic spurs." These incentives to negotiate are designed to motivate a stubbornly silent spouse and include both rewards and whips. In one example of offering a positive incentive, the spouse seeking support offered to label all dollars received "family support," thus providing a tax deduction for the paying spouse. This only slightly expensive act of goodwill (she would be taxed on the income, but her tax bracket at the time was quite low) opened the negotiation door, and soon her spouse was offering some concessions of his own. Other spouses obtain high temporary support orders (by agreement or via court order), then offer to settle for a more reasonable figure if the paying spouse will enter negotiations in good faith, and perhaps allocate other assets to the payee. This approach illustrates the truism, "He or she who has often gets."

In an example of a negative incentive, a husband who needed child support started selling off his wife's favorites from among their community property assets. Within hours, she called and offered to come over for a sitdown session.

In a third case, the wife and her boyfriend plotted for three weeks to raid her husband's construction company parking lot. They confiscated his five heavy-duty trucks and the pink slips (the papers that certified his ownership of the vehicles) and sold the dust-coated quintet to pay the married couple's creditors. Mrs. Contractor explained, "I knew that if I did nothing, he'd sell the firm and its assets, spend or hide the cash, and flee the state and perhaps the country. I'd end up paying all our community bills from the very few assets that would have remained." Relieved of pressing money worries and usurped of his power to singlehandedly control his business, this husband entered negotiations with his wife, and the two quickly agreed on the remaining issues.

In a fourth case, one mate entered court via a preliminary hearing and presented such convincing evidence of her spouse's earning ability that the judge ordered her husband to pay four-fifths of the wife's court costs, appraisal expenses, and attorney fees. Faced with financing his own demise, this husband bowed to reason and opened his records and his mind in negotiation sessions. (Your state probably does not require you to impoverish yourself or expend your separate property to pursue your claims in a divorce case. To give a less-well-heeled spouse legal muscle, judges can order that all fees be paid from a joint account reserved for that purpose or that the higher-earning spouse bear some portion of the poorer spouse's fees. To obtain such an order, produce detailed time records for legal work already performed, accurately estimate coming costs, and support—with evidence—your claim that your mate's income or earning power far outstrips your own.)

Sometimes a mate offers to negotiate and, if turned down, plays a waiting game. In these cases, the open-minded spouse knows (or suspects) that another party will soon find that former mate attractive. This newcomer will soon grow eager to establish a "meaningful relationship" without the trailing problems presented by the unfinished problems from a former marriage. Since separated men typically form new partnerships more quickly than women do, wives often benefit by the arrival of another woman, who often wants to start a new partnership, perhaps becomes pregnant, and who begins applying pressure to obtain a speedy settlement.

If your spouse says that he or she wants to negotiate but wishes to do so through a lawyer, *save funds by helping your mate obtain a skilled, experienced family-law practitioner*. You will profit from dealing with a lawyer who is (1) probably a reasonable professional, accustomed to negotiating for out-of-court settlements; (2) a practiced advocate who knows what the courts consider fair, who will exercise control over a mate who seems greedy or emotionally unbalanced, and who can diminish or eliminate excessive demands or abusive behavior from your spouse; and (3) a business person practiced at dealing effectively and informally in the exchange of information necessary for settlement, thus reducing the costs you may have to pay in underwriting adequate counsel for your spouse.

If your spouse insists on counsel before negotiation can begin, resist retaining the toughest attorney in town—for either of you. First, you may end up fighting everything out in court because some "superadvocate" lawyers view settlement as personal defeats. Second, if your spouse obtains a lawyer with a reputation for being nasty, *your* attorney may charge you a premium rate to deal with unpleasant or abusive opposing counsel.

While you negotiate, learn as much as you can about your spouse's new life. Under relatively new legislation in California, for example, the law presumes that a mate's live-in lover contributes to household expenses, freeing up more discretionary cash. As a result, California courts want to know why more money isn't available to pay more of the community bills, or to make larger support payments to a spouse and children still at home. Even if your state doesn't have such a law on the books, this "more cash" theory remains good common sense, so use it in negotiations with your spouse. Even if your spouse is now supporting (or helping to support) a new love, you can argue fairly that these funds should instead go to your past joint creditors, to the children, and to you.

Since most states divide property, allocate debts, and arrange support without regard to wrong acts by one of the divorcing parties, it may seem contradictory when a legal forum considers a paying spouse's romantic roommate in setting support. For example, it might seem at first gasp that such courts are moralizing by "punishing" an erring spouse. Not so. The judge or commissioner looks only to the amount that a live-in lover contributes to a moved-out mate's normal living costs. Will a court (or you) be able to consider that entire second salary? No, only the portion the second wage earner uses to pay household costs that your spouse would otherwise bear singlehandedly. As a result, your former roommate *should* possess more spendable funds to lavish on any children and you.

While you can certainly use this theory to *ask* for more dollars in support following separation, in order to prevail you'll need to document such contributions. In order to maximize your profits, establish the level of the live-in lover's earnings and the degree of his or her financial aid to your mate's new household. By following one (or more) of the following suggestions, several spouses have boosted their support allotments even months after the separation date.

One precocious teenage daughter called her father's new residence. Pretending that she had reached a fellow student, this high-schooler began discussing a homework assignment. In the process of correcting her error, this youngster elicited the full name—and even the employer—of Dad's new heartthrob. Duplicitous and unfair to use a child for such a task? Daughter cooked up the scheme, carried it through with aplomb, and reveled in her success! With the information thus garnered, Mom made some discreet inquiries of friends in the heartthrob's field, and accurately estimated her earning power. Faced with this knowledge, husband admitted receiving monthly aid, and voluntarily agreed to pay a bigger share of the previously incurred community bills.

A young husband, at first shattered when his new wife moved out, used his anger to fuel long hours of informal "shadowing" to establish the nature of his partner's new liaison. By switching cars with a friend and rearranging his work schedule, this husband tailed his spouse until he determined where she lived and with whom she shared the new quarters. At a safe time, he investigated the mail boxes in her new apartment complex and learned her roommate's name. In several early-morning telephone calls he then asked for that party by name, thus confirming the living arrangements he suspected. Once he'd proved the relationship to a sufficient degree to negotiate effectively, he trailed his wife's new lover to ascertain his occupation and working hours. Calling a friend in the executive search business, he uncovered the lover's probable salary range and suggested a "kitchen-table" compromise of the figure Wife originally requested for support.

Though Sheila rated as a real beauty, she knew that women found her a good companion as well. Charming, quick, and full of vitality, Sheila used these skills to make friends with the new woman in her moved-out spouse's life. Though Sheila never hid her status as Ike's wife, she formed a sincere friendship with Ike's inamorata, who soon revealed all of Ike's generous contributions to the new household's budget needs. Armed with specifics, Sheila "suggested" that Ike realign his monetary loyalty and doubled her monthly receipts with a single, short conversation.

Though all of these scenarios feature a lover, a romantic roommate may not prove necessary to utilize this support-boosting technique. So far, even California requires that a sexual liaison exist between an ex-mate and a roommate before household contributions affect support dollars due at home, but outside of court, legal constraints need not apply. If the more-money-to-spend theory fits your case, should it matter whether the new roommate ranks as a lover, as a business associate, as a household stranger, or even as a disliked convenience? Probably not, for if the "cohabitation" increases available income, it lowers a bottom line, making more funds available for you.

Let's consider what happens if you lived with your spouse before marriage—if *you,* in effect, constituted the "romantic roommate." In addition to profiting from your spouse's new live-in lover, you may also reap real benefits from the weeks, months, or years that you and your mate spent in unwedded bliss. In California, for example, a divorcing mate can sometimes "tack on" to the marriage years the time he or she lived with a spouse before the wedding day. Though this theory sounds like a sailing skill, it probably springs from attorneys' habit of stapling the civil suit for financial recovery (based on an express or understood contract claim) to the family-law petition for dissolution of the marriage. While not applicable in every case, if the facts show an expressed promise to provide for a lover, or the couple's financial habits show that they owned property together as contractual partners, the court will consider the cohabitation years as a portion of the partnership. As a practical matter, a mate must pursue recovery under the promise or contract theory in civil court, but to facilitate a single hearing on all related matters, California's family-law courts usually agree to weigh all the issues arising over the entire period. Considering *all* factors, such forums then attempt to reach an equitable decision regarding the couple's property, obligations, and support.

As a result of this tacking-on procedure, a spouse can often spoon more assets into the community pot because that couple formed a partnership for a period of time exceeding the marriage years. Establishing a longer partnership can also legitimatize children born before the wedding, can facilitate the collection of child support for children born "too soon," and can even spur a spousal support figure higher to offset the longer period of time that one mate may have devoted to another's career at the expense of his or her own.

By now you know that it doesn't matter if *your* state endorses such a principle. If you are negotiating an out-of-court settlement, let fairness serve as your only guide. If limiting your recovery to the property or support rights acquired during the "legal liaison" would prove inequitable to you, introduce the tacking-on concept and bargain for some repayment for your premarriage efforts and contributions as well.

With this advice, you can garner goodies from the years you cohabited and from an absent spouse's new live-in romance, but don't stop here. By following the example set by California's Mrs. Baragry, perhaps you, too, can orchestrate a scenario that will harvest assets for you long after your spouse first packs a toothbrush and moves out.

> When Mrs. Baragry's husband bid her good-bye and vacated their home, did she throw out his belongings, change all the locks, and scream, "*Never* darken this threshold again"? Not at all. Ever pleasant, she welcomed Mr. B. into the family home whenever he chose to drop by. Though he lived with his secretary on a yacht in nearby Santa Barbara harbor, Mr. Baragry frequently showed up at the family home.
>
> He came for dinner, for chats, for birthdays, and for Christmas, too. He joined in family activities and even delivered and picked up his laundry at his former residence. This course of behavior continued for approximately four years.
>
> At the close of that period, Mr. B. marshaled his thoughts and filed for divorce. He asked the court to divide or allocate the Baragry asset values *as they had stood on the day that he first left home.*
>
> "No, no, *no*" said a California judge. "We don't consider yours a true separation, and we intend to weigh your asset values as they rank today." In other words, Mr. B. could not enjoy the benefits of married life then insist that he'd left it behind in order to keep for himself alone the benefits of community assets, which had risen dramatically in value since his "separation" day four years before.
>
> Given a new—and more valid—date of parting, Mrs. Baragry profited enormously.

If your spouse keeps hanging around, keeping a separation date fuzzy at best, make him or her feel as welcome as other members of your family. Don't loose the Doberman until *you're* ready to set the valuation date. If you're extra smart, you'll keep track of those assets on the rise and act when high values and your mate's incipient recovery from "homesickness" threaten to coincide.

While you're waiting, it rests with you to determine the rising (or declining) value of these jointly owned assets. A spouse who feels that he or she has effectively severed your partnership may recognize no duty to reveal to you the true worth of even commonly held property. In fact, California courts recognize a separation as the severing of a community, putting an end to any fiduciary obligation to disclose financial or other asset information. For example, Tony and Regina acquired stock in a privately held corporation during their married years. After separation, this couple entered negotiation to evaulate their assets and reach a marital settlement agreement. Though Tony knew that this private firm planned to go public, he disclosed nothing to Regina, and the court held that he labored under no duty to do so. As a result, Regina transferred her shares to Tony at a property-exchange price that excluded the firm's expansion plans.

A delighted Tony pocketed a lot more than half of the marital wealth—legally.

While you're plotting your retirement, remember that if assets rise because of a spouse's efforts after separation (rather than because of a natural growth in the property itself), that increase may be considered separate property, because "perspiration" after parting constitutes separate energy and separate property. In other words, encourage a later parting date if the asset itself promises to rise in value without any additional care or effort. If, however, your mate will need to devote considerable skill and time to this property to increase its value after separation, the resulting profits could well prove separate in nature, and you may as well get on with setting a value and dividing or allocating this goody to provide yourself with needed funds.

In some cases, it may prove costly to sell an asset to a third party or on the open market. (Perhaps the costs of sale will run high; perhaps demand currently runs low). In addition, any suggestion of dividing this property will trigger a fight and delay settlement of other issues. Parties facing this situation often include couples who own sculptures, valuable pets or livestock, a gaggle of antiques, or unusual or valuable home furnishings. You can avoid tantrums, stubborn demands, and unreasonable delays and still profit if you offer to safeguard the items until a later date, when you can agree upon division, allocation, a trade or a sale. For example, two highly educated art lovers who sought a divorce agreed that she would retain possession of their 13-piece collection of modern works. She would benefit by hanging the collection in her new condominium and bear the minor costs of insurance and care. Husband and wife agreed that no sale, trade, or loan (in which the art would serve as collateral) could occur without each giving his/her prior written consent.

While you're gathering asset information, offering to care for jointly owned property, and considering your most profitable separation date, take a few hours to arrange an up-to-date will. Under your former will (or under your state's intestacy laws, if you do not have a valid will), your now-absent mate may inherit your share of any commonly or jointly owned property, should you suffer an untimely end. Of course, if you're sure that the stress of even a friendly divorce will threaten your mate's well-being more than yours and you know that you're named in his/her will and hold certain properties in joint tenancy (with rights of survivorship), you'll want to leave things as they are, and remain a legal spouse as long as it could prove profitable.

In fact, whether to obtain almost immediate freedom or remain legally wed can prove a potentially profitable issue in itself. To decide which avenue could prove most advantageous for you, consider *bifurcating* your case. This confusing-sounding term embodies a rather simple concept: you agree to end the legal tie between you, but specifically reserve issues involving property (and sometimes custody and support) for later negotiation, court hearing, or trial. If you (and/or your mate) yearn to breathe free of marriage's constraints, bifurcation will terminate your status as husband or wife. Your state may not endorse (or provide for) such a maneuver, but remember that you can probably *agree* in your living room to divide or allocate the debts and assets at a later date.

Now, while this concept remains simple to grasp, weigh bifurcation's pros and cons carefully before leaping to end your marital status. Study carefully all of the pluses and minuses—both emotional and financial—listed below.

Advantages of Bifurcation

(Divorce Decree Then Property Division)

Terminates legal and emotional ties to speed healing, encourages a new start

Both parties free to remarry (useful when an impatient lover awaits, or you discover an unplanned pregnancy)

Ends bar against spousal testimony (after bifurcation, one party could testify against the other regarding civil or criminal liability). Also allows mate to marry a witness crucial to your case (bookkeeper, CPA), then claim spousal privilege to block such testimony at hearing or trial

Federal tax on the transfer of depreciable real property may be capital gain instead of ordinary income

Each former mate can file a new joint return with a new spouse, if desired ("new" joint returns are protected from discovery in later hearings regarding assets or support modifications, and available only for enforcement of support in California; other states may also limit access)

Permits one person to take the once-in-a-lifetime tax forgiveness of $125,000 without affecting the other party's ability to claim this right at a future time

Spouses may qualify to file individual tax returns, thus possibly realizing maximum tax relief

May help spouse to avoid "marriage penalty" (higher taxes for couples with comparable incomes filing jointly)

Losses on property may be recognized in a transfer of ownership between "legal strangers"

Advantages of Usual Procedure

(Property Division Before or Concurrent with Divorce Decree)

Retaining spousal status can lock in insurance coverage and guarantee Social Security derivative rights (if marriage lasts ten years or more from wedding day to final decree)

Protects your power to take as surviving spouse, and ensures retention of your inheritance rights if mate dies without a valid will. Qualifying as a spouse at mate's death can also preserve any right to death benefits, trust interests, pension benefits, wrongful death suit recoveries, worker's compensation payoffs. Remaining wed until all asset issues have been decided helps preserve your state courts' right to divide or allocate all the "marital" property

Enables spouses to more accurately fix the value of an asset in flux over a period of time

Helps to ensure that "community property" will retain that character until its division or allocation date

Enables spouses to file a joint return if they wish to do so

Preserves a Chapter S corporation if the firm has exactly 35 investors before the divorcing couple become two entities

May preserve the gift tax marital deduction until the final decree

Ensures that any "interspousal" exchanges of real property title will not trigger a tax reassessment under California (and perhaps your state's) law

Ensures that date of asset evaluation will be date agreed to in marital settlement agreement, or will be date of hearing or trial

Witness who could testify against your spouse to your benefit cannot marry your mate and plead a spousal privilege to avoid taking the stand

If you do obtain legal assistance to guide you through negotiation (or to do the bulk of the negotiation under your direction), take a minute or two throughout the case to notify your lawyer *before* you make any major decision. Checking before signing, agreeing, spending, or lending can save you dollars, grief, and time. In addition to preventing costly errors, seeking interim advice can even enhance your position during negotiations. Even if your lawyer has proven accessible, and you're good on the phone, try to write instead of calling. It forces you to marshal your facts, convey information concisely, and gives your counselor a permanent record about your course of action. If you can include enough facts to elicit well-informed advice, even a postcard's worth of information ending in a question mark will do.

Writing for advice ranks as particularly important before you take a job, agree to accept a certain figure for child or spousal support, sign any documents relating to the house or other property, or transfer or sell any assets. Now that you've got the idea, let the postal service help you out before committing yourself to a loser's role.

During these weeks and months following your parting, you may want to consider one, several, or all of the suggestions below to boost your child and/or spousal support payments—whether informal or ordered by the court. Using these techniques can substantially increase your support-dollar harvest even as you negotiate with your spouse or attend court hearings to divide property or allocate your debts. Each of the following ideas can boost the current or future support for the children and/or for you:

1. Include *coming events* in your negotiated or court-filed request for child/spousal support. Such expenses include those not immediately due, but that loom so near in the future that they need to be weighed for a realistic setting of support amounts. These "threatened costs" can include eyewear, orthodontia, surgery, or medical treatment for the children or for you; badly needed house repairs; and even a planned move to a different environment that will require a bigger budget for clothing, heating, transportation, etc. To use this method effectively, draw up a detailed, substantiated estimate of these rapidly approaching costs.
2. Formulate a *re-entry program* if you haven't worked outside the home for some years and will need retraining or additional skills to compete successfully for today's profitable careers, or merely to land a decent job. A reentry program works best for a nonemployed or underemployed spouse who longs to upgrade his or her earnings in order to provide more (or all) of his/her own support. If you present your spouse—or the court—with a carefully thought out, detailed, and sensible plan for retraining yourself or upgrading your skills, you can dramatically increase your chances of mastering new career tools at your mate's expense. This "scholarship program" won't last forever, so be reasonable in your requests. Obtaining court or spousal agreement for your plan rests with developing a feasible goal and a sensible plan. (Seeking a degree in computer programming, for example, will probably net you an "Okay" and a monthly sum to cover schooling and living costs. Professing your determination to rank as a leading neurosurgeon in fifteen years will cause your "banker" to clutch his/her salary check and faint away.) A reentry program can benefit both of you: the "student" gains self-esteem and a money-earning skill; the bankroller anticipates the end of this underwriting period and looks forward to years of reduced support payments as the student gains financial independence. The latter makes this approach a highly salable one even to reluctant, uncooperative, or especially stingy mates.
3. Find your own "surrey with the fringe on top": document or establish your mate's fringe benefits and convert these job extras into your vehicle for a better single life. Heavy fringe benefits often mean that a mate can spare more cash for support every month. After all, today's employment fringes can include health and life insurance policies; access to company-offered tax-shelter

plans; financial counseling; psychological analysis or therapy; use of a company car; home-owner, car, and legal insurance coverage; free or discounted meals; day-care services; a liberal expense account (sometimes permissibly padded in lieu of a raise); discounts on company services or merchandise; free or subsidized parking; use of a company plane or recreational vehicle; access to a resort or hunting/fishing/skiing lodge; health and social club memberships; low-interest loans; subsidized or reimbursed schooling or other educational aid; and travel passes and travel discounts. According to one source in a recent business publication, "the average American worker gets $4,000 worth of fringe benefits a year." Make sure that you get a part of this "salary overflow" in the form of increased support. You might also arrange to participate directly in these benefits wherever—and for as long as—possible. When dealing with employee fringe benefits, however, remember that these rights remain personal to the employee spouse. Even a good-faith promise to let you share in a goody after your divorce may not prove enforceable against any employer unwilling (or unable) to comply once your final decree ends your status as legal spouse. Therefore, *never* trade a here-and-now asset for a promise to let you share in a future benefit flowing from and contingent upon the continued employment of your mate.

In profiting from your spouse's job, keep in mind that under some of the new fringe benefit plans, employees choose the benefits they require or desire from a sort of "menu" offered by their company. Those benefits not selected fall into a cash cache that remains available to the working spouse. Upon parting, or afterwards, include the value of any such unused benefits in your asset list, along with sick pay or vacation pay earned during the marriage years but not yet paid out.

4. When timing the start or setting the amount of child or spousal support, look ahead to establish when some monthly payments will end, thus increasing the amount available for support. If your mate will send in March his/her last check for the Cadillac, the winter cruise, Johnny's braces *and* the poodle you purchased on your MasterCard, the amount of cash available in April will markedly rise. Until then, make do by drawing on other commonly owned money sources or by seeking voluntary money allocations from your spouse while you wait for that higher-cash month to set a firm figure for your (and/or the children's) support.

5. Look around for items of property that can serve as support substitutes. When money feels short, consider exclusive use and possession of the family home for a designated period of time as a form of support. To figure out the exact dollar benefit, establish the fair rental value of your living quarters and see if there's a discrepancy between what such quarters would cost you on the open market, and what you're paying now. If you're paying top dollar for your pad, and *you're picking up all the tab,* this approach won't help. But if your mortgage or rental payment remains low while loan or rental rates have risen, you could recognize a nice "paper savings" by helping your mate move out and remaining at home. Remember that one half of this "use benefit" belongs to you anyway, so don't give your spouse too much credit for this exclusive-occupation right.)

—Exclusive use of the family car or truck if the family owns only one vehicle.

—Exclusive use of a jontly-owned bank or savings account for the payment of reasonable living costs (mate to live on earnings after separation, usually considered separate property anyway).

—Exclusive use of furnishings and furniture in the family home for a predetermined or indeterminate time (applicable whether you remain in the house or move the items elsewhere.)

—Exclusive right to operate a family business and to keep the proceeds, while spouse finds employment elsewhere for a set or open period of time.

Finally, offer to continue sharing the family home, but (whether you're male or female) offer to perform the duties of housekeeper, cook, errand-runner, babysitter or child-care employee, laundry expert, etc. *for a fee that will support you* in addition to receiving free room and board. Remember that you'll be residing in a dwelling that may rank as partly yours anyway, so set the price of your services at a reasonable but adequate amount. Such an approach may appeal greatly to a spouse who would otherwise have to hire help for these chores, or spend evenings and/or weekends doing them him- or herself.

6. Keep more of the support dollars you're paid by *avoiding taxes.* Remember that child support is neither taxable to the receiving party, nor tax deductible for the paying party. Our concern lies with spousal support, which operates as a write-off for the supporting spouse, but which remains reportable by the supported spouse. However, the Internal Revenue Service will not tax you on such funds, in four cases. First, the amounts paid bear the name Spousal Support, but the payment plan is not contingent or does not last long enough (more than ten years) to qualify as deductible under IRS standards. Second, you have parted, and your mate pays you spousal support dollars following separation but without a court order to do so and without any written agreement between you that these dollars are deductible by one and taxable to the other. Third, in the eyes of the IRS, your parting does not constitute a sufficient "separation." This third requirement foiled the tax plans of Mr. Alexander. He and Mrs. A. decided to end their connubial relationship but, because of the high cost of living apart, agreed to continue to share the family home. When Mr. A. claimed on his income tax the amounts paid to his spouse over the months that they "cohabited," the IRS disallowed any deduction, insisting that the parties had not, indeed, parted to a sufficient degree. Fourth, one mate pays the other clearly-labeled spousal support, but the couple files a joint return at the close of that calendar year. Since one mate's deduction cancels out the other's tax tariff, no tax assessment befalls the recipient spouse.

7. Deduct child-care expenses from your net pay when demonstrating your inability to finance alone the cost of child rearing. The gap between your available cash and even the reasonable costs of keeping a child fed, clothed, educated, and healthy can mean additional child-support dollars from a spouse who is forced to see clearly what is needed and why.
8. Keep generous temporary support orders or agreements in effect for the longest possible time. Because initial dual-household costs run especially high, such temporary orders usually exceed final support amounts (the monthly amount set until a child reaches the age of 18, for example). Unless the court changes such orders, or until you agree to accept less, the paying mate remains on the legal hook for the *higher* amount of child and/or spousal support. Although the court sets a higher support figure to ease the financial transitions that the custodial or more financially dependent spouse must make, this more generous figure is supposed to last only a few months. As a practical matter, court forums often remain so crowded that the parties won't appear

LOS ANGELES COUNTY SUPERIOR COURT
FAMILY LAW DEPARTMENT

GUIDELINES FOR INITIAL ORDER TO SHOW CAUSE

The schedule set forth below represents a consensus of suggested amounts which counsel may care to use in negotiations and in consultation with clients on temporary support matters. The figures and text are not binding upon the court or the parties.

SPOUSAL AND CHILD SUPPORT

The following support schedule is based on total net monthly income after the usual standard mandatory deductions.

NET MONTHLY INCOME	SPOUSE ALONE	ONE CHILD ALONE (MORE THAN ONE, NOT OVER AMOUNT IN COLUMN 6*)	SPOUSE AND 1 CHILD	SPOUSE AND 2 CHILDREN	SPOUSE AND 3 OR MORE CHILDREN
$ 400	$100	$ 80	$100	$100	$100
500	150	100	150	150	150
600	200	150	250	250	250
700	250	175	350	350	350
800	250	225	375	400	400
900	300	225	400	425	450
1000	325	250	450	475	500
1200	400	275	500	550	600
1400	460	300	560	630	700
1600	530	325	640	720	800
1800	600	350	720	810	900
2000	650	400	800	900	1000
Above 2000	33⅓		40%	45%	50%

In order that employment not be discouraged, if the petitioning spouse is employed, approximately one-half of that spouse's net earnings will be deducted from the indicated spousal support and will be considered in setting child support. Other benefits or compensation from whatever source will be considered. Child care costs for the working parent will be deducted from gross income in calculating the custodial parent's net earnings.

Car, furniture, credit union payments, real estate taxes, and other similar payments and financial requirements will be taken into consideration and may affect the schedule, as will the total assets and liabilities.

*Support amounts per child for more than one child may be less.

Dated: January 28, 1981

Billy G. Mills
Supervising Judge
Family Law Department

before a judge (who will probably reduce the support figure) for up to a year or more. If the person receiving this temporary support refuses to agree to a lower figure, then the paying party must fork over the higher amount until a judicial officer rules otherwise. These higher support obligations, even if reached by negotiations out of court (but embodied in a writing and filed with the court) cannot be reduced unless the court orders it or unless you agree—in another writing—to accept less. If you have or contemplate drawing up an informal agreement with your mate regarding the payment of such support, or if you have drawn up a contract that neither party has filed, you possess a promise to pay support that is only as good as the paper that it's written on. Insist that your agreement be filed with the court, so that the judge can review the terms in setting permanent support, and so that you can enforce the agreement's terms if your mate doesn't pay.

An example of California's temporary spousal and child support guidelines chart, applicable to Los Angeles County courts, appears on the previous page. Permanent support figures usually do not total these amounts. You will note that the earnings of a spouse seeking support will affect, in these courts, the sum suggested for spousal support. Earnings of a parent with custody, however, normally will not affect child-support requirements or amounts.

9. Encourage a voluntary payment pattern if your spouse makes generous voluntary contributions from time to time; this establishes an ability to pay high and continuing support. While only *current* circumstances usually dictate the amount, frequency, and duration of support, such a preexisting pattern provides strong evidence of a party's willingness and ability to allocate such an amount from earnings. A mate already adapted to even a high figure of support will often prove amenable to continuing a familiar outlay. Clearly, the longer such voluntary contributions last, the greater the inertia to keep matters as they are.

10. Suggest that some of your mate's after-separation salary (his or her separate property) go directly to pay balances owed mutual creditors. Since you also remain liable for such bills, your mate's reducing these obligations with his or her separate property (earnings after parting) can benefit you enormously. In these traumatic weeks your mate may feel better about paying a third party than you! Such "support" can reduce past bills (leaving more for division between you), pay your current living expenses, and/or slowly pay off monthly obligations to free up more cash for a later higher support payment for the children or for you. There are two warnings to heed: check periodically with your creditors directly to ensure that your mate is keeping his/her word by sending regular checks, and make sure that creditor payments aren't flowing from a joint account. Clearly, if your mate is using your mutual savings to pay community debts that have been assigned to him or her, then your spouse is getting full credit by using monies he/she owns only in part. If he/she is using your joint account to pay support directly to you, then your mate is paying you with funds that are already half yours.

11. If you live in California and are likely to qualify as the paying party, you can ask the court to order that your mate see a vocational training consultant before any monthly sum for spousal support is set. These experts evaluate a to-be-supported spouse's employment skills and probable earning ability as it is currently, without further specialized training. The counselors may also suggest additional schooling or an apprenticeship to increase that party's ability to move toward financial independence. In fact, even amounts needed for child support may decline once a retrained payee spouse can contribute more generous amounts. Even if your state does not offer such a provision, what path around obstacles have you memorized by now? Negotiate for such a work-skills assessment before agreeing to permanent child and/or spousal support amounts. If vocational training consultants don't operate in your geographic area or if money remains extra tight, suggest a skills or earnings-assessment test at a local community college or career counseling or information center. For further inexpensive but effective experience, help your mate arrange to spend a day or week tagging along with a professional whose occupation you think he or she might enjoy. Planning for a career can steer a spouse clear of an inappropriate fantasy, guide him/her toward the right position, and even land a job offer if he/she acts at the right time instead of just looking on. Suggest that your spouse ask a local reference librarian for a guide showing the duties, pay scales, and pitfalls of various occupations.

If you anticipate needing financial aid for expenses and living costs, consider sources other than your mate to further increase the support dollars flowing to you. While you should tell your spouse if you're receiving funds from another source, he or she may agree to pay you a reasonable sum anyway. If he or she wants to reduce support payments because of your other income, consider offering a promise (applicable only to spousal support) that you will not seek a higher figure at a later date, or that you will wait a certain length of time before seeking an increase in support, or that your spousal support will last only a given length of time, or that any built-in increases will lag behind the usual rate standard, the cost-of-living index. If your spouse earns little cash, ranks as exceedingly stingy, or has never managed money well, you could enhance the amount and certainty of receiving support by turning to other avenues for your spousal support until you're able to earn a comfortable living on your own.

These additional income sources include the following:

Adult children Children living at home can pay reasonable room and board; those supporting themselves can contribute as a family obligation; those away at school or college can begin paying more of their own way, thus relieving you of costly cash drains.

Boarders Respectable but shelterless members of your community may welcome the opportunity to rent a bedroom and bath, a fixed-up portion of the attic, the sitting room in the basement, or the one-room nest over your garage. If you cannot pay for needed household services or fear receiving extra cash because this might result in a permanent reduction of your support award, exchange housing for child-care services, gardening expertise, cooking or cleaning duties, or for a seamstress's skills.

Tourists and visitors If you live in an area featuring hiking trails, hot springs, summer concerts, or winter sports, fun seekers and vacationers can provide extra income if you offer meals, room and board, or gift items.

An asset Review your property, both personal and real, liquid and locked in, to determine if you can reallocate one or more assets to produce more income for monthly bills. Perhaps funds sitting in a low-interest savings account or earning nothing in your checking balance could flow into a money market fund, a mutual fund, or even a second or third trust deed to produce some profits for you. Review any investment thoroughly, and base your decision on objective evidence (like an investment's track record) instead of on the charisma of a salesperson or counselor. In addition, try to avoid locking your funds up for more than a year's time (in fact, some avenues—like money market funds—can be ideal because they pay high interest and are relatively safe but allow you to withdraw part or all of your monies immediately upon demand).

In addition to increasing your income during these months, you will probably want to think about selling some of your "worthless rights" for money or assets *now*. This approach means getting cash or property now for those elusive rights that might benefit you in the future, but whose cash potential is uncertain and whose value is often difficult (if not impossible) to enforce effectively as time goes by. In short, consider selling all of those expected goodies that, in all candor, you may never receive anyway. For example, let's say that you are legally entitled to receive monthly spousal support sums. In reality, obligor spouses (legal parlance for the paying spouse) often fail to make these payments, make erratic payments, pay for only a short time, or pay grudgingly and with such "strings" that you'd soon rather forget your money rights entirely. In addition, entitled spouses almost never exercise any later right to seek spousal support. Of course, you may prefer to hang on to your hopes rather than cash them in, but weigh these facts of financial life before you decide to bank on hope alone.

The first of these rights involves the decision about whether or not to file a joint tax return. Frankly, either party, even while legally wed, can file separately. But it usually benefits the higher-earning spouse to file a joint return, particularly if that party earns markedly more than the other. While both of you will benefit from a higher refund check, you must agree to cooperate in the filing—no rule says married people must file a joint return. If filing jointly will net a higher refund, then bargain now for your signature by asking for a larger share of the return, or some other piece of property now. You may come out ahead with just an even split, but consider an agreement to use the entire amount to reduce mutual bills, or to prepay some of the mortgage (if you're living in the family home). If money's short, suggest that the refund flow only to you as a form of support (but do not forget that at least a proportionate share of this sum already belongs to you). If the idea of "buying" your signature doesn't appeal to your mate, prepare (and even file) a separate return, paying your lower tax assessment yourself. Leave your mate to pay his or her higher assessment alone. If suitable concessions come your way, you can amend your return to file jointly: *once you file a joint return, however, you cannot "withdraw" your signature.* Because of this one-way street, play it savvy when contemplating your earnings, your mate's salary, and the requests of the IRS.

If your state recognizes the bifurcation process (dissolving the legal ties of marriage now and resolving property and debt issues later on), suggest your taking an extra asset now in return for your cooperation in agreeing to a bifurcation. It's true that one spouse can apply for, and probably get, a bifurcation of the proceedings. Some delaying motions may prove possible, however, and your agreement will certainly speed matters along (a crucial consideration if your spouse has a new lover who wishes to marry, who is pregnant, or who's simply tired of sharing a partner who feels tied to you). For these reasons, try "selling" your cooperation in a bifurcation for an immediate transfer of an asset that you agree will not affect any later division, or trade your okay for cash now.

Since courts consider child-support amounts always modifiable, parents can do little to bargain between themselves to limit such amounts or obligations. Adults can, however, arrange spousal support amounts, schedules, periods, and form of payment as they wish. In other words, you can bargain, in setting the level of spousal support, for a termination date, for a ceiling on amounts, for the tax deductibility of all payments, for a nonmoney form of payment, and even for a clause that bars any later modifications at all. In cases where both spouses earn an adequate living or where spousal support otherwise appears an unlikely (or very limited) possibility, weigh the wisdom of waiving any present and future rights to such support in exchange for assets here and now. Don't know the value of waiving such an intangible? Don't worry, because no one else does, either. This "elastic" value, in fact, can turn out to equal the appraised price of your favorite chiffonier, your mate's share in a joint savings account, or your spouse's 20 shares of AT&T. In other words, anything goes that seems fair to both parties. While you can never reclaim waived rights, only a small percentage of women today receive spousal support awards for any length of time. An even smaller number of obligor spouses pay in full, on time, and for the full term of such ordered support. Weigh these alternatives and take the more profitable path.

Even if you're unlikely to receive spousal support, there are still two ways to weather a rainy day by using related support concepts effectively. The first of these ideas involves a concept called, in

California, a "retention of jurisdiction over the issue of spousal support." This means that the court will "hold the courthouse door open" if your circumstances change and you later require such support from a former mate. If you fall ill, suffer an accident, or cannot support yourself for some other reason, you can reenter the court and ask that spousal support be awarded you in some necessary sum. Usually such a right is deemed reciprocal—your mate would also be able to approach the judge to seek funds from you at a later date if circumstances or earning abilities change. In negotiating with your spouse, you may agree that this "open door policy" shall apply to only one of you, and you can bargain to set the length of time that you wish such a policy to remain in effect.

In the second instance, you may choose to waive (give up) any right to receive spousal support—now or in the future—from your spouse. If your marriage ranked as quite short (two or three years), your health remains good, you possess good earning skills, and there are no small children at home who might prevent you from working, then you're unlikely to receive even a retention of jurisdiction over the issue of spousal support (the judge will shut the support door as of the day of trial). However, if the factors laid out in Chapter Two indicate that you should receive such support, or if you're likely to enjoy the open door policy for a period of time, *then consider selling your rights to your spouse for a tidy sum.* What is such a waiver or a closed court door worth to your mate? Well, men rarely return to court to ask for support, but most fear that a wife will do so. According to statistics, few spouses of either sex ever request later support, but your mate probably does not know this and foresees financial ruin looming near. This fear can enable you to sell your right to receive support (or your right to reenter court) for an extra asset, for the right to spend more years in the family home, or for more than your fair share of the common cash.

While all this trading and selling goes on, keep your eye on who's occupying the family home. If you have moved out so that your mate and/or children can occupy the family home, and your mortgage requires only low payments, bargain to pay a low support sum based on his or her or their exclusive use and possession of your family home. While your mate may pay all the mortgage obligation and any costs of maintaining the home, and you can arrange to share equally in the net proceeds of any ultimate sale, in the meantime (which can stretch over several years), you must finance or rent other digs, and you must put off using the funds that remain tied up in the family home. After balancing all these factors, you may want to press for a financial offset for allowing matters to continue as they are, instead of pressing for an immediate sale. Such a credit may take the form of a lower child or spousal support payment, extra property for you in any asset division, or even the allocation to you of an income-producing asset to offset your interim loss on the use of those mutually owned funds.

If you're an in-house spouse who's paying the mortgage during these months or years, be sure that you claim all payments as deductions on your income tax. And if you're an in-house mother and are uncertain about finances or your ability to pursue career or educational needs while raising your children alone, consider asking your mate to occupy the family home and care for the children. You can offer help via a liberal "drop by" schedule. If you suffered severe twinges when you read about this concept in an earlier chapter and still feel that transferring custody may not suit you, consider the following information, drawn from an article by Nicole Yorkin that appeared in the *Los Angeles Herald* (April 5, 1982, page 1 of Section C) "Help for Women Who Face the 'Kramer vs. Kramer' Syndrome." The piece describes and quotes numerous mothers who have "chosen to live apart from their children" and who have joined a group called Mothers Without Custody to better deal with the age-old stigma of the mommy who transfers the care of her youngsters (however briefly or however painfully) to another adult. Since its founding in Boston in 1982, MWC has started chapters in 106 cities. Members gather regularly to "battle the myths surrounding mothers without full-time custody and to provide a support system for those who often feel stigmatized as a result." Members make up just some of the one in every 20,000 women who live apart from one or more of her minor children—a total that will surely increase as transferring custody gains respectability, and the fathers' rights movement gains momentum. Many of these mothers have had to work hard to accept the "realities" of single parenting: low income, strained health, the needs of the child, and the additional personal sacrifices a solo parent must make. F.M. Margolin, a Newport Beach psychologist who specializes in marriage and family counseling, says, "[I've long felt] that women should be reconsidering the whole custody matter. Sometimes the father is the better parent [and] I think that's very difficult for women to understand." No member of MWC claims that a switch in traditional custody allocations has proven easy, and many cite a "bittersweet" experience. All four women interviewed in the Los Angeles area said that the group "helped them become much clearer about their own situations and the positive aspects of living apart [from their children]."

If you feel that a nontraditional custody arrangement could benefit all of you or you would at least like to explore this possibility, contact Mothers Without Custody, P.O. Box 76, Sudbury, Mass. 01776 to find out which chapter is closest to you.

While straightening out issues like custody can prove draining, you'll find that it can pay to devote as much care and attention to the successful resolution of these purely emotional differences as you would to allocating your property and dividing your debts. In addition to the obvious financial repercussions of custody decisions (support, possible extended use of the family home, etc.), unresolved emotion-laden issues like custody can sap energy and sometimes destroy common sense, making any discussion of legal or property issues a waste of effort and time. If you suspect that custody (or another high-blood-pressure but low-financial-value issue) may turn out to be a major concern in your case, make early and concerted efforts to resolve this matter. If you don't, even energetic negotiations may get nowhere, and sensible proposals may meet with a blank and stubborn stare. In short, when a reasonable, fair, well-presented proposal for settlement fails to win acceptance, there's an excellent chance that an unresolved emotional issue is at fault.

Once you deal effectively with these heart- or psyche-triggered roadblocks, move on to the items with more easily recognized price tags. If some of these prove intangible (like the advanced educational degree or certification, or the goodwill in a spouse's business), consider using an "elastic estimate" to even out your after-divorce division of property. When you've allocated the assets between you, added up the pluses, then subtracted the debts you've agreed to pay and those attached to "your" assets, balance the two bottom-line totals by assigning a reasonable but negotiable value to all those "worthless rights" described earlier in the chapter. While considering these possibilities, do not yet relinquish an asset like a military pension, which federal courts recently declared the separate property of the earning spouse. Since that determination, several states (including California) have drafted bills to reassert some state control over this asset and to compel a more balanced division of such property.

Such judicial changes show why jurisdiction should be retained if an expected legislative or case-law change could benefit you.

If you'd rather not guess at an asset's or right's value (and I strongly suggest that you do make an *informed* division of assets), you'll want to consult with specialists and do some spadework of your own to unearth the true worth of your communal property. In evaluating these assets, remember that in most cases you'll be able to see, feel, smell, weigh, measure, or hear the items involved (perhaps your mate gets residuals for every sale of that hit song.) In other instances, a shared ownership in an "invisible" asset or an intangible right can produce profits for you. Even well-informed spouses frequently overlook unfamiliar property, or fail to pursue an asset that *appears* to have little value. If a mate hasn't taken an active interest in the other's business or family investments, then he or she faces a difficult decision: probe unknown territory or give up on possible assets and reap long-term regret. Clearly, only the first can prove profitable, even if the amount of detective work may seem a little scary. While it will take you a while to learn all that you'll need to about these hidden or unfamiliar assets, you needn't work without direction or help. Both informal and well-schooled, professional experts abound and are discussed below. You may find that some educated guesses from the former can provide you with a free assessment of an asset or business's value. In addition to choosing some of these methods for your detective work, you might want, at this time, to review the list of appraiser sources outlined in Chapter Three. While no informal assessment can be as reliable as an appraisal by a schooled and practiced professional appraiser, professional appraisers do charge (sometimes hefty) fees, and a money shortage may limit your investigations to whatever free sources you can find. In such cases, *some* information about an asset's value remains better than none; every sensible estimate can help you negotiate more effectively. Consider calling on the following professionals and using some of these tips to unravel business interests, open corporate coffers, uncover buried treasure, and get your fair share (or more) of any mysterious marital assets.

"Informal" business or asset appraisers included the following:

1. A business associate, competitor, or person in the same field or profession as your spouse, provided that he or she is knowledgeable and has conducted business for a sufficient period of time in a neighbor-

hood or professional community similar to that of your spouse.

Even a supplier or creditor who deals with numerous other businesses like your spouse's may provide you with an accurate "guesstimate" about the worth of a business, company, professional practice, or going concern.

2. The bookkeeper, CPA, or public accountant who keeps your spouse's business records, books, and/or prepares the company's tax return.
3. You, if you have worked in your mate's profession or business or one like it for a sufficient period of time.
4. A local storekeeper, repair expert, hobbyist, or trader in the product or asset that you need evaluated.
5. A used-equipment dealer (but beware if the quote seems too low; the dealer may anticipate purchasing the goods and want to ensure a sufficient profit margin in a later sale).
6. A realtor or real estate sales person experienced in dealing with the sales of businesses in the geographical area of your mate's business or company (particularly important if your spouse owns the firm, and the firm owns its building; or if your mate and his/her company own no real estate but hold a long-term lease at below-market rates).

Formal and professional business or asset appraisers include the following:

1. Actuaries, who are skilled in assessing pension values, retirement plans, and the present worth of even sophisticated annuity plans or other formalized programs designed to assure future payments after a certain time period or in special circumstances. Appraisal fees vary; in Los Angeles an actuary will charge about $175 to appraise the present worth of a single retirement benefit plan.
2. Certified public accountants, who can review records, ledgers, and even tax returns to estimate—from current income, inventory, and past performance—the present value of a going concern. Have your professional add in the intangible value of goodwill, an existing credit line, or other invisible asset of your spouse's business.)
3. Business appraisers, who sometimes deal in the sale of businesses and firms; others only evaluate the fair market value of a company.

Whomever you select, furnish your expert with *all* the information necessary to a well-informed appraisal of the asset involved. Necessary records can include any or all of the following:

- Financial statements, both personal and professional/corporate.
- Individual income tax returns for at least the last three years.

- Corporate, company, or partnership tax returns for the past five years, if possible.
- Any buy-sell agreements between members/partners in the firm.
- Any partnership agreements and related documents.
- Any leases for premises, autos, and equipment.
- Notes payable, trust deeds payable, and conditional sales contracts owed by the firm, professional, or partnership or payable to it or them.
- Documents relating to any acquisitions and obligations connected with real and/or personal property investments of the professional and/or his or her firm.
- Records describing the form and contributions to date to any pension plan, profit-sharing program, or retirement benefit schedule.
- Depositions and answers to any interrogatories (if your attorney has already conducted some formal discovery relating to an asset's value).
- Business and personal insurance policies.
- Personal and professional/corporate bank statements and canceled checks.
- Ledgers, financial records.

In directing your expert (remember that he or she is your "employee" for this detecting period), make sure that he or she obtains "office access" for the review of crucial records and books. Office access means that your expert reviews finances at your mate's firm itself. The reasons? A business owner/operator who wants to "sterilize" your expert's audit by moving all records to a separate office, or by denying your appraiser a spot on the premises may want to . . .

—exclude your expert from contact with other company personnel, gossip, and conversations that could help your appraiser form a complete picture of the firm's present value, past performance, and profit expectations (useful in later proving an ability to pay child and/or spousal support), or

—stretch out the time needed for an accurate appraisal while records get shuffled from office to expert and back again (such evasive techniques often backfire because the court often demands that the richer spouse underwrite all or a good part of investigative costs), or

—increase the difficulty of forming a complete picture of the company's or firm's financial health, or

—feed your expert only the information that your spouse wants him or her to see.

In contrast, an on-the-spot appraiser may prove able to gain access to books of original entry, general ledgers, the corporate minute book and stockholder communications, accounts receivable, unusual or overly generous inventory, esoteric or expensive office equipment, work in progress, and even the presence of unusual experts on staff who might signal an especially profitable project for the firm.

If you hire a professional appraiser, you will receive a report estimating the fair market value of the business or asset involved. But if you've gathered information from more informal sources, you'll want to know how the experts (and the courts) evaluate professional practices and companies. The following paragraphs offer only general guidelines, based on California law. Each state varies in applying formulas to estimate worth, and even the following suggestions should not provide your only evaluation for an important asset. Use these approaches to ball-park your joint assets' values, but try to obtain some official confirmation of your best guess before you sign any marital settlement agreement dividing or allocating your marriage's financial harvest.

The fair market value of a medical or dental practice can equal three months' gross receipts, or 20 percent of the average of the previous three years' total gross income. To guesstimate the value of other types of professional practices, try multiplying one year's gross receipts by 125 to 200 percent. The better the quality of the clientele, the higher the percentage figure you may use. To establish the value of other going concerns, experts multiply a firm's gross monthly or annual income by varying numbers, but these multiples differ so much from expert to expert, and from business to business, that even accomplished appraisers can disagree widely on an accurate figure.

To ensure that your approach meets with your state's approval, ask the reference librarian in your local law library to guide you to the most recent cases dealing with the issue of evaluating businesses for divorce purposes. By scanning the court's review of this case, and the court's decision and rationale, you can probably formulate your own, court-guided method of appraising an asset's value by following the appraisal approach set out in the case.

Once you have some accurate evaluations in mind for all of the assets you want to allocate or divide, proceed in a fashion that should net you more than one-half of the communal property. As a first possibility, let your spouse gain "imaginary property" while you take items of *present* value. What does this mean? Perhaps one of the reasons you're parting is because you view business opportunities differently. You, for example, just can't endorse your mate's dream of operating a horse-grooming salon in your suburban garage. She sees this scheme as a prime money maker and agrees to give you cash or property *now* for the right to keep all the earnings and ownership rights to this "promising" business venture, which she began before you moved out. Entrepreneurial egos tend to overvalue their own earning ability; they would see unlimited possibilities if assigned to sell furnaces to Tahitians. Your more realistic, sensible attitude can reap you generous here-and-now rewards.

Second, if your state law resembles California's, you may receive assets, property, or cash to compensate you now for a mate's financially wasteful ways during your marriage years. In short, you may recoup one-half of the funds your mate expended during a prior financial blowout that did not benefit either of you and that you did not endorse. Such activities can include (depending on your state laws) gambling, drinking, drugs, clearly poor business investments, and "loans" to friends or associates that no one could reasonably expect to be repaid. Remember that this reimbursed sum should come to you in addition to your share of any other communal wealth.

Third, try negotiating for an "equitable" (instead of even) division of the family assets. No court would probably object to an uneven split if both parties agree and if both parties' legal counsel review any agreement to ensure that each spouse knows the ramifications of such a contract. To gain your mate's acceptance of such an "unfair" deal, mention the children; your lower earning ability; any physical, mental, or career disabilities; a lower professional standing (if applicable); and any other valid reason why you should receive more than half of what you've acquired together.

Fourth, promise your spouse that you'll pay the community debts (in part or entirely) *if* you get most of the common assets to offset this assumed liability. Since your action frees your spouse of pressures from creditors, he or she may well agree to provide you with more than a fair share of the communal property to help you pay such bills. Negotiate with those creditors to stretch out your payments. Consider using your services or trading an asset you don't need to pay off some of the debts. See which obligations may be affected by the passage of time (so that a statute of limitations erases your legal responsibility to repay). Review all debts to determine if any really constitute gifts that you won't have to repay, or loans by friends who will wait perhaps months for payments to start.

In truth, you will probably remain liable anyway on debts incurred during your marriage, regardless of which of you made him or herself liable. In such circumstances, if your mate doesn't pay his or her assigned share of such debts, your creditors will surely come knocking on *your* door. If you're divorcing a fiscally irresponsible spouse, better that you should obtain most of the common assets and all the debt than that you take one half of the assets and end up paying *all* those mutual obligations with limited funds, while your former mate kicks up unburdened heels. In addition, freeing your spouse from monthly bills will give him or her more discretionary income with which to pay child and/or spousal support to you.

Fifth, obtain more than one-half of all the commonly owned property by giving an equalizing note for the difference. Such an equalizing note accomplishes exactly what its name implies—it's your promise to pay to your mate one-half of the difference between your two totals, so that after payment in full, you will both end up with comparable amounts of the jointly owned property. A few recipient mates will accept such a note with just the payer's signature for security, but other spouses will ask for additional security. Such security might be a second trust deed against an asset assigned to you, or a lien on other property allocated to you. Under the terms of such a note, you can pay the asset difference over time, on terms favorable to you. For instance, with your spouse's agreement, you may stretch your payments to him or her over a lengthy period of time, pay a below-market interest rate, or provide for interest-only payments—or no interim payments—with a complete payoff months or years away. While the law provides for your mate to get an inflated note (to compensate for a discounted sale to a third party), a fair interest rate, and possibly at least interest-only payments before payoff, your mate may not know of these financial protections. But even if your spouse knows about the terms that he or she *could* demand (or if your conscience demands that you inform your spouse), the two of you can agree that one will wait for a payoff bearing low interest, and even wait for a generous period of time. If you can reach such an arrangement, do so, for you immediately gain present-day assets that you can sell, trade, or borrow against. Meanwhile, you will repay that note with cheaper dollars, greenbacks that will consistently purchase less in future years. Your spouse immediately gains a promise of future payment that he or she cannot sell without discounting (reducing) the face value of the note dramatically. In fact, your mate may prove unable—given these biased terms—to sell your note at all.

If you still feel uncomfortable about negotiating this arrangement with an unsuspecting (or even agreeable) spouse, make your "note-for-goods" offer more attractive by adding to the deal an asset that may hold little value for you but that you know your spouse desires. A good example of such an asset might be granting your spouse the sole right to continue holding and using the credit cards you both obtained during marriage. If you're a male with good earning power, you'll face no problem renewing credit for yourself. If you're a woman eager to resume a maiden or former name during divorce proceedings, you'll need to apply for new credit anyway. Remember that when you do so, you're entitled to rely on any good credit history that you and your mate established during your married years.

Sixth, your objective situation may legally entitle you to most or all of the marital property, depending on state law. Research the code in your state under an appropriate heading (like marital property, community assets, etc.). California legislation, for example, allocates a more-than-fair share of the community property to just one spouse in either of the two following circumstances:

> If the community contains few assets but overwhelming debts, all the communal obligations can be awarded to the higher-earning spouse. If that's not you, you can probably take your share of any common assets free of debt.
>
> If the net value of the community property totals less than $5,000 and even diligent efforts cannot locate the missing spouse, the filing party may receive *all* of the community property.

Seventh, if your mate paid property taxes or other charges on his/her separate property during your marriage, you're probably entitled to at least a reimbursement of the amount expended (assuming that you can show you didn't intend a gift of these sums). You may also be able to claim a proportionate share in the profit and equity growth of the asset involved. Whether you receive a straight reimbursement or a percentage share in the asset's increase in value, be sure that you pocket this amount *on top of* any other asset rights that you may take under state law.

Eighth, bargain for more than one-half of all the marital assets in exchange for accepting a lower spousal support award (or for waiving the right to claim spousal support entirely). If you're anticipating that an inheritance, a great job, a raise, a boarder, remarriage, or some other event will boost your income in the near future, consider limiting or selling your spousal support rights for additional assets in the here and now. You should lose nothing, for when any of these events (or any other that draws more financial aid into your life) occurs, your spouse will probably ask you or the court to reduce his/her support obligation dramatically. If you're facing such a reduction anyway, why not give your mate a break on monthly payments now, and take more of the joint assets to compensate yourself for this "sacrifice"?

Ninth, if you have been living in the family home and you both agree to sell to a third party and divvy up the net proceeds, remember to do the following:

- Purchase a new residence within two years that costs as much or more than your 50 percent share of your gain from your former residence's sales price, in order to protect your profits from capital gains taxes levied by the IRS.
- Consider taking the once-in-a-lifetime tax forgiveness of $125,000 if you've reached the age of 55 and have lived in your home three of the past five years, and you do not anticipate needing this tax break later on in life.
- Consider taking payment from your buyer in installments, so that you suffer taxes only on the amounts received, when received.
- Consider taking your share of the house sale in a lump sum, but average your income over the allowable number of years so that a sudden bulge in receipts does not force you to pay a hefty tax bill.
- Consider letting your spouse have any (or most of the) cash from your buyer, while you take a second or third mortgage at a healthy interest rate and receive more funds, over time, than your spouse receives. If you select this option, check your buyer's credit rating and do not extend more credit than the house is really worth.

With any of these options, you will initially recoup as much from your home sale as your mate, but over a period of time, your after-tax share should exceed his or hers substantially.

If you do not wish to sell the house but can't muster enough cash, separate property, or communal assets to buy out your spouse's share, try to persuade your spouse (or the court) to let you remain in the family home (with its probably low mortgage) for an extended length of time before a sale occurs. The following arguments often prove effective. Choose those that you can apply in your case, and sit down at the kitchen table with your mate to see if you can work out the details. Look your spouse right in the eye and calmly suggest that:

a. It would prove detrimental to the children (and to you) if you had to move out of the family home immediately and find suitable housing. Such a move would be more costly, would place the children in a less safe part of town, would separate them from their school, their friends, their community commitments, and their social activities. The longer you have all lived in your home, the stronger the appeal of this argument. In such cases in California, the courts have balanced the detriment to the spouse forced to find other housing and wait for any sale proceeds against the potential harm to any children and a spouse who is primarily a homemaker if they are forced to secure alternate housing immediately because of a quick sale. Depending on the factors applicable to each side, courts have often ordered a sale delayed for one, two, three, or even five years or more.

b. It would prove fruitless and wasteful to offer the house for sale in this (slow, poor, high-interest-rate) real estate market. Why not hold on to it and both profit from a later sale under better financial conditions?

c. You could both continue to live in the residence like two roommates, sharing common expenses and both benefiting from the lower-than-an-apartment monthly payments.

d. You'll not only help him/her move out *and* share furnishings to make a new place less expensive and more like home, but you'll take on the day-to-day chores of keeping the house and grounds in order. You'll also perform minor chores and repairs, prevent vandalism, handle the family-oriented correspondence and bills (with some financial aid for the latter, of course), and in general protect your mate's investment in this property. Your spouse will receive one-half of any net proceeds in an ultimate sale, or a predetermined profit share.

e. You pay the mortgage and relieve your mate of sharing in this obligation while you reside in the house alone, then promise to split equally any net proceeds from the future sale.

f. Offer to give your spouse a bit more than half of the mutually owned assets in exchange for an agreement that you alone will occupy the family home for a set amount of time; agree to share equally the proceeds of a later sale.

g. Refinance the house for a lump sum that you can comfortably repay, then give that sum to your spouse to compensate him/her for waiting for a later sale, after which you would divide any net proceeds in an equitable way. If you have a Federal Housing Association-insured mortgage on your home, consider refinancing with a new FHA loan to obtain a better-than-market interest rate. Under a new program of the Federal National Mortgage Association (Fannie Mae, the government-chartered corporation that buys mortgages from lenders), you can borrow up to 90 percent of your (residence's) market value at two or three points below market rates. To find out if you qualify, ask the bank that issued your present mortgage.

h. Pledge a set amount from your separate or allocated share of any property to make needed improvements or repairs to your jointly owned home. When the house is sold you will claim no right to reimbursement, but you and your ex-mate will share equally in the higher sales price that the improved residence should bring.

i. Offer your mate a credit on child and/or spousal support payments if you and/or the kids can continue to live in the family home for some time. While adults cannot "bargain" away their offspring's right to adequate support, California courts often consider the exclusive use and possession of the family home, over a period of time, as a "partial payment" of such support. Of course, if you feel safe in waiving any present and future right to spousal support, you might also offer such waiver in exchange for inhabiting the home for a certain period of time.

j. Agree to "freeze" your own share of the home's value at a current sum. Exact a return pledge that you can live in the home for several months or years. Both agree that you will receive only that figure from any net proceeds, and that your mate can garner all remaining monies from the sale.

k. If you merely want to hold onto the house but aren't set on living in it, suggest that you both rent the house out, splitting any net monthly profit and sharing in any negative cash flow if the income doesn't meet mortgage and related expenses. A later sale — provided the market rises — can net you both more cash, or perhaps enable you to obtain financing, savings, or a personal loan sufficient to buy out your partner's share.

If you *do* wish to own the family residence yourself by purchasing your spouse's share, keep in mind that this asset will continue to rise in value. In other words, the longer you wait, the more you will have to pay your mate for his or her share. If your earnings aren't going to rise dramatically, and if you're not anticipating a large inheritance within the next few years, you'd do better to buy out your spouse at your earliest possible opportunity. If a buyout looks impossible, try to reach one of the following agreements with your spouse: you will let him or her occupy the house for a period of time, and help pay the mortgage; in return, you will have the right to purchase his/her share of the house at a price equal to the home's value at (for example) the separation date. As a second option, consider waiving any right to receive spousal support if your mate will sell you the house at its present value—even though you will be completing the sale some months or years in the future.

Now, if neither of these options will work for you, and you cannot transfer enough cash, communal assets, or separate property to your spouse to take full ownership of the family home, begin now to cooperate in getting top dollar for the house. (One couple low on cash did this by spending two weekends meticulously cleaning their residence before their realtor's open house.) In addition, begin researching the financing options for other, less expensive shelter. Penny, for example, worked for low wages and realized that she would qualify for only a very small mortgage loan. When she and Harvey sold their residence and divided the proceeds, she floated that small loan and purchased a modest mobile home. Because retirees abounded among her trailer mates, Penny easily arranged day care for Sherry, her little girl. Though her surroundings are much more simple than her former home, she says, "At least all that I survey is mine, all mine!" Investigating and deciding on this housing alternative gave Penny confidence. Shortly after her move, she landed a promotion and a raise and started saving for a traditional home.

As a second warning, keep in mind that if you *do* reach an agreement about the use of the home that seems advantageous to you, rush your terms onto paper and into court, or you'll be holding little but a memory if your mate (financed with your additional gifts of cash or property) changes his mind and petitions the court to force an immediate sale.

While one of these housing options may suit you, and these (true) tales can instill the courage to proceed, you may feel your creativity and courage fading under an onslaught of monthly bills. These of course arrive regularly, whether you and your mate remain together or not. Duplicate household costs further diminish funds available to satisfy creditors. In order to survive financially during these months, can you escape paying your share of past family bills? Of course you can. However, every benefit bears a price. You'll want to think hard about the consequences before taking one of the escape routes listed below. Before considering these possibilities, remember that (in California and probably in most other states) *both* spouses remain liable for debts that either one incurred for the benefit of the family before the date they parted. (Obligations incurred after separation normally are considered the obligation solely of the incurring party.) Because of this mutual and continuing liability it is unfair to saddle your spouse with these bills while you dash off debt-free. While *149 Ways* may not have shown heretofore much concern for your mate's welfare during divorce, this guide does not endorse shafting your spouse when you know that those expenditures benefited you both and that your mate will suffer greatly without your monetary aid. Keeping these thoughts in mind, consider the following avenues to see which could lead to your financial rescue from past obligations:

1. Ask for your spouse's pledge to pay all (or most of) the common bills, but give him/her more than half (almost all, or all) of the jointly owned assets. If you take this option, remember that such pledges officially are mere promises unless the terms are written out and filed with the court. Memories can fade, and only a written, filed agreement will allow you (or your attorney) to enforce the promises exchanged. Remember also that if under your state law you remain liable for such debts regardless of who assumes what in a marital settlement agreement, you *could* end up owning little property but owing all the obligations if your mate later refuses (or becomes unable) to pay. For these reasons, consider this avenue only if your spouse seems in good health, works in a secure job or industry, and has proven fiscally responsible in the past.
2. Work with your spouse (or on your own, if you manage the family funds) to reduce all outstanding balances before you say goodbye. You'll both share in the higher net assets of your marriage, and your mate will have more funds with which to pay support, or with which to support him- or herself.
3. Consider filing for bankruptcy . . . but think long and carefully about this option before taking such a step. If your mate files for bankruptcy, you may be forced to do so as well, since your mutual creditors will pursue the nonfiling party for full repay-

ment. While new bankruptcy laws make it possible to exit a debt-ridden situation with more assets than ever before, the personal costs of bankruptcy run high: damage to self-esteem, difficulty in obtaining later credit, and damaged self-confidence in handling finances effectively. If your marital community is truly insolvent, however, file for bankruptcy before dividing and/or allocating any property or debts that survive the procedure you choose.

While you're researching, weighing, deciding, and pursuing the various suggestions outlined throughout this chapter, save a little energy to sidestep some of the common, costly traps that often do people in just when matters appear to be nearing a profitable resolution. Some of the following pitfalls will seem obvious (when you see them laid out below), but others remain cleverly hidden and exact a later price.

a. Don't confuse spousal or child support payments with any right to receive a monthly payment designed to equalize the property division over a period of time. If you're entitled to receive funds to support yourself and/or any kids, if your mate wound up with more than half or most of your communal property, *and* if your spouse gave you an equalizing note that entitles you to receive payments over a period of time to even up that asset allocation, make sure that you keep careful records and that you get all that's legitimately coming to you for support and for any property.

b. If you're receiving or are entitled to receive property equalization payments *and* support, consider postponing the receipt of the asset equalization allotment so that its receipt will not reduce any support dollars. In other words, in considering all circumstances, a court (or your spouse) could well conclude that with other income, you can get by on a lower figure for support. In fact, in these economic times, a spouse may not prove able to pay an adequate support amount *and* a property equalization payment each month. To sidestep reduced support or missing payments, suggest that you take the full support figure now, but reduce the monthly support sum as each child reaches his/her majority, or contingent on some other event that lessens your need or increases your income from another source. As your support figure dips, the property equalization payments can kick in, so that your spouse slowly pays off his or her obligations to you at a feasible rate, while you suffer from no reduction in income from this source. Don't worry that you're offering too easy a path for your mate. You can ask that interest accrue on the note's unpaid balance, and meanwhile dramatically increase the possibility that you will receive pay in full by giving your spouse a reasonable financial break. Mates saddled with heavy payments often fail to make any at all.

c. If you're entitled to receive child and/or spousal support, make sure that it comes from a "safe" source, or you may simply receive payments from an asset already belonging to you. (If you're arranging for support before any division or allocation of marital assets, insist that such payments flow only from your mate's future earnings, or from property already characterized as your spouse's separate asset—received prior to marriage, or received during marriage by gift or inheritance. Don't agree too quickly that an asset "really belongs only to him/her." When all is said and done, you may rank as a co-owner.) Whenever and however you arrange support, consider these sources, listed from most preferable to least attractive for you:

- Your mate's earnings after separation (if such earnings rank as separate property in your state).
- Income from an asset or property allocated to your spouse in the marital settlement agreement or by the court.
- Your jointly owned or community property (remember that one-half of such assets or funds may be yours anyway).

d. If your spouse refuses to agree to pay support, but wants to handle monthly bills from joint creditors, pay the mortgage, or lavish necessary goodies on the kids, don't rock the boat. It's very possible that such payments will be declared by the court to constitute the equivalent of support, or that your spouse will admit to such in a saner, cooler moment. If either occurs, you will not need to return these amounts. In addition, you'll have a record of (hopefully) high voluntary payments to show that your mate can well afford a generous support allocation in coming months. Many parties rush into court to obtain an order that their mate pay support. In reality, they often risk

—receiving a lower amount because their spouse is voluntarily paying more than he or she can really afford at this time.

—alienating a spouse so that later negotiations grow tense or halt altogether, and a previously tractable mate grows suspicious, stubborn, and bitter.

—setting a pattern of problem solving that involves a stranger (the court) and usurps from the parties any ability or motivation for reaching creative solutions on their own.

e. Don't accept future benefits (like spousal support) in lieu of assets owed you here and now. Agreeing to such "over time" payments puts you at the mercy of Paying Spouse, keeps open a channel that often conducts negative "emotional charges" as well as money, and keeps you at the mercy of Paying Spouse's financial ups and downs. In fact, some spousal types spell special trouble if you count on receiving rights or property at some future date, or over an extended period of time. Such personalities can include mates with wanderlust, profligate spenders, and spouses who philandered during marriage and already boast one or several new romantic liaisons (it's unrealistic to expect a new love to endorse or encourage the payment of healthy support allotments to you). Other former partners who don't make good risks for future payment include people who have never managed money well, those intending to move out of state (absence makes making payments somehow more difficult), and some entrepreneurial types who rarely possess enough funds for the next financial daydream, let alone you.

f. If it appears that you will star as Supporting Spouse, consider limiting your earnings during these first months of separation in order to limit your obligation for support. Some favored tactics include:

- Limiting or eliminating overtime
- Asking that a promotion or bonus be delayed
- Utilizing few (or none) of available fringe benefits (personal use of a company car, allowable personal purchases on the expense account, exercising stock options, etc.)

g. Spouses who have moved out and face paying support sometimes find that they can lower support obligations by "using up" discretionary income in realistic, reasonable, but hefty living costs. These life-style expenses often encompass a nice (but not lavish) apartment or house (large enough to accommodate any offspring on overnight visits), adequate furnishings and furniture, and a quality of life resembling that enjoyed during the marriage years. As one middle-aged husband put it, "I didn't buy a Rolls Royce, but I made sure that there wasn't a lot of extra cash around when we sat down to set spousal support."

h. If you're paying support after "separation," make sure that you've moved out of the marital residence, and that any spousal support is paid within the framework of a written agreement, so that you can deduct these amounts on your tax return. To do this, your spouse must understand that he/she will have to pay taxes on any amounts received.

i. Regardless of which role you play, don't bring your new love to negotiating sessions or to court while your divorce proceeds. Doing so will

—appall your new romantic partner.
—spoil any fresh start with above.
—confuse your children.
—suggest a new source of support (or of contributions to your household expenses) that could undercut your demands for financial aid.
—hamper your dealings with your lawyer, your former mate, the court, and opposing counsel.

In fact, don't flaunt any new love(s). In other words, "Don't anger the alligator till you've crossed the stream." One man reached a swift and fair settlement with his longtime wife, then flew off to a Miami convention for construction firm owners. In about 10 days he returned . . . with a redhead who moved into the family home in their relatively small town. Enraged and hurt, Mrs. Contractor tore up that settlement and announced that she would sell her cooperation only at a celestial price.

If you occupy the family home, don't leave your lover's clothing or personal effects lying around the bath, the bedroom—anywhere. Spied by a spouse, such indiscretions can ruin a previously smooth visitation schedule with any children, upset even a good support payment schedule, spur your spouse to hide or spend mutual assets, and even reduce your support allotment, if it appears that New Love contributes to your living costs or to household expenses so that you benefit thereby.

j. If you end up selling your house to your spouse and taking a promissory note to be paid over time, don't limit your interest rate because of state usury laws or the legal rate of interest allowed in your state. Because you will rank as a seller instead of a lender, such interest ceilings do not apply to you, and you may set any financing terms that your market will bear. Buying a mate's argument that you can't charge him or her more than the legal rate of interest (now set at 10 percent in California), or some other lesser figure will needlessly cost you hundreds over the term of your note.

k. If you choose to bifurcate your procedure (snip your legal ties before dividing your assets and debts), the filing of a final divorce decree will cut off any rights you might otherwise enjoy as a spouse. You'll recall that these can include coverage under a spouse's health insurance plan, the right to receive workers' compensation or wrongful-death awards, and rights to any survivorship benefits as a legal spouse. In addition, a decree that becomes final before the marriage has lasted ten years will terminate your rights to collect derivative Social Security rights under your mate's work history in the years to come. In other words, weigh the outcome carefully before rushing to terminate the legal ties that bind you to a marital twin.

This postseparation period can prove a crucial one in setting the stage for your later financial, psychological, and personal success. Though you may feel rather down and out at this stage, consider Thomas à Becket's words to King Henry II in the movie version of Jean Anouilh's *Becket:* "In despair there is strength." For just when we fear that all may be lost we recognize that every step beyond this point can prove a gain. If loss appears certain if we do nothing, then we're bound to gain *something* with any effort at all. While it can appear mighty attractive to relax now and take a backseat in determining support, custody, asset allocation and debt division, giving up all negotiating or litigating responsibility to your lawyer or your spouse can exact a stiff price. Even a still-caring mate will eventually grow more assertive and less interested in providing for you. Even a capable and caring attorney cannot afford the time and attention to minor details that will gain you every advantage you seek. Therefore, *only you* can ensure a positive outcome from divorce, and you can do so only by risking some uncomfortable feelings as you arrange terms, and by investing personal energy in the settlement or litigation process. Though these suggestions call for the expenditure of a great deal of energy at this difficult time, they promise a greater chance of success. On the other hand, taking a passive role will almost guarantee you an unsatisfactory divorce and a financial struggle for years to come. Now that you're committed to doing right by yourself, consider that expending energy in a meaningless, random way will net you nothing. Even a person willing to devote effort and risk emotional discomfort will need some guidance and a practical philosophy for proceeding profitably. For that reason, follow carefully all the suggestions in this book that could possibly apply to you and take just a few more moments at this time to scan the following tips. The results should more than repay your energy expenditure.

Consider these guidelines suggested by psychologist Dr. Priscilla Partridge-Rankin, a California therapist, to help you through this painful period:

- Find one person to talk to who will not judge you, and who will love you no matter what you reveal about yourself or your feelings of inadequacy.
- Get everyone out of your life who is not supportive of you and what you're trying to do. Keep the energy givers and avoid the vampires who weaken your self-determination and contaminate your actions and thoughts.
- Fuel your body and mind by eating right: avoid sugar, caffeine, red meat, and white flour to keep your machinery running smoothly. Leaning on an artificial sweetener or a raw sugar can reduce the hyperactivity and nervousness that many nutritionists feel is caused by a high intake of refined white sugar. Eliminating refined white flour from your diet may constitute no loss—numerous dietitians now insist that this ingredient lacks the vitamins needed to maintain a well-functioning nervous system. Instead of processed white flour, consume more complex carbohydrates like potatoes, whole grains, and brown, long grain rice. Caffeine, though it can warm and motivate, often makes already-tense people excessively anxious. To learn more about how diet can affect your well-being and ability to cope in stressful situations, pay a few visits to a trained nutritionist, enroll in a local adult education class, or visit your local library to bone up on Adelle Davis's *Let's Eat Right to Keep Fit* (The New American Library, 1954) or review another similar guide. Get more than enough sleep; tension can wear down your resolve, but dreams can refresh us and provide a shortcut to insights at this time.
- Listen to your feelings—they can tell you when a spouse is fibbing, when a path will prove beneficial for you, and when a course of action is likely to hurt more than help.

- Play more! Play renews us, and activities with cultural overtones lift us from an animal state, call forth our better natures, and keep even pressing problems in perspective.

Take some minor risks in other areas of your life to experience the payoffs and pains of trying something new. If you've always gone bare-headed, for example, try flaunting a fedora, or sport a scarf wrapped like a turban, to some social event. If you've never dined alone, treat yourself to brunch or dinner at a nice restaurant. Make the first move in inviting a person who interests you over for a chat, or out for coffee or lunch. You'll enjoy the wins when you reap praise for your actions or ideas; you'll grow more practiced at handling rejection or failure when your attempts just don't pan out. To gain maximum benefits, give your flops an instant replay and study—as an objective observer—how you could turn these into successes on the next attempt. If you keep your risks reasonable at this stage, either outcome can prove a plus.

View the divorce process as a whole. Don't fret about the skirmishes; concentrate on the final outcome. If your mate seems to gain a temporary or minor advantage, don't panic. Instead, figure out how to turn his/her gain to your advantage and how to bargain effectively from your new position. You'll find help in this approach if you consider the next suggestion.

Stay in a "bargaining mode." Every step of a divorce involves a bargain of some sort. "If you take this, I'll settle for that. If you'll pay Trapp's Department Store, I'll pick up your car payment for the next six months." Looking at every asset, debt, custody wrinkle, and potential or future right as one-half of a bargain will help you make savvier deals. You'll also find more goodies to trade, for this approach will help you perceive unusual or seemingly worthless items as bargaining chips. Taking an "I'm-ready-to-bargain" stance can also help you empathize with your spouse because you'll elicit proposals and deals from him/her. Mate-suggested bargains will reveal what the other side craves, and this knowledge can lead to creative exchanges and profits for you.

To make this strategy really pay, strengthen your negotiating skills. It's not enough merely to suggest a deal, you must carry through with terms favorable for you. Start small and give yourself homework assignments to build up your negotiating ability. If a friend wants to meet at a certain place and time, offer a plus to get her to change the location or hour. The next time you shop, suggest a discount for cash. Insist that your dry cleaner pay for a ruined coat or say that you'll take him/her into small claims court—and mean it!

Obtain professional aid, if you need it, to develop your communications skills and raise your "assertiveness quotient." If money is scarce, look for a county mental health office, enter group therapy, or seek out a counseling center that will accept payment from your health insurer or that charges on a sliding scale, depending on your take-home pay. Make a foray through your largest local bookstore and/or library to scan books on shyness, on negotiating effectively, and on asking assertively for what you need and want. Check with local schools and colleges for adult or continuing education classes designed to enhance assertiveness skills. Attend faithfully, fulfill homework assignments, and ask for a referral to other therapy or for extra classroom help if you need to.

Vitalize passive habits by thinking of yourself as a powerful person who can affect others and make things happen in your favor. If you've always used a passive tone in chatting with yourself, start using active, positive words to emphasize your responsibility for what happens to you. For example, instead of thinking, on an especially hectic day, "Why does everything happen to me?" say to yourself "I'll need to allow more time for these errands in the future." Make a comment—out loud—that puts you in control, even if it means taking the blame for scheduling too much or starting out late.

Refuse to play the victim role any longer in dealings with your mate or the world at large. Stop waiting for people to do things *to* you and begin acting for yourself. As a management consultant acquaintance once relayed, "When you're unhappy with things as they are, *act*, don't *re*act." Once you begin to take action in your own best interest, instead of plotting revenge or responding in kind to some outrageous act of another, you will begin to value your worth more, and to move ahead toward your own goals regardless of the hurdles others throw in your path. If you've played some rather neurotic games with your mate for several years, don't expect to achieve clear, independent thinking overnight. If you've always responded to your spouse's goads, it will take some time to escape an automatic reaction to his/her old game-playing tactics. Keep in mind, however, that you *can* begin to act in your own best interests, free from your spouse's (however clever) controls. Whenever you find yourself *re*acting, take a moment to cool down. Consider what action you can take for your own good, given a change in facts or circumstances, then carry through. Whenever you find yourself thinking clearly, sanely, and exclusively about what actions will prove most effective and profitable for you, *reward* yourself with a sundae, a movie, some flowers, a small shopping spree, or a congratulatory chat with the bathroom mirror.

"Work out" mentally to build your problem-solving muscles. If you're psychologically flabby at figuring out solutions to daily obstacles, you'll need to pump some mental iron to handle the issues raised in divorce. To exercise effectively, imagine yourself facing a problem. Choose a hassle that seems possible, but not overwhelming at this stage. Your catastrophe could include a broken arm, a lost job, a small claims court action against you, or a tyrannical friend who seems to take more than he or she gives. Flesh out a scenario that makes your imaginary headache seem real, then set about finding *at least* five solutions or approaches in dealing with that wrinkle in your life. Over time, you will develop new skills—and rebuild old ones—that will minimize even large problems. You'll also develop, eventually, a Problem-Solving Approach applicable to the most complex divorce issue or intractable spouse. Building such musculature will also make you feel less like a victim and more like a vanquisher as time goes by.

Take an active role in your divorce. All of these suggestions (and, in fact, this entire book) call on you to participate in your own divorce by investigating, negotiating, and resolving the issues that divorce presents. Don't wait for your attorney to suggest strategy; consider your mate's predilections, fears, and desires. Don't dump a grocery bag full of records and paper scraps on your lawyer's desk—go through the file cabinet and other record caches at home and figure out the income, the outgo, the creditors' balances, and the location and nature of most (if not all) of the property yourself. Don't wait for your mate to finally appreciate you and return home; pursue some new interests that spell benefits for you, particularly if these activities offer income-enhancement possibilities. Instead of waiting for your spouse to open negotiations, draw up a property and debt list and suggest a meeting. While you shouldn't sign any agreement or let go of spendable assets without consulting with your legal counselor, you can complete a great deal of discovery and some basic negotiations without waiting for another's push.

It's often said that divorce courts deal in equity—they do what *should* be done. But another popular legal saying is: "Equity aids the vigilant." Don't wait and hope that your lawyer or the court will "rescue" you from both your spouse and poverty. Play a vital role from beginning to end in your divorce. Do the best job—for you—that you can do. Your financial gains should prove to be only one of your rewards.

8

How to Win Financially at Trial

WITHIN a few months after separating, or perhaps sooner, you or your mate will begin thinking about going to court to formalize the termination of your married state. Considering such a step can trigger feelings of remorse, regret, depression, and loneliness. Perhaps only a few close friends know of your parting, or you may feel that everyone around you appears happily wed. If you live in a family-oriented suburban neighborhood, most of your neighbors probably *are* married, and you may indeed form a minority in your community.

You may feel better, however, after learning that you have plenty of company. In a May 10, 1982, edition of the *Daily News*, Sylvia Porter's column (headed "Little Comfort in Divorce Laws") appeared on page 2 of section 4, and informed readers that "A full 50 percent of today's marriages, including second marriages, end in divorce." When the July 20, 1981, issue of *U.S. News & World Report* ran "A Look at America's Divorced Population" on page 54, it revealed that more than 80 percent of all men in the U.S. work force have been divorced, and that almost three-quarters of the women workers are divorcees. In short, you may feel lonely right now, but you're far from alone. When you prepare for the formal ending of your marriage, remember that thousands have preceded you, and all have survived.

Of those thousands, however, some have survived better than others. Invariably, those who feel most satisfied about their divorce experience include people who officially ended a marital community without undue assistance from their lawyers or the court. These participants played an active role in determining values, dividing property, allocating bills, assigning custodial duties, and in setting support. They relied on legal counsel and court personnel to safeguard basic rights and to perform the necessary legal procedures, but for little more. In fact, many never visited a courtroom, faced a judge, or took the witness stand.

Depending on the forum in which you file, you may be able to avoid unnecessary court time as well. In some states, like California, parties can submit a marital settlement agreement and one spouse can make the necessary "appearance" by simply signing a printed affidavit relating certain facts and filing it with the court. In other forums, you may be required to make a brief court appearance, even if you've resolved every issue in negotiations and can present a detailed, signed marital settlement agreement to the court.

In *all* forums, however, you will have to go to court if you cannot resolve all the differences between you by means of negotiations between your lawyers and/or yourselves. If you choose to ask the court to play a major role in your divorce (and the choice *is* yours), you will probably emerge with adequate support and property, since most states subscribe today to an equal or equitable division of marital property. But your gains will remain limited to 50 percent of any jointly held property, and your trade-offs and bargaining power will consist of only those assets and rights recognized by your state; you may not be able to "sell" those imaginary rights and properties discussed previously. Finally, *you may forever lose several valuable personal assets* if you abdicate decisions regarding your divorce terms to that (however kind) stranger on the bench.

You could lose on several fronts. You could lose a good (or at least neutral) relationship with your spouse—fostered by continuing communications; clouded or curtailed when all information gets exchanged between attorneys or in the formality of court.

You could lose your self-respect if you give all responsibility for the outcome of your case to your lawyer or to the judge. This option always appears attractive because we can blame our legal counselor or the hearing officer if matters don't go well for us. Shouldering some duties means that you may feel deeply any disappointments, but you can also rightfully garner some of the credit for any ground gained.

You could lose your self-confidence if you expect your attorney to deal with all those third-party professionals (like realtors, appraisers, business experts, etc.) who may have always frightened you. By working directly with these people, who will function, after all, as *your* employees, you can build communications and negotiation skills that will aid you for years to come.

You could lose your self-esteem if you do not investigate your property, your debts, and your options for yourself. If you allow your spouse, your lawyer, or the court to dictate the assets allocated to you, the amount of support you're going to receive, the date when you must return to work and/or become self-supporting, and other highly personal decisions, you risk living an inferior life with a matching attitude.

In order to avoid most of the above losses, insist on working as an active participant in all phases of your divorce. You will increase your chances for a profitable divorce and do better at avoiding these and other losses if you try every possible avenue to effect a favorable settlement out of court. If you have tried everything you can think of, and your spouse's actions or uncooperative attitude dictate a court hearing to resolve your differences, consider the following suggestions for orchestrating a "cooling-down period" or for detouring your action to a friendlier, more open forum in which you can take a last stab at negotiating creatively:

1. Arrange to bifurcate your proceeding, so that you obtain a divorce immediately but divide property and debts at a later time, when cooler attitudes may prevail.
2. If you've been married just a short time, and assets remain few, take advantage of any simplified divorce process offered by your state, and let your spouse know of the time, energy, and fee savings if you can file such a form and attach a written agreement settling all the issues between you.

In California, for example, you could attach such an agreement to your Petition for Summary Dissolution (a streamlined divorce process) if your case meets certain requirements. (Checking to see whether your state may provide such a simplified process can save you legal fees, discovery costs, and courtroom hassles.) While Californians applying for a Summary Dissolution must still wait six months for a final decree, neither party needs to make a court appearance, do extensive discovery to establish assets, or hire legal counsel *if* . . .

- You have both read and understand the summary dissolution booklet (provided with filing papers for this procedure).

- You have been married less than five years from the wedding day to the date of filing.
- One of you has lived in California for at least six months and in the county of filing for at least three months preceding the date of filing.
- There are no minor children born of your relationship before or during your marriage or adopted by you during the marriage, and the wife, to her knowledge, is not pregnant.
- Neither of you has an interest in real property anywhere.
- Except for obligations with respect to automobiles, you owe no more than $3,000 on debts either or both of you incurred during the marriage.
- The total fair market value of all community property assets, excluding encumbrances and automobiles, is less than $10,000.
- Neither of you has any separate property assets, excluding all encumbrances and automobiles, in excess of $10,000.
- You have no community assets or liabilities *or* you have signed an agreement listing and dividing all your community assets and liabilities and have signed all papers necessary to carry out your agreement. A copy of your agreement needs to be attached to the petition.
- Irreconcilable differences have caused the irremediable breakdown of your marriage, and both of you wish to have the court dissolve your marriage without anyone appearing before a judge.
- You both give up forever any right to receive spousal support from the other party.
- Upon entry of the final judgment of summary dissolution of marriage (available in six months' time from the filing date), you both give up any right to appeal, to request any findings of fact or conclusions of law, or to move for a new trial.

The petition also provides for the restoration of a wife's former or maiden name, if she desires it.

3. Even if you've accumulated more assets, have children, or have been wed for longer than five years, you can often avoid a court appearance in California by signing an affidavit under oath that states the same information that you would have revealed on the witness stand. The information involves the length of time that you've lived in the state and in the county where your matter was filed, the fact that irreconcilable differences have caused a permanent marital breakdown, and other factors dealing with support, asset and debt division, and the custody of any minor children. If your state provides such shortcuts through the legal sys-

tem, and you can utilize them by working out your own agreement for presentation to the judicial bench via the mail, do so.

4. If your matter is set for trial, or is about to be, you can suggest to your lawyer, to the court, and especially to your mate that you all visit with conciliation court personnel to resolve whatever differences remain. (Though you may recall the discussion of conciliatory court procedures in an earlier chapter, you may find it helpful to study this court's additional services, as outlined here.) All courts in California are empowered to institute such services, and many of the counties that do so house conciliation court staff members within the courthouse structure itself. Conciliation court people consist of trained therapists, social workers, and counselors (who sometimes rank as lawyers as well). These professionals see the parties and other involved persons (like children or a relative) in informal office settings to work out issues in a friendly fashion. In some court systems, these counselors open their doors only to parties facing custody or visitation issues in a divorce. But in other counties, conciliation court people will work with a married couple experiencing marital difficulties even if a legal separation, divorce, or annulment has not been filed. If the parties' problems threaten the well-being of their child, the adults need not be wed to seek counseling aid.

   In conciliation court sessions, the therapist will usually see all the parties together (sometimes with their lawyers as well), and then interview individually every person involved (including any children). If their efforts result in an agreement, the parties sign the written terms and a conciliation court staffer presents the stipulation for court approval and then—if it is approved—for filing. Once filed, an agreement gains the weight and power of a direct order from the bench.

   Everything discussed in conciliation court sessions—including admissions, damaging statements, and offers to settle—remains confidential. Neither party can introduce anything said there as evidence at any later hearing or trial. Such county-by-county services are offered to families free of charge, so long as one party is a county resident.

   To find out whether your state offers such services, call your local court hearing family or domestic relations matters. Ask the clerk of the family-law or domestic relations department if the court offers counseling, family mediation, arbitration, or any other informal-but-binding means of resolving, out of court, intrafamily disputes triggered by divorce.

5. Call the family-law clerk at your local courthouse (or ask your lawyer) to investigate the possibility of scheduling a voluntary settlement conference with a judge, commissioner, or hearing officer whose schedule will allow such a gathering. If the presiding chief judge agrees, this jurist may agree to meet with you to resolve remaining issues in his or her chambers, which is usually an office just a few feet from the courtroom itself, where judges work on cases, do research, and conduct settlement conferences when not sitting on the bench.

   Generally, such attempts at settlement involve the attorneys, the parties and sometimes their children, and any necessary third parties (like a pension plan administrator, an appraiser, someone with an ownership right in some of the community property, or perhaps a person who holds title with one of the parties to an asset that will be disposed of in the case). The hearing officer will review the paperwork filed in the case, ask questions of the people involved, and suggest some terms of settlement. Sometimes a judge will indicate how he/she is likely to rule on a particular issue in the case. After hearing that judge's opinion on an issue, one party will often concede a point or agree to a previously objectionable term. If you haven't retained a lawyer, then you will address the judge in his/her chambers and take an active role in reciting the facts of your case when the clerk or other court employee indicates that the judge, the commissioner, or the hearing officer wants to meet with you.

6. Your court system may require that a mandatory settlement conference be held—which all parties and necessary third parties *must* attend—in order to attempt a settlement without a full-blown trial. Such a policy has proven popular in Los Angeles County, for example, because it results in a high percentage of resolved cases, which court personnel can then remove from the calendar. In addition, provisions reached via conference tend to rank as more creative, more realistic, and more closely followed, since both parties can unburden themselves to a robed decision maker, but both contribute in formulating any settlement terms.

   These conferences, even though not held in the courtroom itself, can exert great pressure on a stubborn spouse because the judge will provide frank answers that can deflate one party's unreasonable demands. Hearing the judge reiterate what one (or both) lawyers have counseled and being given the face-saving device of abdicating to a judge's "suggestions," even a recalcitrant mate will often become tractable in a mandatory settlement conference.

7. If you'd like to avoid anything even slightly resembling a courtroom (and few would blame you if you did), try suggesting to your mate that you visit a divorce mediator. This relatively new professional category includes therapists and sometimes lawyers who help both parties reach their own decisions about the division of property, custody, support, and any allocation of debts. These neutral moderators sometimes ask the lawyers or other specialists to sit in on sessions and often provide referrals to other experts (financial counselors, vocational trainers, real estate professionals, etc.) to aid the parties in reaching resolutions. While even therapist-mediators do not offer psychological counseling during these sessions, they can help to uncover the hidden needs, fears, and angers that divorcing parties often carry inside. If one or both parties feel that personal therapy would help speed the process or aid emotional health, they can seek separate counseling from another therapist—sometimes a professional on the mediator's staff or one who counsels nearby.

   The mediation format works well when a couple feels evenly matched in asset knowledge, earning power, and psychological strength, so that neither can manipulate the other unduly during these sessions. But even when one party has a history of intimidating or manipulating the other, a therapist-mediator's special training can help minimize such games and keep all discussions on track.

   Sometimes a couple uses mediation to resolve the more personal problems of divorce (who will have custody, how will visitation schedules evolve?), but each party consults with an attorney to settle the strictly legal aspects of their case. If you use a mediator, have all terms reviewed and explained by your attorney before agreeing to a settlement.

   You can find more information on mediated divorce from these sources: "Divorce Mediation," an article in the Spring 1981 issue of *Family Advocate*, an American Bar Association publication for lawyers available at any law library. It contains survey results of participants' reactions to private mediation projects; *Di-*

vorce Mediation: A Rational Alternative to the Adversary System by Howard H. Irving (Universe Books, New York, 1980, $11.95); *Sharing Parenthood After Divorce* by consumer advocate Ciji Ware (Viking, New York, 1982, $14.95).

8. In some jurisdictions, private parties can retain a retired member of the family-law bench to hear evidence and decide the terms of a divorce. The parties may hire a reporter to transcribe all testimony or keep no records, as they choose. Parties who can afford the $500 to $750 daily judicial fee can schedule hearings when and where they choose, can keep all matters confidential, and can select a jurist with special knowledge if the case involves a complex business or other esoteric asset. While private judges preside in more informal surroundings (some people even schedule sessions in their living rooms), and the parties and all witnesses undergo swearing-in ceremonies, all rules of evidence prevail.

To find out if your court system endorses this private adjudicator system, call the presiding judge of your family-law court. If your county provides for such services, ask for a list of the available judges and select one unknown to both of you but skilled in any particular area of family law that your case may require.

9. You may also obtain an out-of-court hearing in a friendlier, more-conducive-to-settlement setting by contacting the nearest branch of the American Arbitration Association. Many AAA offices offer a panel of mediators and hearing officers skilled in the family-law field. Fees are extremely reasonable, and the parties can decide in advance whether the decisions will be binding on them or whether either may seek a new hearing by applying for a regular court trial. Arbitration sessions can occur almost anywhere and often take place in the office of an AAA-suggested neutral lawyer selected by the divorcing pair.

10. Third-party intervenor. This unbiased party should be someone you both trust, but could include a clergyperson, therapist or a mutual friend.

Even if none of these ideas works for you, you may prove able to "break up," alter, or shorten the course of even a full-fledged trial by utilizing one or all of the following strategies.

Suggest to your counsel (and/or to the court) that the lawyers join the judge in chambers to obtain a quick decision on a point of law or judicial policy that does not involve the taking of evidence or the presence of a court reporter. Sometimes such a "judicial reading" on a seemingly small point can speed matters or settle related issues. Such a minimeeting might revolve around the admissibility of a certain piece of evidence, the court's view on a similar case in another jurisdiction, or the judge's policy on calling teenagers to the witness stand, interviewing children in chambers, or on refusing to see such impressionable parties at all.

Even if you do succeed in involving your intractable mate in out-of-court negotiations by means of one of the types of mediation just described, you will most definitely need the services of able counsel to advise you during both the negotiation and court phases of your divorce. Choosing the proper counsel is a very important step.

What happens when a divorcing party chooses not to retain counsel, but to conduct a hearing or trial by her- or himself? Participants usually run little risk in representing themselves if the matter is a simple one. If you're making a technical appearance only, and your respective rights, duties, and obligations are detailed in a marital settlement agreement filed with the court, you're probably risking little or nothing, *provided that your attorney has reviewed your agreement and explained all its terms and ramifications to you.*

Note that your protections rest upon retaining your own counselor. This does *not* mean the attorney who handled your wife's business incorporation, or the lawyer who's always handled your husband's trust. It means an independent professional accountable only to you, who doesn't feel any obligation or friendship toward your mate, and who is experienced and skilled in the family-law or domestic relations field.

If your matter appears at all complex (real estate, one or more pension plans, a child custody disagreement, or exotic or extensive personal property), consult with your lawyer (and make sure that your spouse sees his or hers as well) before signing any final terms or proceeding to trial.

While judges make special efforts to provide a fair hearing or trial for unrepresented parties, they cannot run your case for you, suggest evidence, or guide you through the labyrinth of procedural pitfalls. Hiring professional assistance will prove far cheaper, even in the short run, than losing an important point or extensive asset because you wanted to save a few bucks.

What do you need to know to hire the right lawyer for your situation and for you? To begin with, consider these don'ts to save money, sanity, and time. First, if you don't have a great deal of property, you've decided who should primarily care for any children, and the noncustodial spouse agrees to pay some reasonable amount of support, then you probably don't need the most prestigious attorney in town. A professional with an up-to-date knowledge of family law in your state should easily suffice. Second, you don't need a shady legal counselor who wants you to hide or diminish assets to cheat your spouse. Most people know what is fair, and a counselor who encourages—or lets you give in to—such low desires will cause you heartbreak and lowered self-esteem during the proceedings and for years afterward.

Avoid an attorney who wants a doormat for a client. One male client switched attorneys because his first counselor kept urging him to give in to his wife's unreasonable demands for excessive child support. Watch out for attorneys whose religious or social beliefs may affect their ability to furnish you with objective services. In the example above, the husband's attorney was Jewish, and the client felt that the counselor had a strong sense of duty to provide for a wife's every desire believing that her needs outweighed the husband's right to retain enough assets and earnings to begin a new life. In another case, Jenny and Peter wanted to end their marriage, but her Catholic attorney refused to finalize the terms of their marital settlement agreement, hoping that they would reconcile. Every time Jenny called him to urge matters along, he found some excuse for his delays and billed her for the call.

Beware the attorney with high overhead. That fancy office and cast of employee thousands costs money, and guess who's going to foot the bill. Don't hire a costly lawyer with the impression that your spouse will have to pay for him or her, while you gloat over your mate's financial ruin. In these more modern times, you'll need to review these monetary facts of life:

Both of your lawyers may be paid from joint savings, or

Your attorney will hold you personally responsible for your fees, but will *try* to recoup them from the other side, or

You will be ordered to pay your own lawyer out of separate property, or out of some of the communal property that's been allocated to you, or

The better-paid spouse may be ordered by the court to *contribute* to the lower-earning mate's legal fees (such an assessment may be based on the comparative amount of take-home pay each party enjoys).

In short, any lower-earning spouse who trusts the bench to order a mate to foot his or her entire legal bill is living in the past. As a rule, it's wise for both parties to keep legal costs as low as possible, for each may well wind up paying his or her gladiator's entire fee.

Avoid a lawyer who takes on every type of legal case. Even if your case appears simple, you'll want a counselor with a more-than-passing knowledge of family law in your state. Both legislatures and judges have produced such a volume of legal changes in this field that you should probably consider an attorney who devotes more than one-half of his/her practice to the domestic relations field. It's impossible to overstate the importance of in-depth knowledge in this field. California law experts often say that more changes have occurred in this field in the last five years than in the previous three hundred. Bringing your divorce to your second cousin (who's great at corporate law) will cost both of you valuable time and possibly the successful outcome of your case and even your friendship.

If you choose an attorney who focuses on more than one area of law, try to select a counselor with complementary—instead of competitive—fields of practice. A lawyer who deals routinely with real estate, business sales, debt collection, estate planning, contract drafting, or tax consulting, for instance, can bring valuable skills to bear when resolving issues arising in your divorce. An attorney whose practice involves a great deal of criminal law, however, must put those clients first because they're entitled to swift hearings and trials under state and federal Constitutional safeguards. In other words, an attorney with a heavy criminal caseload may have to appear frequently in court on short notice—just when your negotiations have reached a crucial stage.

In addition, beware an attorney whose other legal matters usually require settlement only in a legal forum, so that he or she discounts the importance of negotiation and elevates the gavel's power. Such professionals often grow accustomed to solving every problem through a court appearance; they sometimes tend to employ emotional tactics successful with juries but detrimental to clients already traumatized. This refusal to negotiate can hike client temperatures instead of cooling them and makes for much wasted legal energy, since judges decide family-law matters and juries are never involved.

Lila chose an attorney famous for pursuing every issue in court. She wanted a gladiator who would "fight to the last possibility," as she put it, in her case. From the first, this lawyer's litigious personality so intimidated Lila that she hesitated to ask for explanations of confusing terms and strategies. In addition, this counselor's abrasive attitude so angered Lila's husband that he refused to consider even reasonable settlement terms, because, he said, "I'm not giving in to that bastard, no matter how long this divorce takes!" Increasingly uncomfortable with her attorney's personality, no closer to a settlement than when she retained him, and frazzled from dealing with a spouse who started fights whenever he arrived to pick up the minor children for visitation, Lila fired her gladiator. Claiming a right to immediate payment for his $4,000 (but undocumented) bill, her former attorney promptly served her with papers and forced her into court to collect his fee. "I'm not really surprised," admits Lila, "since rushing to court has been his answer to every issue."

Enough of the negatives . . . what qualities indicate a good potential advocate and some extra advantages for you?

First, explore your prospective employee's philosophy of divorce to determine whether it meshes with your own. Just asking a lawyer to formulate his or her theories about divorce and how it should be handled will tell you a great deal about the person you're considering. Will he conduct a hard-fought battle? Does she claim skills as a good negotiator? Can he give examples of creative problem solving in previous cases? Does she offer evidence of a broad knowledge of business issues? Does he believe in a "team approach" that would involve other community resources, therapeutic assistance, or your active participation in your case?

Consider a lawyer who utilizes others' strengths effectively, so that he draws on each member of the firm for his or her area of expertise, and you save funds whenever possible. In one case, a lawyer who loved courtroom work paired with another who, enjoying research, interviewed clients, discovered assets, and prepared the paper side of each case. In other firms, paralegals operating at lower hourly rates interview clients, draft documents, handle research, and gather evidence to prepare a marital settlement agreement or a case for trial.

Lean toward attorneys whose personal objectivity will help keep you on track and who will tend to devote their high-priced energies to the *important* issues in your case. Though all attorneys receive training in advocacy—that is, dedication to pleading their client's case and to pursuing all avenues that further the client's interests—some lawyers feel their client's emotions too deeply. These professionals lose their objective outlook, often fail to guide the client effectively, and sometimes refuse to accept fair settlement terms even when they're offered by the other side. A cool-headed counselor, on the other hand, can devote most of his/her energy to the major issues in your case. This concentration will limit your fees and tend to speed a resolution of your case, as clients become more amenable to compromise after settling their case's more important points. Such a professional will also bring an objective viewpoint to issues you may not see clearly due to anger or despair.

Assuming that you choose a lawyer who's right for you and that you work well together as a team, still, don't expect to become friends. (Some clients and their attorneys start out as friends, and others become friends in the course of an action, but count this as a possible extra benefit, not a probable one.) Consider the well-regarded Beverly Hills family-law attorney who orchestrated a huge party for all his past clients. Almost nobody came. Though they appreciated his work, another family lawyer opined, "Those clients probably didn't want to recall a time when they acted like neurotics or crybabies, attempted dirty deeds, or at the very least operated with diminished capacity. In addition, they were no doubt ashamed to meet again the person who'd lived through that period with them."

But even if you don't forge a friendship, you *can* maximize your power as a winning team by following the following guidelines in working with your legal partner on your case:

1. Secure a fund for payment of fees, court costs, and investigation and appraisal of any assets that you haven't yet found. Monies may come from a relative or friend, from your separate property or savings, or (best of all) from your spouse's earnings after separation or from a community-owned account. Knowing that you have sufficient monies to mount a good case can, paradoxically, lead to an early out-of-court settlement, as the other side gets no negotiating advantage from delaying and hoping that your money runs out. In addition, remember that lawyers are business people, and it's human nature to work on those cases in which payment appears assured.
2. Save your lawyer's time and energies by offering to help out in

your case. Negotiate directly with your spouse to obtain settlement on as many issues as you can (always check with your conselor, of course, before you commit yourself to even a minor point). Arrange appraisals and evaluations of some or all of the property at issue in your case. Complete some or all of the legal research related to a new or unsettled issue raised by your divorce. In California, you yourself can even serve subpoenas on witnesses, etc. and save the service-of-process fees.

3. Treat your lawyer with respect and value his/her time as you do your own. Marshal your thoughts and questions before each meeting. Complete—promptly and thoroughly—whatever homework he/she assigns. If necessary, visit a therapist to bitch and moan about the personal injustice of this situation, so that you can concentrate on business when you and your lawyer communicate. (Besides making you a stronger person, a therapist can save you cash, for therapy on a sliding scale beats incurring legal fees running from $90 to $200 per hour.) Don't confuse the case by sending your spouse around the emotional bend by punching his buttons, or pulling her old strings. If you show yourself able to help your case along however you can, you may well obtain a bill that contains some "soft edges" for your cooperation. Attorneys respect fair treatment, and many will reciprocate in a way that may leave more in your pocket when your case ends.
4. Always tell your lawyer the *whole* truth. The most skilled practitioner or creative negotiator cannot overcome the harm caused by a damaging truth that you "forgot" to convey. If you physically or psychologically battered your husband, let your counselor know. If you really separated at any earlier date that cuts off some of your right to share in acquired property, tell her that, too. More than one potentially profitable case has crumbled at the introduction of a fact or facts unknown to counsel. Don't let your case join that group.
5. Obtain your lawyer's court schedule and attend those hearings and/or trials that bear some resemblance to your matter. Watch him or her in action. Study his pace and personality when performing in court. Learn how she prefers to structure the evidence and draw out testimony. Pretend that you're sitting as the client in the case you're observing. Think how *you* would be of assistance if this were your trial. Does the client impress you as trustworthy? Is he or she dressed appropriately? Is the client's

body language undercutting his/her testimony on the stand? Could that client have taken a more active role in preparing exhibits crucial to the case? Has this client revealed *everything* to his (and your) attorney, or has the lawyer been caught by surprise in presenting a crucial issue? Is this client's behavior showing disrespect to the court, or irritating the judge? (It doesn't take much with some hearing officers—one divorcing woman dropped her pencil in disgust after one of her spouse's statements from the witness stand and received a swift, harsh reprimand from the bench.)

6. Visit the courtrooms in your area and observe other hearings on cases similar to yours. This time, concentrate only on courtroom procedure and etiquette. How do the witnesses address the bench (a rare but possible occurrence)? How does the judge react to the way the parties and the counselors are dressed or groomed? (Most judges hide adverse reactions based on personal appearance extremely well, but the jurist that you're observing may let a reaction slip through body language or through a passing expression—watch closely and learn.) Listen for the type of evidence that the attorneys try to elicit from the parties and other witnesses on the stand. Watch the procedure for introducing documentary evidence like photographs, records, letters, trust deeds, etc. Are some items not admitted into evidence? Why? (If you're not sure, consider asking the *other* attorney in the case during a courtroom recess, before court reconvenes, or in the courthouse cafeteria, if you're not interrupting a lawyer-client talk.)

6. If you can determine which hearing officer will hear your case, visit his or her forum and observe proceedings similar to yours. By combining this exercise with the previous one, you may pick up valuable insights without investing excessive time. How does this judge show acceptance or displeasure? What signals show that testimony interests or bores him? How does she show disbelief in a witness's testimony? Which indications reveal that he considers some evidence to be weightier than other during a case? Does he/she run a formal or informal court? What parts do other court personnel play—the bailiff? the clerk? the reporter? anyone else? After a few hours of watching, it's possible that the judge may recognize you when you finally appear for your hearing or trial. He or she may well feel impressed by a client willing to sit through courtroom procedures to learn more about how justice operates.

If you're a working person with a crowded schedule, ask if any night or Saturday sessions encompass family-law matters. If you can learn what you need to know only during working hours, make careful inquiries of the courtroom clerk about the matters scheduled, so that even a few half-days of forum attendance can prove productive.

8. A final benefit of following this advice: your growing familiarity with the courthouse will take some of the trauma out of appearing in your case. You'll listen with a sharper ear, observe more, and prove more helpful to your counselor because of your more relaxed and capable attitude.

After studying these ideas for making you and your lawyer a more effective team, you may get some idea of the importance that *documentary* evidence plays in a successful case. Knowing or suspecting something does not count. The court is not interested in what you feel to be true, only in assets that you can *prove* you acquired during marriage, deeds that show you own property together, or agreements or written contracts that embody any understandings you formed as a married pair. Nothing constitutes such proof better than documentary (physical) evidence.

Here are some other tips that can improve your legal teamwork. Help the court help you by making sure that the other party is personally served. As you may recall, personal service consists of notifying the other party effectively that you've filed a case against him or her. What constitutes personal service varies from state to state, but it is acceptable everywhere for the other party personally to receive the required court papers via personal delivery by a person (not a minor) other than you. Personal service enables the court to obtain jurisdiction (judicial power) over your spouse.

File in a forum near important witnesses, necessary evidence, and you. If this forum proves inconvenient for your mate, its location may speed early out-of-court settlement, since commuting to court can prove expensive, tiring, and detrimental to a job or career.

If you plan to testify, pay attention to the following points:

- Review records and other documents to refresh your memory before you take the stand.

- Make sure that you've done nothing to compromise the foundation that your lawyer must lay before the judge can hear documentary evidence (more about this concept later on).
- If your testimony will concern an event or observation that occurred a long time ago, review any reminders you've retained of the event. Study any photographs. Return to the location of the event. Close your eyes and picture the event exactly as you observed it. If you gave a written statement to a third person (as in police report or a sales contract) review the writing before taking the stand. Relive the event with anyone else who was present, to see if you've forgotten an important detail.
- Dress neatly (a dress or suit; sports coat and slacks), but do not attempt to look like Ms. Bucks or Mr. Destitute.
- Behave with respect; no gum chewing, smoking, loud laughter, swearing, threatening behavior, etc. in the courtroom itself (most courthouses provide snack bars, cafeterias, lounge areas, or ample outside grounds for these activities if you feel you must indulge).
- Stand straight, take the oath in a strong, clear voice, and stay relaxed but alert in the witness stand. Don't fidget, and keep your hands away from your face, as this gesture shows indecision and could undercut even strong testimony.
- Tell the truth. If you have already revealed all to your counsel, you have little to fear. In fact, a good lawyer will sometimes volunteer somewhat negative information in order to undercut the other party's case. (One attorney, for example, not only readily admitted that his client was a recovering alcoholic, his client and the other spouse met at an AA meeting! In another case, the headwaiter of an extremely expensive restaurant testified under oath to receiving only minimal take-home pay. The woman judge hearing this case ordered him to pay his wife and children support totaling four-fifths of that pay. When husband's attorney protested at the apparently excessive award, this jurist leaned over the bench, looked husband in the eye, and said, "I think I know perjury when I hear it.")
- Make sure you understand each question before you begin your answer. Answer candidly and fully, but do not volunteer more information than the question calls for. This last warning applies to queries by your own lawyer as well, for your "help" may destroy the impact or purpose of a carefully planned line of questioning.
- Wait to hear the full question and any objections from opposing counsel before beginning your answer. If the judge, your attorney, or opposing counsel interrupts you, stop immediately. No jurist can effectively follow more than one conversation at once, and wordy overlaps drive court reporters crazy.
- Remain polite to the other attorney, even if you feel that he/she seems

abusive or intimidating. If you get nervous, grip the witness chair, press your feet together, or push a toe down into your shoe to relieve the internal pressure and siphon off emotions that may confuse you.

- Testify only to what you know from personal experience. What you think happened, or learned from others, or said or heard out of court is usually not admissible (study the list of objections to evidence that appear later in this chapter). Your conclusions or opinions in most cases cannot be considered by a judge either, so keep them to yourself unless your lawyer specifically asks you for this information.
- If you realize that you made a mistake in something you said earlier, or it becomes clear that your testimony was understood incorrectly, or you did not reveal important information and your omission makes your previous answer inaccurate, correct yourself, on the stand, as quickly as possible.
- Giving extended testimony can be very fatiguing. If you grow tired or cranky or feel willing to give any answer that will help you leave the stand, ask the judge for a short recess or for a drink of water in order to gather your strength and retain your perspective.

Now that you've reviewed how *you're* going to behave in court, give some thought to your "supporting cast"—the witnesses whom you think you're going to need. If your case appears relatively simple and your assets straightforward, encourage your mate to exchange income and asset worth information with you so that few—if any—expert appraisers will need to appear at the trial. Even if your assets deserve careful evaluation, decide on a single expert to appraise each different type of asset (the house, any pension plans, antiques). This approach can slash appraisal fees and eliminate the need for your expert (and opposing experts) to appear at your hearing. With costs for expert testimony running into the hundreds of dollars per day, does it make any sense to hire a heavyweight appraiser (or several) for each side, then pay them to sit around, waiting to testify? Of course not. Whether your expert(s) appear or not, an updated appraisal can add thousands to the value of an asset, and in California, at least, most communal property gets evaluated at or very close to the date of trial.

Occasionally, the "testimony" you're looking for will appear in the other party's filing papers, or in later forms submitted to the court. Since your file remains a public record (unless sealed by the judge), you, too, can visit the courthouse and review everything within its manila covers. Because the material in all filing papers is considered information submitted under penalty of perjury, every fact contained therein constitutes a sworn statement by your spouse. Don't waste money and your expert's or your own time trying to establish that an asset belongs to both of you, if your mate already so indicates; or that the family home would sell for $60,000, if that estimate of value already appears in the file. While a party can amend his or her filing papers, bank on what appears. If new evidence crops up, merely ask for additional time to deal with any unfavorable new information.

Sometimes parties embroiled in a custody battle want to subpoena the children's teachers, neighbors, relatives, family friends, therapists, doctors, any police officers involved in domestic violence calls, and assorted other professionals who could give testimony regarding a child's well-being in the care of one party or the other. Try first (and sincerely) to resolve the custody issue through mediation and arbitration, or with the help of counselors within the court system. If you still can't agree on how custody should be allocated or shared, at least agree on utilizing one private service, one court-endorsed psychological/psychiatric group, or the custody-investigation services provided by your court. These professionals will gather material, interview all interested parties (including children of sufficient age), and make a single report to the court. If you both agree to this, you needn't spend thousands to collect reports from varied sources to be considered by the court.

Parties sometimes ask family members or relatives to accompany them to court. Such people can provide moral support and offer an open ear for settlement offers during trial that a distracted you might not hear. You can enhance these benefits by inviting to court a cool-headed, savvy relative or friend whose judgment, business acumen, and personal insights you admire. More to the financial point, relatives can sometimes testify as to surrounding circumstances at the time that a family member passed along an asset to your mate or you. Was the property intended as a gift to only one of you? Was the transfer really an inheritance (separate property in many states)? Can this family member or friend give testimony on your mutual conduct regarding that piece of property? Did he or she attend the birthday party where you received the antique emerald pendant that your spouse now insists ranks as an investment owned by both of you, or by him alone? Utilize these people who care for you to help prevail on issues of property ownership and related matters.

Once you've obtained their cooperation, let the other side know that you intend to introduce such evidence via credible witnesses. If opposing counsel agrees that you can introduce the information into evidence without requiring actual personal testimony (via an affidavit, for example), you will save hassles and time and therefore fees and witness costs. Even if the other side won't accept this approach, you may spur a settlement if your evidence appears strong or if your mate for one reason or another does not want that friend or family member called to the stand.

Flip through your Rolodex or address book to find any friends (and especially new loves) whose special skills can aid you and who will expect no pay for their services. Such contacts might be real estate brokers, insurance pros, or art dealers. Make sure that this party is qualified in his or her field. Consider the example of Nancy. Soon after her separation from Mack, Nancy began dating Randall, a successful insurance salesman and investment counselor. Since Mack also worked in the insurance business, Randall could estimate Mack's income from the husband's probable gross earnings, business overhead, client roster, and lengthy commercial history. By adding his expertise to the financial details that Nancy had gathered in the weeks before separation, Randall was able to draw detailed charts. These showed Mack's probable income, expenses, and a heavy cash flow from some income-producing community assets. Faced with Randall's credibility and the chart's "factual overview," the judge ordered a far more generous spousal support figure than he would have, had he relied only on Mack's testimony. Be warned, however, that you open your "expert" to charges of bias if your selection springs only from a personal relationship with someone whose knowledge is not of expert caliber.

Review all evidence with your counselor prior to trial, and offer to illustrate as much of it as possible. This means getting out your glue, construction paper, felt-tip markers, camera, or graph paper, and polishing up any dusty graphics skills. By converting concepts to pictures, you can refresh your memory on the stand and make even a complex argument immediately clear to your hearing officer. For example, if you want custody and you know that your mate does, too, show some pictures of your home (including photographs of the child's room, complete with toys, hobby material, and any unfinished projects). Display a color 8×10 of the family pet, especially if it's comfortably ensconced at your place and wouldn't fit into your spouse's city condominium. Introduce a map showing your part of the city, suburb, or town. Highlight the safe paths to school and the proximity of parks, playing fields, friends' homes, the Cub Scout meetings, or the Sunday school class. Draw a circle encompassing all the locations your kids enjoy; show your home at the center point. To boost your support award, follow Randall's lead. Draw up charts showing your mate's gross income, net earnings, and monthly cash flow. Detail your family expenditures over a three-month period prior to separation to show the standard of living that you and any children enjoyed.

If your concern focuses more on gaining generous spousal support, and you've spent most of the marriage caring for home and hearth, take advantage of any state law that requires your court to weigh your impaired ability to earn a living for yourself. Several state legislatures have recently recognized that a woman often gives up important career-training opportunities to care for a husband, several children, and a house. Because of this lost time, a wife may deserve extra spousal support until she can learn marketable skills. In addition, more legislators seem to agree that performing home-care duties makes a distinct and valuable contribution to a marital partnership. To translate such contributions into dollar values, consider the South Carolina case of *Parrott v. Parrott,* in which that state Supreme Court ruled in June, 1982, that a housewife must be compensated for her homemaking contributions when divorce breaks up a longterm marriage. According to Chief Justice J. Woodrow Lewis, who wrote the opinion, the issue rested on one question—whether Shirley Nadine Parrott, who stayed at home to care for her family over a 20-year marriage, could share equally in the real and personal property owned by the primary wage earner, her spouse. As Justice Lewis put it, "We hold that such an award of property is a matter of equity. [When one marital partner] has foregone career opportunities at the behest of the primary wage-earning spouse, and throughout a long marriage has remained in the home to rear children and provide a suitable environment for the family, the home-maker spouse shall have an equitable interest in real property acquired by the wage-earner spouse in the marriage."

But how can you arrange for accurate compensation for family care and household drudgery? Researchers in the University of Alabama's consumer science department discovered that "at 1982 wage scales it would cost close to $12,000 annually to pay for the services provided by the average American homemaker" (quoted from "At Work," *Changing Times,* May 1982, page 18). Yet in spite of a woman's expertise in 11 job categories, her annual marital contribution measured in cash dollars remains disappointingly low because "the majority of a homemaker's tasks pay only a minimum wage in the job market. . . ." Still, the study shows that cooking, kitchen work, housecleaning, tutoring, child care, family nursing, marketing, laundry and ironing, special clothing care, financial management, special house care, gardening and other household chores could easily have been worth $1,000 per month. Why not suggest that such a monthly allotment would seem fair spousal support until you can master new skills? At that support rate, your "take-home pay" would far outstrip most spousal support awards.

As an aside, it's interesting to note that the value of a homemaker's services depends, apparently, not so much on the duties performed, but on the person evaluating them. For example, the October 1981 issue of *Changing Times* exerpted the following material from *The General Mills American Family Report 1980–81:*

> *Question:* If you had to place a dollar value on the job of a homemaker, what do you feel fair wages would be?
>
> *Answer:* Total men: $12,700
> Homemakers: $13,700
> Total women: $13,800
> Working women: $14,000
> Family movement leaders: $19,600
> Feminists: $21,500

It's clear that, compared to these responses, a value of $12,000 per year for homemaker services appears low. However, only the study performed at Alabama University compared the duties performed with pay earned for the same activities on the open market. On the other hand, the responses in the General Mills survey appear to spring from opinion alone. For these reasons, it seems safest to bank on an overview that provides you with a strong foundation for the value suggested, a fair market value that the court could justify using to provide you with adequate support.

But whichever report you present as evidence shows that caring for a family and home represents a financial contribution to a marital partnership. However, you will maximize your award only if you can show your spouse's ability to pay the amount you require and can prove that you need this amount of spousal support each and every month.

Even if your state does not require judges to consider time expended specifically as a homemaker, it probably asks its hearing officers to consider the California equivalent of "any other factors that the court deems just and equitable." This open door encourages you to introduce any evidence (via testimony or documents) that should be considered in a decision about spousal support. Do your adult children still live at home in order to afford college? Are any grown children developmentally impaired, so that you will have to provide custodial care for years to come? Does your schooling lead toward a career but prevent you from holding down a demanding job at this time? Review your needs and gather some of these factors to boost your support.

Whether you're seeking support, property, or proving a point important to the outcome of your case, bear in mind that the court can consider only evidence that you present in a *proper* fashion. While forum rules differ, the following list can provide a good overview of the objections an opposing attorney can raise to admitting evidence; you'll need to steer clear of them in presenting testimony or documentary evidence. Each of these objections, if sustained by the judge, will bar your evidence. The list is designed not to send you to law school or into a catatonic state but to show you the importance of gathering proof and of presenting it effectively. You can help by keeping some of these "excluders" in mind when you gather and prepare the records, ledgers, charts, and other facts that you'll need to present.

Testimony and other evidence can be excluded from the record if it is elicited from a witness in the "wrong" way, presented without certain prior steps, or offered by the wrong witness, among other reasons. Consider the following grounds for barring evidence and try to set your "evidence stage" correctly in order to prevail:

Argumentative question. Query or series of queries that appear likely to trigger an argument between inquiring counsel and the person on the stand.

Asked and answered. The information sought has already been provided by this witness.

Assuming facts not in evidence. The question or the answer is based on previous testimony or documentary evidence that was excluded by the court or that has not yet been introduced.

Beyond the scope (of direct testimony). The question asked during cross-examination deals with a matter or information not introduced during direct testimony by the witness on the stand (since cross-examination questions may only probe a witness's credibility or explore matters introduced in direct testimony).

Calling for a conclusion. Asks the witness to draw an opinion from the facts, an activity reserved for the judge after hearing all the evidence.

Compound and/or complex. Question likely to confuse the witness because it asks for more than one answer, combines several queries, or is convoluted or hard to understand.

Cumulative evidence. Answers from the same or a new witness that merely repeat prior testimony, or that add nothing to evidence presented previously.

Hearsay. Evidence not springing from the personal knowledge of the witness but from what he has heard others say. Includes testimony that does not derive its value solely from the credit of the witness but rests mainly on the truthfulness and competency of other persons not in the courtroom and not under oath. It is "secondhand" evidence and is admitted only under special, clearly defined circumstances.

Immaterial. Testimony or documentary evidence that is not essential or necessary, not important or pertinent, not decisive, of no substantial consequences, without weight, or of no significance.

Improper impeachment of one's own witness. Questions that argue with, or call for a contradiction from, the attorney's own client or from a witness favorable to the party's case; also, questioning the veracity of one's "own" witness. An opposing counsel may raise this objection to bar testimony if it appears that the lawyer questioning a witness is attempting to elicit favorable evidence by contradicting or contesting the words of his own client or a witness called to aid his case.

Incompetent. The witness testifying is not capable of giving believable evidence on the matter at hand because he did not observe an event, has too little information or experience, or is perhaps so biased by money, friendship with, or dislike of a party that any testimony should be disregarded.

Irrelevant. Not relating or applicable to the matter at issue; not likely to prove or disprove any issue involved.

Leading and suggestive. A question that instructs a witness how to answer; puts words into a witness's mouth to be echoed back; a query that suggests the answer desired.

No corpus delicti. Not so much the absence of a body (an objection that might be raised in a criminal trial) as a lack of substantive evidence showing that the party ever committed the act(s) in question. For example, since bad acts can play a role in custody or visitation issues during a divorce, opposing counsel might raise such an objection if you insisted that your spouse was a junkie but could produce no recollections of drug deals, no drug paraphernalia or other evidence of his or her condition, and never observed your mate taking narcotics or appearing drugged.

No proper foundation. Insufficient testimony or other evidence showing the credibility or authenticity of the item to be introduced. For example, is the copy certified? Was the evidence sent to the court directly from its source, so that no party could tamper with it? Will the photographer testify that this photograph is an accurate portrayal of the event in question?

Not the best evidence. The original instrument is itself always regarded as the primary or best possible evidence of its existence and contents; a duplicate item, or the recollection of a witness, would be secondary, or not the best, evidence. No substitute evidence, like a copy of a document, will be admitted if the original evidence can be had. A court will accept secondary evidence only if adequate testimony proves that the original document or evidence has been destroyed, has disappeared, is in the possession of the other side, or is missing for some other valid reason.

Opinion by a non-expert. Objection to testimony from a person not experienced enough in the matter to draw an informed opinion relating to the case.

Privileged communication. The evidence that the spouse-witness intends to give involves a conversation, agreement, or act that would incriminate an accused spouse who declines to take the stand. The spouse on trial owns the right to bar such testimony, and he or she must waive the protective privilege before the mate not on trial can offer potentially damaging evidence. In a divorce action there is no longer any "community" to be preserved so this rule may be relaxed in certain circumstances.

Probity outweighed. The "proving power" (probity) of the evidence offered is less useful than the time that would be consumed in hearing or digesting the evidence, the confusion that would result, or the harm that this testimony would do to the other party.

Self-incrimination. The witness is being asked to admit to a matter that would expose him or her to prosecution for committing or being involved in a criminal act.

Self-serving. Testimony or evidence that so patently favors the witness that it is barred as probably slanted, highly colored, or altogether useless.

Unintelligible. Question and/or answer cannot be understood by the witness, the court, the court reporter, opposing counsel, or all four.

The next chapter offers a review that will help you to solidify your gains. You gain little for all your efforts if you cannot compose—or help compose—those final terms that lock in your benefits.

9

Final Terms That Lock In Your Benefits

WELL, HERE WE ARE, several months after announcing that painful decision to leave. We've probed earnings, uncovered property, appraised assets, arranged conferences, written letters, and dialed one index finger to a nub. But even all this is not enough — a crucial step still looms large.

For even if you've achieved an out-of-court agreement, you'll still need to get those favorable terms in writing to preserve your gains.

If, on the other hand, you've arranged only a partial settlement or cannot get together on a single remaining issue, you have much to do before you can finalize anything. If this is your situation, it's normal to feel discouraged at your apparent lack of progress. For despite all your efforts to reach creative compromises with your spouse, that date on your calendar appears your only reward: a fast-approaching trial. Your stomach churns at the thought of this courtroom confrontation. You anticipate the gavel's tap introducing to the public the squabble that you've sensibly been trying to keep private. You envision a stern, robed stranger who will decide — without feeling or understanding — all those personal issues that took courage to raise in private with your spouse. You may well feel angry, frustrated, and too discouraged to go on. Should you give up and settle for peanuts right now? Or should you give up trying to communicate with your spouse, withdraw your previous settlement offers, and fight for half (or more) of the communal elephant?

Your postdivorce net worth depends on your not doing either one.

In fact, an open attitude at this time can net you rewards before your trial begins. Because courtroom confrontations cause stress to everyone, compromises often occur in the courthouse corridors, lounges, elevators, cafeterias, and conference rooms. Even a mate who's staunchly resisted every settlement offer to date may crumble on the courthouse steps.

So, if your adversary shows signs of wavering toward a settlement on even some of the issues in your case, keep these handy tips in mind to negotiate a profitable deal:

a. Matters agreed to by the parties out of court need not appear in a public record—the court file—in intricate detail. While the record of a property division arranged by the court may include financial details, net worths, asset values, and other private information, marital settlement agreements need not reveal such details. You may be able to settle some (or all) matters outside the courthouse door by pointing out this fact of legal life to your spouse.

b. Put those items you agree upon in writing; don't rely on the judgment to contain all that you discussed. Many of the agreements that spouses forge involve personal promises of a contractual nature that the court may or may not deem proper to include in the final judgment. An agreement between the parties can—and often does—contain mutual warranties and representations that underlie the division of property, support obligations, and any allocation of debts. Regular court action outside the family-law forum remains available to enforce these "foundational understandings," thus ensuring the rights and assets you bargained for. If a personal reminder does not encourage your mate to keep such promises, you can pursue a breach of contract action in civil or municipal court for any damages that you sustain—but you must have a written contract.

c. If the debts one of you incurred prior to separating is an obligation for training, schooling, or education received by just one of you, your state law may require that the mate receiving the benefit repay the bill . . . without any credit, offset, or aid from the other spouse. The California Civil Code harbors such a clause. Unless allocating all of this debt to one party would prove manifestly unfair, then the party gaining the educational advantages has to pay the freight. If your state's code or a prior case decision dictates such an outcome, make sure that you aren't paying a monthly stipend for that greater earning power that your mate alone now enjoys. Further, if you allocate this preseparation debt to your spouse, make sure that he/she pays it from earnings after separation (or with other separate property), and not from a mutually owned fund or joint account.

d. If you can agree on a base amount for child and/or spousal support but worry about rising costs in the future, arrange for a cost-of-living boost to the base figure every year or so. Be sure, however, to key the rise to an objective standard (like the cost-of-living index or a preset percentage of any salary increase) that either spouse can check and neither can manipulate. If you choose the second method, make certain that the percentage isn't linked to an amount that your mate can control (like commissions or overtime earned).

By proposing either of these solutions in the following way, you'll show even a stubborn mate how you *both* can win:

> With built-in increases in support amounts, the spouse receiving funds can benefit without costly or traumatic trips to court and without having to prove that circumstances have indeed changed since the last court appearance that set (or altered) such support.
>
> The paying spouse who obligates him- or herself to share a preset portion of any salary increase (or to pay more under the spur of inflation whether earnings improve or not) may actually fare better under an automatic increase plan. If the paying spouse faces a rapid career rise and will probably receive generous raises in take-home pay, then he or she may actually save dollars by adhering to a gradual support increase keyed to the cost of living, rather than pay support via a plan keyed to actual salary sums.
>
> While a supported spouse could refuse to honor such an agreement calling for automatic raises, and reenter court for a modification exceeding the preset amount, this mate could face an uphill fight. After bargaining in good faith for the protection of automatic increases, this party may appear too greedy to be rewarded by the court.

e. If your mate has been a successful entrepreneur, consider basing any support figure on his or her past, demonstrated, ability to earn, rather than on actual income, which may vary dramatically over the years.

f. If your enterpreneur needs a lot of room to maneuver and doesn't want to be tied down, consider taking other common property and allocating all of your spouse's business to him or her. A nonfounding party who insists on owning a share of an individually run company asks for double trouble. First, the company president will resent sharing any growth with a former spouse. Second, the continued, shared ownership will promote acrimony, diminish corporate profits, and perpetuate emotional dependency for the mate less knowledgeable about running a commercial concern.

g. If you come to an agreement on the courthouse steps, make sure that you have your attorney recite—in open court in full detail—those matters agreed upon, so that a reporter can put your mutual pledges into the record. Later on, one of the attorneys in the case will compose a written agreement (stipulation) reciting those reciprocal promises. You will both then sign this document and have it filed with the court, so that the writing binds both of you to the terms recited.

Whether you agree on provisions before your matter begins, or only grudgingly accept those that the judge hands down, you'll need to describe all those agreements and orders in terms that protect your newly won rights. After arriving home from the courthouse, pour yourself a toddy, put your feet up, crank up the stereo, and settle back to review the day's (or week's) events. Mentally review each of the issues on which you prevailed or on which you gained ground. No one wins every point, but you probably gained much on the courthouse steps or in court that you won't want to lose in the final step: drawing up a judgment that preserves and makes enforceable your gains.

Whether you've added to your assets and rights via negotiation, trial, or both, consider the following suggestions to solidify gains by drafting judgment terms that lock in those benefits.

If possible, label payments your spouse owes you—for whatever purpose—as support. Support obligations will usually survive any later bankruptcy filed by your spouse, but such a filing would probably erase all other debts, including any property equalization payments claimed by you, as a "creditor spouse." If your mate is supposed to pay your attorney's fees, call this amount support as well, in order to preserve your right to receive these funds.

Consider, however, that if you call every obligation support, an event like your remarriage may automatically end your right to receive such payments. Make sure that your state law would not call for such a result, or that you clearly provide for continued payments in the event of your remarriage or the payer's untimely death (the estate would continue the payments).

Even if you can squeeze what you're owed under the support

banner, seek some security for your debt, and spell out your protection in your final terms. For example, if your mate is to pay you monthly installments for your share of the family residence, take out and record a second trust deed against the property until you've received payment in full. Such a document protects you because it gives you the power to foreclose on the residence (force a sale to a third party) if you must do so to recoup the funds your spouse owes to you. When you have received payment in full, you can reconvey this second trust deed to your mate, who then must pay off only any other lenders to own the home free and clear. When a savings and loan extended you funds to purchase your home, it took back a first trust deed. If you are extending credit to your mate and awaiting payments, you would take out and hold a second trust deed to ensure your power to foreclose on the residence if your spouse does not pay. In the event that your mate fails to pay either the first lender or you, then either of you can call for a public sale of the property, and collect the amounts due from what the new buyer pays. Because earlier first trust deed holders must be paid in full before later trust deed holders will realize any funds from such a sale, it is clear that succeeding trust deed holders enjoy ever-decreasing protection. For this reason, if your family residence is heavily encumbered by past loans, you might do better to seek other security for your spouse's payments than to accept a deed of trust that stands third or fourth in line.

If these terms puzzle you, it's likely that your state offers these protections under a different name or form of security. To gain the financial security that you need, investigate through your library, take an adult education class in real estate, or ask a local real estate agent to explain your state's procedures and terminology.

But whatever the nomenclature used, keep in mind that if you're depending on a fiscally irresponsible spouse to make monthly payments to discharge a support obligation or to equalize a property division, or both, arrange to put your faith in more than your mate's promise to pay. Consider seeking some security to ensure that you will receive your funds . . . in full and on time. For example, you might have the court (or your marital settlement agreement) compel your mate to furnish you with one of the following to guarantee the result you desire:

- *A performance bond,* so that the insurer pays if mate does not.
- *An insurance policy,* so that if your mate expires before the payment schedule ends, you can collect a lump sum to compensate you for your

loss. (But your spouse can always change the beneficiary of such a policy, and in the case of a National Service Life Insurance policy, neither you nor the court can bar his or her right to do so at any time.) To prevent such a change in a civilian policy, send the insurance company a copy of the court decree ordering your spouse to maintain you as an "irrevocable" beneficiary until the payment period expires.

- *An irrevocable provision* in your former partner's will, so that you're paid in full if your creditor passes away.
- *Ownership or possessory rights to property* or an asset until you receive full value on the obligations due (you could hold title to a building, the pink slip on an auto, or some stock certificates, with the understanding that you'll hand this asset over upon receipt of your final payment).
- *A deposit in the amount due you,* deposited to the court, is in an escrow service, or is with a trusted friend. Your spouse can reduce this sum, of course, as the outstanding balance diminishes.
- *A lien on an upcoming judgment or award* due your mate (but be certain that your creditor-mate will prevail).
- *A trust fund* with sufficient property and/or income to meet the obligations and the principal sum due to you, perhaps with income being paid directly to you.
- *A joint tenancy in property,* so that ownership of that particular asset would immediately be turned over to you if your obligor died. Of course you would want additional protections, so that your mate could not destroy the joint tenancy and sell all or part of the asset to an unsuspecting stranger, thus cutting off your rights.

Even if obtaining an annulment of your marriage seems important to you, consider filing for a divorce instead. In your state, a judgment of nullity may terminate the court's authority to enforce payment of alimony/spousal support. If you still want to seek an annulment, consider receiving all of your future spousal support funds in a reduced but present amount, so that you need not wait for future payments.

If you agree to a step-down schedule of support payments (steadily diminishing monthly payments) and you subsequently find that you need more money, recognize that you will bear the emotional and financial burden of returning to court to halt the declining amounts or even to increase your support. To succeed in this, you will have to demonstrate a change in your circumstances or the failure of an expected event to occur. A steady schedule of payments, on the other hand, requires that the paying spouse petition the court if he or she seeks a reduction or a change.

Include all property—real, personal, and even intangible—in your marital settlement agreement or your final judgment. If an item or right to receive payment does not appear, the court cannot order enforcement by citing your spouse for contempt for noncompliance. Nor can the court order that part of a mate's earnings be paid directly to you, or send a marshal to impound and sell a mate's property in satisfaction of the debt.

Spell out carefully all payment schedules and exchanges of properties, including the dates that you both must complete such duties. If you don't provide sufficient definition and details, the court will not be able to enforce your rights. Help, rather than sabotage, yourself.

Wherever your agreement or judgment deals with real property, include the following items:

- Legal descriptions as well as street addresses.
- The specific date(s) upon which a title or ownership share transfer should occur. A sale between legal strangers (after the divorce is final) may lead to a new and costly tax assessment on a family residence for the new sole owner. Also, any gain on an interspousal sale after the final decree may trigger an ordinary income tax assessment on the profits, but sales between those still legally wed may instead receive the less costly capital gains tax treatment.
- Specific documents that either of you must sign.
- Exhibits such as photographs if the property is unusual or difficult to describe or identify.
- Notarized signatures for each of you on any marital settlement agreement (or you will not be able to record any terms in your order).

If your final judgment deals with the ownership of, or ownership rights to, real property, record those segments of the judgment with the recorder of the county where the property is located. If you do not provide such public notice of your share in real estate, your spouse may orchestrate a sale. An innocent buyer, having no notice of your ownership even after a title search, would owe you nothing. If your mate then took the sales proceeds and disappeared, your position could prove bleak indeed.

If your judgment calls for the sale of personal property and an equal division of the proceeds, designate the best marketplace for the pieces you're conveying. Sell important art and antiques in major markets like New York, Chicago, San Francisco, Los Angeles, Houston, Boston, Philadelphia, or London. Put items of regional importance or historical significance in your area up for auction or sale in a local forum. You'll get a better price in each case. Don't break up a pair, a collection or a set of items; sold together they are worth more.

Don't end your marriage too soon. In addition to terminating any right to Social Security benefits, you could

—face deportation, if you married a U.S. citizen to gain lawful permanent residency in America but obtain a divorce after less than two years of marriage.
—lose the chance to file a joint tax return with your spouse, and pay more taxes than you would otherwise.
—lose important health insurance coverage that your mate's employer supplies to the *spouses* of employees.
—lose your right to insure cars or other vehicles under a "family plan" at reduced rates.
—lose other valuable benefits that you reap as a "legal partner" but that terminate upon the filing of a final decree.

Keep your marital settlement agreement or your judgment handy and let a trusted, levelheaded friend know where you keep it. Until the final decree, you're wed to your mate. In the event of your death, he or she could claim inheritance rights that have been terminated by the judgment or by the terms of the agreement that you signed. Your other heirs could suffer if the truth doesn't come to light in time.

Even though some terms will save you funds only in the future or provide benefits only years from now, it's important to establish your rights right now, within the framework of these same final terms. Weigh each of the following considerations to determine which relate to you.

Designate which parent will bear the fiscal responsibility for a minor's accidents or misdeeds. If you're not the better-heeled spouse, you'll want to suggest that your mate agree to underwrite any fines, uninsured damages, or repair bills for the damage wrought in the future should one of your children turn out to be a delinquent.

On the other hand, you may want to arrange an agreement in advance that you (or both of you) will serve as guardian(s) *ad litem* (adults who would speak for a minor in prosecuting or defending a suit). Such an arrangement would allocate this in the event that some occurrence involving your child causes an action for damages to be assessed against another party; any monies recovered can belong to you (or be divided between you).

Try to gain a pledge (included in the settlement or judgment, of course) that your mate will contribute child support or other aid after the children reach their legal majorities. Such fiscal assistance could go toward schooling, professional training, sports involvement, or for some other anticipated expense that you know your spouse will endorse or support. To ensure that the kids or you receive such support, it might help to arrange payment by diverting, now, the money from a trust or an income-producing asset. If the mechanics of such a trust are arranged now, the income produced will begin to flow now to the receiving spouse. This solution provides two advantages: first, the support payments arrive in full and on time; second, a mate tends to forget that he or she is paying such sums because they don't flow through the monthly budget or require the writing of a periodic check. It's easy to see that your mate could well "forget" his or her generosity until the agreed-upon termination date.

If the child-support payments in your case appear in a stipulation (agreement) without any information included about how such figures were reached, you're more likely to obtain later increases without having to show any change in circumstances, so long as future facts would justify more money.

Ensure your right to increase spousal support by including the right to modify such support if your needs change (and your spouse's income rises) in the years to come. While child support always remains open to change, adult parties can bargain for an end to alimony, a diminishing schedule, or a mutual waiver; you can also agree to fix spousal support at a figure that will never increase—or to leave the question open in case the need for an adjustment arises later on. Such an agreement as the latter must be definitively worded; even so, bars to modifications can creep into seemingly innocuous phrases in your settlement contract with your spouse. If you cannot specifically keep this support door open with detailed phrasing, at least review your judgment carefully to make sure that no one could reasonably read in a fixed-rate provision limiting your right to seek more spousal support in the future.

A good marital settlement agreement and/or judgment will provide for the division or allocation of community assets discovered after the settlement. Such a property might be the bank account you hid from your spouse, or the five acres of jointly owned desert land that your mate inadvertently overlooked in listing all the assets. Such a provision normally provides that if one party uncovers an overlooked asset, the nonholding mate will share in one-half of that asset's current value and and will have, for example, up to two years from discovery to insist on a division or sale. In addition, the spouse forced to pursue such a property through legal channels can also recover reasonable attorney's fees and court costs.

If you take an equalizing note in return for giving your mate more than half of your common property, make sure that your note's terms include the following:

- An inflated face value, so that if you sell the note to another party (which will bring you only a discounted price), the money you get will equal the amount actually owed. In one California case it was estimated that such a note is worth perhaps only 50 to 60 percent of its face value to a potential buyer, who must accept the risk that the borrower will not meet the obligations due. If you're wondering why anyone would purchase this I.O.U. even at a hefty discount, consider that the salability of such a document depends upon the credit-worthiness of the borrower, and whether or not any security (besides the borrower's signature) goes with the personal note. Even if there are no guarantees of payment like those outlined earlier, remember that many banks extend personal loans on the strength of a signature alone. If your mate's credit is excellent, and if you've arranged for other security to back up the note, then you stand a good chance of recouping cash, via a sale, on your paper rights.
- A competitive interest rate—the same rate that a stranger could command in the open market for advancing the same amount of credit, property, or cash.
- The right to receive at least interest payments until the full balance falls due. Of course you can agree to accept only a fully amortized note, so that each payment includes interest *and* a portion of the principal, reducing your risk with each payment received.

If *you* are obligated to pay on such a note, suggest a contract that shows only the amount owed and no interest. If this isn't accepted, offer a lower-than-market interest rate, and do not offer to make any interim payments or interest-only payments, in order to forestall your financial pain as long as possible. Even if your mate realizes that he or she could demand better financial treatment, a spouse may agree to such terms because they lessen the financial burden on the spouse occupying the family home while caring for the parties' minor children.

If you're going to be the "out-house" spouse, make sure that the terms of your agreement provide for you to share equally the net proceeds of the ultimate sale of the family home. In addition, try to insert a provision allocating to you an additional portion of the sales proceeds as compensation for foregoing immediate enjoyment and control of the dollars sitting in that house. If this threatens to send your spouse around the bend, seek a reduction in the child and/or spousal support you will have to pay, arguing that the use of the house should operate as a form of credit in providing such support.

If you've purchased your home just a few months before the parting, and you've agreed on an immediate sale, it would be a good idea to delay the final sale until you've held that house for two years or more. If you do not hold the property for this minimum amount of time, neither of you will be able to gain by buying a new residence within the two years *following* your sale. Once you receive the funds from your sale, consider keeping them in an insured but interest-bearing account to keep pace with inflation over the ensuing two years.

If your mate's indiscretions or bad business judgments have produced a number of debts that creditors have converted to liens against the family home, try to allocate payment for such debts from your *mate's* portion of the proceeds from the sale of your home so that payment is *not* drawn equally from money due both of you.

If you've paid for the repair or maintenance of a jointly owned asset after separation out of your own income or with other separate property, make sure that the terms of sale of that asset include a repayment provision for you. Better still, if the asset seems sure to rise in value, make your repayment a proportionate share of the sale proceeds (otherwise, you'll be repaid in tomorrow's buy-less dollars for today's costly expenditures). If you can't bargain for either treatment, at least retain the sole right to add your interim costs to the basis of the asset to limit any tax consequences you will suffer when you sell.

To fully understand this concept, consider Trudy's experience in a similar situation. Trudy and Omar owned a getaway cabin as joint tenants. Purchased during the marriage, they paid off the mortgage balance with Omar's earnings out of their joint checking account. Everyone agreed that each party deserved an equal share in any proceeds of sale. An economic downturn, however, made an immediate sale unlikely, so the parties agreed to discuss possible sales terms in another six months. They further agreed that Trudy, who had remodeled their family room, would visit the cabin periodically and repair the storm-damaged roof, replace some cracked window glass, and re-wall the lean-to shelter protecting the fireplace wood on the cabin's south side. Wishing to recoup some individual profits for her after-separation investment, Trudy asked to keep 60 percent of the sure-to-be higher net sale proceeds in return for performing those chores. Omar objected, saying he'd rather suffer a potentially lower sales price for the cabin's damaged state than see Trudy receive such a gain. Omar insisted on a fifty-fifty split, even if it meant that both parties would receive less in a sale. A rather stubborn man, Omar even refused to agree to repay Trudy a reasonable wage for her efforts, or to allow her any reimbursement for materials used. The two at last hit upon this solution: though each would receive an equal number of dollars from the sale, Trudy alone would claim all repair costs on her next tax return, so that the difference between her *total* investment in this asset and its sales price would be smaller, and her taxes, therefore, less.

If your sale will involve the family home or another large asset, keep your canceled checks and receipts for work done and improvements added. By adding these later costs into the price you paid for your residence, you raise the tax basis (total cost) of your house. When you then subtract this higher figure from your sales price, you'll see a smaller profit margin on which the IRS can base a tax assessment. For maximum benefit, add to your original cost your charges for state and county transfer taxes, appraisal fees, assumption expenses, attorney's fees, credit report costs, mortgage origination expenses, notary fees, property inspection charges, recording fees, title examination bills, title insurance costs, utility connection expenses, amounts owed by the seller that you paid (such as part of the sales commission, back taxes, or overdue mortgage payments and interest), and all improvements or major repairs to your property.

When divvying up property to form two "equal" totals, consider the tax consequences of any anticipated sales. Compare totals with such assessments in mind to determine whether you and your spouse's after-tax totals remain comparable or not. Remember that you'll be filing a separate tax return after the final decree and that you will be coping with a different tax bracket and a different collection of deductions as a single citizen. Apply this new financial pattern to the assets allocated to you to see if you should receive more or less than half of all the joint assets to obtain a truly equal division of the property. (If you do receive more than half of the common goodies, remember to figure in the taxes you'll need to pay on those assets that exceed 50 percent.)

If your spouse gains more than one-half of your common assets and offers to pay you off over time with earnings after separation or with some other separate property, you can ask for additional funds to help you pay the taxes on those receipts.

If you can't obtain your mate's promise to help pay such an assessment, insist on final terms that outline an installment payment plan. In other words, instead of receiving these separate property assets in a lump sum, arrange to receive only a portion of the funds due you each year. If you're a cash-basis taxpayer (one who declares income only when it's received), you can soften your tax blow by stretching out your receipts, so that your income in any one year doesn't bring heavy tax consequences for you.

As long as you divide community assets equally, you'll get a yawn from the IRS, since such divisions don't rank as "taxable events." Because of this, you'll want to divide with your mate any assets which now rate as valuable but which cost you little originally and in which you have little or no additional investment. Such property has a low tax basis, because you spent little in acquiring it, and you've invested no or few additional funds in improving that property—in other words, your cost (tax basis) in the asset is low. If this asset would sell for a lot, however, the difference between your investment (low) and your sales price (high) would trigger a hefty tax bill because your profits would be generous. You can avoid such a taxable gain by dividing the asset "in kind" and sidestepping a sale. If you need quick cash, agree to sell those items that would bring in about as much cash as they originally cost (again, consider later payments that increase the funds you've actually invested in the asset), because your taxable profit from such items will be small. Divide any proceeds equally. Each of you will pay only a small tax and keep the maximum sum for yourselves. In fact, your final terms can designate certain items for sale because their proceeds would receive preferential tax treatment, leaving more funds to divide or allocate. Such assets include those held for over one year (subject to the lighter burden of long-term capital gains taxes), and any property specifically exempt from taxes. Finally, you can specify a tax-free exchange of property with a third party before dividing or allocating all assets. Let's assume, for example, that together you own an office building but would prefer an apartment complex so that one of you can obtain free lodging in return for managing the real estate. Making a trade with an apartment-building owner may result in a tax-free exchange. With that apartment complex "in the family," you can allocate common assets in a way that will give that unit and managerial job to your spouse, and other commonly owned property to you. Following this path should legally avoid taxes for both of you.

If you own property together that was held for investment or profit that has lost value, "sell" it to each other in dividing up assets *after* filing your final decree and declare it as a business loss. The IRS will disallow such losses between married parties but will allow you to take an ordinary income loss if the depreciated asset was not held for personal use.

Get a tax break via your legal fees by

— adding the fee you paid to obtain an asset to that property's basis to reduce later taxes on any profits when sold, and
— deducting any legal fees that helped you obtain taxable funds (like spousal support or an income-producing property), and
— deducting all expert and legal fees relating to tax advice (how to file, when to pay, which deductions to claim).

If you decide to continue co-owning some personal property that will remain in the custody of the other party, remember to label such goods clearly. A vengeful or forgetful former spouse could otherwise sell these goods to an unsuspecting buyer. In California, property in the possession of a party who dies four years or more after the final divorce decree goes to that person's heirs as the deceased's separate property. Make sure, therefore, that a possessory mate's will provides for the return of such items, or that the paintings, gems, antiques, cars, or hand-blown bottles in your ex-mate's custody bear some sign of your ownership share.

Include in any final terms a provision dictating how the two of you plan to resolve future disputes. You may be able to save massive court costs and legal fees in years to come by specifiying that if differences arise, you agree to first attempt a resolution through arbitration, mediation, or by referral to a disinterested party whom you both respect. Further, you can agree in advance that if such a step fails to knit your attitudes together, you will seek an in-court judgment in a legal forum (but make sure that it's a court system convenient to you, and with laws that would tend to favor, if possible, your anticipated point of view).

Whatever you do, remember that at the end of each financial path lurks the IRS. While *evading* taxes will put you in jail, legitimately *avoiding* taxes ranks as one of America's favorite sports. To help you prevail in the first annual tussle in April that follows your divorce, consider the following aids:

1. Showing that any tax consequences are "immediate, specific, and [incurred] in connection with the dissolution proceeding" will encourage the court to order your mate to pay you one-half of the tax burden you will bear. If you can provide an accurate estimate of your anticipated tax bill and obtain one-half of this amount from your spouse, place the funds earmarked for paying the tax in treasury bills, in money market funds, or in a short-term, high-earning deposit to earn maximum interest while awaiting your date with the IRS. You can offer to take a reduced amount from your mate if interest paid in the interim will sufficiently increase the basic sum, or you can offer to return any excess interest income to your spouse after you pay the tax assessed. Although it's clear that this procedure may profit your spouse as well as you, note that a court may not require a mate to produce the cash to aid you with your tax bill until the IRS actually mails you a bill. During the wait, an irresponsible or malicious mate could spend his share of the assets or depress his income, so that you could never collect on your right to financial assistance from that source. If you resent the fact that your spouse may benefit more than you if you profitably invest the funds in advance of their due date, remember that your mate may *deserve* a profit because he or she has lost control of those monies in any interim months, and because he/she has helped to provide you with financial peace of mind.
2. If you or your mate has celebrated the 55th birthday, and you've lived in your residence for at least three of the past five years, consider taking the once-in-a-lifetime tax forgiveness on up to $125,000 of your share of any sale proceeds. However, you should *wait until after filing your final decree* to apply for this tax break, and make sure that your spouse does the same. As long as you're legally wed, the tax people consider you one entity. This means that if your mate qualifies for this deduction and takes it, *you* could not claim the tax forgiveness for yourself in later years, even if you applied as a divorced home owner and otherwise qualified. Further, claiming such a deduction as a couple would limit you to a total write-off of $125,000; claiming

separately after your divorce can shelter $125,000 worth of gain for each of you.

3. If you want to claim the $125,000 deduction or want to shelter your gain from the sale of your home by purchasing another principal residence within the two years following your sale, remember that you can do so only if you sell a *principal residence*. Moving into an apartment and filing a separate tax return from your new address means that your family home no longer ranks as your principal residence. Renting out your home for an extended period of time prior to a sale may destroy its character as your principal residence. In short, don't take a step that will bar you from claiming either tax shelter without careful consideration of the tax bill you'll pay.
4. If you've already moved out and will face a harsher tax assessment on your share of profit from the sale of that family home, consider receiving your payments in installments, taking more of the commonly owned other property to compensate you for this impending loss, or arrange to have one-half of your tax bill borne by your spouse.
5. If you qualify, file as a head of household to enjoy a lower tax bill than if you filed as a single. To file in this category, you must have obtained your final decree, maintain a household that is at least one qualified dependent's principal residence, and pay more than one-half the cost of maintaining that home.
6. Watch the income earned by any children over 19 whom you intend to claim as dependents, or you could lose the $1,000-per-dependent tax deduction. In general, you will lose an exemption if a dependent's gross income tops $1,000, but you needn't add in scholarships or Social Security benefits received or interest on municipal bonds owned by your child. In addition, there's no limit to the amount each dependent can earn if he or she is younger than 19 or enrolls as a full-time student during at least five months of the calendar year.

   To claim a dependent you must, in addition to the above requirements, also supply more than half of that person's support. Gifts, furnishings, clothing, medical care, cars, and the fair rental value of lodging you provide can be included in your proof of such support.
7. If you've worked as a homemaker but now want to enter the open market, you can get a tax credit for 20 percent of all job-related

child-care costs—up to $400 for one child and $800 for two or more. This tax break can provide potent "extra" help, because such credits are subtracted from the actual taxes owed; deductions merely lower the total income subject to a tax.

8. Take every deduction allowable on your paycheck, but consider setting aside enough in an interest-bearing savings account to pay your taxes when they are due . . . The IRS now charges 16 percent interest per year on late taxes.
9. Until you file the final decree, you are still legally wed and as such can file a joint tax return. If thus filing will benefit both of you by providing a larger tax refund, consider delaying the entry of your final decree until after the close of the calendar year.

Even if you utilized every one of these ideas, you could still suffer later if you don't make provisions to keep the court door open for later developments. For example, if your state law remains in flux over an important issue in your case, include a term in your judgment that retains the court's jurisdiction over the issue in question. If new legal developments favor you, you've given the court "permission" to decide that issue under freshly applicable law. Without specifically reserving jurisdiction, you may prove unable to open the courthouse door ever again. In lieu of this provision, consider appealing your judgment's terms so that any ruling unfortunate to you remains unfinalized at the time of a favorable legislative change. (Such new laws do not normally affect court orders that have reached final status at the time of a change.)

For example, California Superior courts for years characterized military pensions as community property, and divided this asset routinely in the course of a divorce. Under a recent ruling, however, the United States Supreme Court declared such pensions be the separate property of the earning spouse, and barred state courts from deciding otherwise. In the months following this decision, California legislators joined with other special-interest groups (like the wives of military men) to create and pass the Uniformed Services Former Spouses' Protection Act, which allows state courts to follow their local laws in characterizing such earnings in the course of a divorce. It's clear that even on the same facts, two non-military spouses living in California and undergoing divorces could receive vastly different treatment, depending on when the parties drew their final agreement, or the date on which each case was decided by a judge. To complicate matters, at times when the law decreed such earnings separate property, a military mate would want a divorce case finalized as quickly as possible. The non-military spouse, recognizing that this portion of the law was in flux, would ask the court to delay characterizing the military pension until these legal disagreements had been resolved. Clearly, a final decree handed down at an inauspicious time could terminate a non-military wife's rights to share in the military pension—often an extremely valuable piece of property. A wife facing this possibility could ask that the court reserve jurisdiction to later characterize the pension. If the court refused, she could—and many did—appeal the divorce court's characterization of this asset so that her case would still be open if legislators passed the pending, more favorable law.

If your state laws seem to flip-flop on an issue important to you, or if there is a conflict between state and federal law that has not yet been resolved, study the situation and estimate the possiblity that legislation more beneficial for you may take effect within the next few months. You may prove able to speed or delay your divorce procedure to maximize your asset share.

Once you've taken every possible step to spell out and preserve your gains, make sure that your judgment accurately reflects your agreement or the orders of the court. A single oversight can eliminate an important gain won through negotiation or trial; check your attorney's work carefully. Make sure that every portion of your marital settlement agreement, and every court-ordered duty, shows up in the final judgment, or the court won't be able to enforce your rights.

If you're a soon-to-be-former wife, consider resuming a maiden or former name. While you can use any name you like at any time (as long as you intend no illegal purpose, like defrauding creditors), your state may well include in its divorce procedures an opportunity for you to take another surname. In addition to providing yourself with a fresh outlook, a new name can help you think of yourself differently, throw off old "emotional baggage" evoked by a married surname, and give you another chance to obtain credit if your payment record as a marital pair could prove detrimental to you now.

10

Profiting in the Year(s) After Your Divorce

It is perhaps depressing but true that the effects of your divorce will always remain with you. The terms you forged in your marital settlement agreement or received during your trial will shape and color your daily life for years to come. Because no party to a divorce ever prevails on every issue or receives all he or she wants, it's important to realize that you can change those "final" terms and even increase your benefits years after you've filed your final decree.

Since your judgment provided for a division of later-discovered assets, and child support is always modifiable, one of your first and continuing activities may be fostering a close-as-possible relationship with your ex-mate. If your efforts to remain in contact prove unsuccessful, at least arrange some means of keeping tabs on your former mate or to stay in touch with people who see him or her on a frequent basis. Building an information pipeline will allow you to learn promptly of property taken out of hiding or uncovered by accident by your former spouse. Some former partners pick up bits of gossip from the rumor mill; others entertain mutual friends; a few listen in on industry scuttlebutt (including a subscription to an industry publication to keep track of a former spouse's career climb); and several merely trust their personal observations (How could he afford that new car? How could she take a month in Europe?). Some inventive people look up a former mate's former employee—especially if the worker left in a huff or in an angry frame of mind—and quiz the staffer about their ex-mate's income, outgo, skimmed earnings, false deductions, or living arrangements, any things that could increase a party's ability to pay additional child or spousal support. A few ex-wives stay in touch by making friends with a former husband's new love, and other parties enlist their children's aid to serve as mini-detectives during visitation periods. (While most parents would cringe, rightly, at sending their children off with instructions to spy, there's nothing distasteful about listening when the kids want to talk about Mommy's live-in boyfriend, or Daddy's new house.)

If your ex-mate is not paying the support ordered in the judgment, or if you think he/she is easily able to pay more, as soon as you've gathered sufficient evidence of this, arrange an informal sit-down session to discuss your need for more funds, and your former spouse's apparent power to comply with existing orders and to pay more. If a friendly chat gains you only denials and you remain convinced that the other party's hiding assets or an increased ability to pay support, consider subpoenaing your ex-spouse's tax return to gain a glimpse of his or her new annual earnings (available if he or she files an individual return and is behind in paying child support). Where a recipient seeks to enforce or alter *spousal* support, these single-taxpayer returns may be available. If you are the party obligated to pay support and you're planning to marry, do so before December 31st: a joint tax return cannot be subpoenaed because doing so would invade the privacy of your new mate.

If the asset you have discovered and want your share of is not money but a particular piece of marital property not included in your final terms, make sure that you obtain an accurate appraisal of the asset before approaching your former spouse. Of course, you'll want to accomplish this in a manner that will not encourage your ex-mate to sell or again hide that property. With estimate in hand, try a straightforward request to share equally. If that doesn't work, you could return to court to enforce the terms of your judgment by seeking a division of the asset or by forcing a sale and splitting any proceeds.

In some cases, you may want matters to continue as they are as long as you hold some proof of your ownership right and can protect your ownership share. For example, if the property consists of shares of stock that give your ex-spouse a controlling interest in a company, and he or she has managed the firm exceptionally well, consider a writing (which you could file with the court) outlining your half interest in those shares and perhaps limiting your recovery to one-half of the highest value those stocks will reach within the next two years. Your former mate thus retains the control so profitable to you both, and keeps safe the power to elect himself or herself to a salaried position in the firm. You in turn will receive an amount equal to your highest possible gain, whether the stock rises or falls within the ensuing two years.

You may also want to establish your rights but remain a co-owner of an asset, even in property discovered at the time of your divorce. This is because the asset in question may be growing rapidly, and your share therefore keeps increasing in value. For example, if you must terminate your account to receive your part of funds deposited under certain terms with a savings and loan, and you will both suffer a penalty for early withdrawal, why not wait to receive your share? To consider another possibility, ask if your spouse participates in a qualified cash or deferred arrangement plan. Under these programs, an employee makes a tax-deductible contribution to a corporate profit-sharing plan in an amount greater than the $2,000 that he or she could direct annually into an Individual Retirement Account (IRA). If your ex-mate worked for a company offering such a plan during your marriage, he or she may have elected to defer receipt of a percentage of any salary due and instead to direct that it be invested in the employer's profit-sharing program. The contributing employee enjoys a tax saving on any amount contributed, the company swells the employee's share by making contributions of its own, and your ex-spouse benefits from several aspects of such a plan at distribution time. These pluses include the following:

- Reaping annual contributions that can far exceed the IRA limit of $2,000 per year (a qualifying employee can sock away up to 25 percent of his or her salary).
- Payments to the plan escape Social Security tax assessments.
- Receipt of any deferred salary, without penalty, before the employee reaches age 59½ (though income tax will be assessed on any amounts received). (If a party withdraws funds from his or her Individual Retirement Account before reaching the age of 59½, the recipient must pay a penalty—in addition to income taxes—on any sums withdrawn.)
- Amounts received in a lump sum can be income-averaged over the ensuing ten years (other retirement-plan receipts may incur a tax on the whole sum in the year received).
- Any amount received will augment any IRA sum, since a taxpayer can contribute to both plans simultaneously.

If you discover that your ex-spouse brought home only part of his or her paycheck during your marriage and deposited a percentage of earnings into such a plan, your legal share may have grown to impressive proportions by the date of your discovery. If the assets involved appear to be well invested and show good growth with relative safety, why not agree to set your dollar share at a fair figure, then plan to harvest that sum (plus interest at a given rate) when your ex-mate retires, or when you mutually agree that the employee party will withdraw a lump sum in terminating the plan.

Once you've reached any agreement whereby the other party keeps control of the property, arrange some means of protecting your ownership rights so that your ex-mate cannot defeat you by hiding the asset or selling it and dissipating the proceeds. If you own stock certificates jointly, for example, you might agree that the shares should remain in the care of a trusted friend or business associate, so that neither party could convey them without the other owner's cooperation or consent.

Make all transfers of property (including money) contingent upon receiving something in return. Don't turn over the bank book unless you receive the deed to the house at the same time. Don't sign off on the Mercedes until you hold the Cashier's Check in your hand. A transfer interrupted by even an hour's delay can leave you holding nothing but air.

If some delay seems unavoidable, arrange for some protection for yourself if your mate does not perform. This need not be a formal undertaking; perhaps holding her thousand-dollar watch or his bearer bonds will prove adequate insurance for the completion of promised acts.

Whether you insist upon an immediate sale or not, take one-half of the property itself, or agree that one of you can continue managing and controlling it. Finalize your solution within the period of time after discovery allotted to you in the judgment, or your failure to pursue the issue will forever bar you from sharing in this extra wealth.

Sometimes an investigating party discovers that an ex-partner has disposed of jointly owned property and spent the proceeds. If this happens to you, and your former mate lacks sufficient funds or property to repay you your fair share, you may be able to recover from a surety, guarantor, cosigner, or other third party involved in the conveyance or the sales transaction. For example, some third parties guarantee that a signature necessary to transact a sale is genuine. If your ex-mate sold assets belonging to both of you by forging your name, this guarantor will make good your loss. The names and purposes of such sureties often appear stamped on the face of transmittal documents; review any sales contracts or conveyancing papers to see if such a seal or imprint appears. By contacting the guarantor company and signing an affidavit of satisfaction, you can probably recoup either the value of the items "stolen" by your former mate or obtain a replacement of your portion of the asset involved.

Even if you both know about every asset and have agreed to continue sharing ownership of particular property, changing circumstances may affect your attitudes toward shared ownership in the months and years following your divorce. Don't let this feeling of "shifting sands" dismay you. Developments can favor you if you can gain additional profits by selling your rights in such assets, or by purchasing the co-owned property from your ex-mate. An item can appear more valuable to one person than another, and an appetite for full ownership of any one asset can wax or wane. If you are aware of your former spouse's changing concerns and goals, you can benefit from offering to sell full ownership of an appropriate asset or right to your ex-mate. Such an asset can consist of *anything* tradable between you. For example, you can obtain money, property, or rights in return for any of the following that your former marital partner may desire: a reduction or waiver of spousal support, access to the family home or to areas within it, your cooperation in making joint business decisions, your proxy as a shareholder in a commonly owned company, or even a change in custody (assuming, or course, that your children will benefit or at least suffer no harm by the change).

In another kind of case, you may currently share ownership, but with the understanding that title will be transferred solely to you within a limited time after the filing of your final decree. If your judgment provides for such a title change, and your ex-mate stubbornly refuses to comply, falls seriously ill. or simply disappears, the clerk of the court can sign the documents necessary to transfer title to you alone. Such an official signature can help you cash joint tax return refunds, give escrow instructions, complete property transfers to a third party, record documents requiring both spouses' signatures, convey stock certificates, and complete other transactions beneficial to you. If the clerk's action results in your sole ownership, protect these ownership rights fully. Record the new document of title at the recorder's office in the county where any real property exists. If the title change relates to personal property, find other means of protecting your full ownership rights (make sure the proper authorities know about change of title to an automobile, for example).

If your judgment spells out support obligations carefully, you can enforce payments in several ways and can secure them with several types of assets—but you may need to employ craft, investigative powers, and determination to collect what's due you.

To begin with, a *former* spouse labors under no fiduciary duty to reveal his or her after-divorce assets or earning power to you. Because your old confidential relationship has ended, and there survives no duty to disclose, you'll need keen observational powers to establish sources for payment, or to figure out when a request for higher support could prove successful.

If your former partner can afford to pay you monies now due and still refuses to do so, then you can take the following steps:

1. Serve papers on your obligor and bring him or her into court on a charge of contempt of court. If you succeed in showing that the party could pay and claims no good reason for not doing so, then a hearing officer will order the erring party to fork over any overdue sums (in toto or vía installments). The court may also fine and/or jail the nonpaying parent for flaunting the order of the court. Because this enforcement procedure requires a court appearance and some prior investigation to establish an ability to pay, you will probably want to retain an attorney to press a charge of contempt. If your funds are low and the overdue sum is hefty, ask an attorney to undertake your case on a contingency basis. You may have to ante up court costs, but you'll pay no legal fees unless your conselor obtains the sums overdue. After a successful outcome, your lawyer will accept a percentage (usually one-third to 40 percent) of any recovery, but you can keep the rest.
2. Ask the court for any papers you must fill out to apply for a writ (a form that compels a marshal, for example, to enforce the terms of an order or judgment of the court.) Because a writ directly empowers an officer to collect funds from a bank account, impound a car, or gather up and sell personal property, it allows you to avoid courtroom confrontations and high legal fees and enables the marshal or other enforcement arm of the court to obtain funds from a party's bank account, to attach and sell a debtor's personal property (including cars, stocks, and business inventory), and/or to funnel to you any fees or payments coming from others to your former spouse. Writs can also order an employer to withhold some of a party's pension plan payment or salary (called a wage assignment or garnishment), and send the funds directly to your attorney or to you.

3. Consider filing an abstract of judgment against the non-paying party's real property. An abstract of a judgment merely restates that portion of the court decision that you now wish enforced. The abstract form will ask for the date of the decision and the number and page where the judgment is filed, and leave you space to fill in the provision(s) of the decision that your spouse now refuses to obey. You may need, for example, to collect some overdue child and/or spousal support. Your mate may have lost his or her job, but may own one or more parcels of real property. Fill out the abstract of judgment form, and file it with the county recorder in every county where your ex-mate owns real estate. When your ex-partner sells or conveys that property, escrow will not close (and your ex-mate will receive no proceeds of the sale) until your claim is paid in full. If you learn that one of your spouse's lots or houses is in the process of being sold, do not walk but *run* to the escrow company or realtor handling the sale. Make sure that the person in charge of clearing all liens against this property before title passes to the new buyer knows of your enforceable claim. You should receive your funds promptly, as title will not pass until you have pocketed all the overdue payments—plus interest—that you listed on your abstract of judgment form.
4. Ask the court to appoint a receiver. Initially, this procedure can be more costly than options No. 2 and No. 3 because you must pay the daily charges of this professional, but you can recoup these expenses from your ex-spouse, along with any funds due. Sometimes a marshal, and sometimes a state-licensed party, a receiver, can vacate a fraudulent purchase of property, can carry a judgment into effect, can dispose of property according to a court order's terms, can preserve property pending an appeal, and can assist in satisfying a judgment by collecting and selling your former mate's personal property.
5. Use the nationwide Uniform Reciprocal Enforcement of Support Act to track a dilatory payer who moves out of your state. The URESA has been adopted throughout the United States and by Guam, Puerto Rico, and the Virgin Islands. Under URESA, your state's governor (working through the district attorney's office) may demand that the governor of another state surrender a person found in that state who is criminally charged in the originating state with failing to provide for the support of any person. If you're not interested in your ex-spouse's being fined, jailed, or

otherwise punished but want only the funds that he or she should be sending along, register your judgment in the state where your payer now resides. You can then enforce your support rights by means of one or more of the measures listed above, depending on the avenues available in your spouse's new home state. Note that you may not be able to attach property or income for obligations currently due, as most such support orders remain open to modification and are thus not considered final by the enforcing forum. However, even another court order will not alter any *overdue* sums, so other state courts normally consider any arrearages final and do not object to enforcing court orders for amounts overdue.

6. Renew your judgment before a decade slips by. If you haven't enforced one or several terms and the tenth anniversary of your judgement date is approaching, take the time and the easy steps necessary to renew your order's terms, for judgments expire (lose their power) after ten years. Such a renewal can prove particularly profitable if you can claim unpaid support still due you from years past. If you're waiting for an ex-mate's fortunes to improve before attempting a collection, don't let your enforcement right lapse by allowing your judgment to grow too stale.

An effective judgment and knowledge of your avenues of enforcement can carry you only part of the way to the bank. Even a well-stocked enforcement arsenal will do you little good without an asset or income target. Therefore, review these payment sources to see if one or more can provide the needed funds:

- An ex-spouse's Individual Retirement Account, a Keogh account, bank or savings accounts, or a matured, vested pension plan (obtainable via a wage assignment or earnings withholding order).
- A former mate's salary (available via a writ for a salary withholding order).
- A former spouse's business, professional practice, or store (collectible via a receiver).
- An ex-mate's raw land, home, rented-out condominium, ski lodge, apartment building, or warehouse space (collectible via an abstract of judgment, which becomes effective upon sale of the property).
- An ex-spouse's anticipated income tax refund check (with the help of your nearest district attorney, but only if you're receiving state aid—discussed on the next page).

- A former mate's current credit cards (the social services department in New York's Westchester County now allows delinquent support payers to "put it on plastic" during a visit to one of their four offices, or by telephoning in a payer's Visa number).

Because custodial parents who don't receive support often cost a state welfare funds, government interests have recently placed a relatively new investigation and collection tool into service. Now unpaid support recipients working through any district attorney can utilize Federal Parent Locater services to track down a nonpaying obligor, *if* the payee has been receiving public assistance to pay family bills. While pending law would offer this service to any party not receiving court-ordered support, only people receiving welfare can currently plug into federal information systems (Social Security, etc.) to locate and financially squeeze a noncomplying parent.

At this point, you may note that some of your most potent remedies require the aid of state-funded litigators, like district attorneys. While their services may cost you no out-of-pocket funds, you will probably have to stand in a long line for legal attention from a district attorney. If you have had to seek financial aid from your state's welfare system, and you ask the district attorney to collect your overdue payments, you may have to assign to the DA (or to another state enforcement agency) all of your rights to recover any overdue sums. These agencies require assignment of collection rights in order to recoup funds laid out from the state treasury for your benefit. If you must sign such an assignment form, realize that, as a practical matter, your case will hold no appeal for a private practice attorney who works to recover these arrearages on a contingency basis (accepts a percentage of the sum recovered in lieu of a fee). Clearly, if your arrearages total a hefty amount, it might prove wiser to consider options 1, 2, 3, or 4, or to enlist the advice of some knowledgeable private citizens, as outlined in the next paragraph.

To provide some assistance to parents somehow making it without state aid, several individuals have joined to aid custodial parents in enforcing orders for child support. For example, 44-year-old Yvonne Prestwich has founded PECOS, an Enfield, Connecticut, group of 25 divorced mothers who call themselves Parents for the Enforcement of Court Ordered Support. About a year ago, several Virginians known as FOCUS (For Our Children's Unpaid Support) lobbied successfully for a statewide wage-assignment law. The Organization for the Enforcement of Child Support, based in Maryland, concentrates on "educating and acting as a clearinghouse for information." The group sends copies of any new laws that might help members collect overdue support. There are branches of the Maryland-based consortium in Long Beach, California, and in Flint, Michigan. In addition, members live in Florida, Texas, Kentucky, Pennsylvania, and New Jersey. For information on these local outposts, call Elaine Fromm at (301) 833-2458.

To do as much for yourself as you can (which is, after all, the purpose of this book), encourage your ex-partner to provide as much informal support as he or she can afford. Encourage your co-parent to attend birthday parties for the kids, send them out together on shopping trips, suggest that the ex-mate contribute back-to-school wardrobe purchases or underwrite a sport activity. Involve your ex-mate in choosing (and paying for) Johnny's summer camp, in Jenny's music lessons, and in Herman's Bar Mitzvah plans. Finally, consistently encourage your co-parent to keep the children for extended periods of visitation time.

To enhance your ex-spouse's fortunes (and therefore your own), consider helping him or her land a higher-paying job. Sound beyond your control? Marty kept the kids, and received regular child-support payments from Caren. This monthly allotment didn't begin to pay half the cost of raising their twins, but Marty knew that asking for more would be useless because of Caren's low-paying job. After quizzing a few of their mutual friends and asking Caren several general questions about her work, Marty drew up a résumé outlining his former wife's capabilities. He sent this off to a head hunter along with a letter, which he signed for her, requesting a confidential search for a better-paying job. Though puzzled when a career counselor called her with several possibilities, Caren quickly saw the benefit in cooperating, and landed a new position within four months that doubled her salary.

If you're the paying spouse, and feel a bit drained by your support obligations, consider seeking a contribution from others who could or should help. You might promise, for example, that your payments would never fall below a minimum sum, and/or that you will not seek to end your payments, if your former partner finds other sources of monthly income. As the paying party, you could safely reduce your monthly stipend without triggering an angry court action by your ex-spouse, and your ex-mate will not lose income from you by attracting it from others, so both parties should profit. Such additional funds can flow from your ex-mate's part- or full-time job, from grown children, from boarders, or from "guests" (new girl- or boyfriend) who reside for long periods of time in a still commonly owned family residence.

In short, keep improving your situation by continuing to negotiate after your final decree. While you must comply with your judgment's terms, you may find some legitimate flexibility in how you meet the duties outlined. In addition, mutually agreeable changes in terms relating to children and co-owned assets, for example, almost always prove acceptable to the courts. Where you can improve your situation with some continuing creative bargaining, do so!

If your postdivorce judgments, suggestions, or negotiations *do* net you additional assets, only by considering tax consequences will you keep the bulk of your gain. For example, you might want to consider some of the following ideas:

Accept any lump sum payment only in installments, so that you don't have to report an income "bulge" in any one year. To ensure eventual payment in full, however, have the full amount placed in a safe, interest-bearing escrow account on the date full payment is due, and have the financial institution make your payments.

Try income averaging if you must accept a large fund in a single year (for details, send for IRS Publication No. 506: *Computing Your Tax Under the Income Averaging Method*).

Reinvest any proceeds from the sale of a principal residence within two years of the sale (for more details, send for IRS Publication No. 523: *Tax Information on Selling or Purchasing Your Home*).

Arrange an exchange of any real estate you got for some you'd like to have. Some such trades don't have any tax consequences until the date of an ultimate or final sale.

Keep a larger share of any income you receive from operating a business or service from your home by writing off a portion of your mortgage, utilities, upkeep, and other home-related charges that are overheads of your work area. You cannot use that square footage for any other activity. You must discontinue this write-off in the year that you sell such a residence if you want to be able to shelter the *whole* sale proceeds when you purchase a new home within the next two years.

Arrange for any insurance coverage on your ex-mate to be paid off in segments rather than in a large sum (such scheduled payments can prevent dissipation of the funds, guarantee an adequate lifelong income, and drastically reduce tax bills).

To *retain* all your profits in the years after your divorce, consider these warnings or risk losing all.

If you receive a less-than-adequate check from an ex to satisfy an obligation of any kind, and it bears a note that says your endorsement constitutes an acceptance of payment in full, don't cash the check without crossing out the phrase, or you could give up your right to pursue any balance due.

Use the rights you gained in a final judgment, or you may lose them. A long-term failure to insist on what's due you may constitute a waiver; your ex-mate may never have to deliver on the obligation owed. "It's amazing to me," noted one family-law judge, "how many hard-won assets remain forgotten in the 'loser's' garage."

If you consider remarrying, make sure that your new spouse can afford to supplant any support that you're receiving under an existing decree, since most spousal support ends with the marriage of the recipient party.

If you consider remarrying, make as sure as you can that this is it, because a later separation, divorce, or even annulment won't reinstate your former support unless your judgment specifically so provides — and such a protection is highly unusual.

If you consider remarrying, consider drafting a prenuptial agreement that spells out your sole ownership rights to the assets you bring into or earn or acquire during a subsequent marriage.

11

Modifying Upward What You Already Have

EVEN IF you've followed every possible suggestion in this book, including negotiating effectively, you may find yourself—just a few years after your parting—without enough child and/or spousal support to get by. Recognizing this possibility, the judicial system will sometimes modify such orders, so that you can receive more funds if your financial need *and* your ex-partner's ability to pay have both risen. Of course, such modifications can also occur via agreement between the parties following discussions or negotiations after divorce. If such an agreement is signed by the court and entered in your court file, its terms remain as binding and enforceable as an order handed down by the judge after testimony at trial. Since this path can provide for more creative solutions, avoid court hassles, and save both you and your ex-mate legal fees, try to reach such an agreement before you rush into court.

Whether you proceed in court or begin by discussing this issue over the kitchen table, you'll want to consider the following factors to help you modify such allotments upward (and block your ex-spouse's efforts to modify them downward).

To begin with, take an objective look at your current dating partners. While few if any legal considerations should affect your choice of romantic companions, you'll need to use some common sense in dating to maximize your chances of increasing your support.

For example, avoid accepting ostentatious gifts from your ladies or beaux. It's a little difficult to claim that you're suffering financially while sporting a post-Christmas three-carat emerald ring and a Tahitian tan in February. If you're seeing a generous person, start your own retirement program with less obvious assets—like a few shares of AT&T.

Avoid openly dating your former mate's biggest business competitor, present boss, or a younger but more successful professional in your ex-mate's field. Since appearing in your former haunts with such a star in tow will probably make your ex-mate feel more angry and inadequate than ever, use a little discretion in laying out your dating itineraries. Don't give your former partner any incentive to close your money pipeline.

Avoid inviting Ronnie or Rhonda to linger on in briefs or lingerie when you *know* your former mate is due at the door. Such an obvious psychological slap in the face can screw up your current payments, cause a visiting parent to take his/her frustration out on the kids, and spur real stubbornness when you seek an increase in support.

Avoid letting either Ronnie or Rhonda move in, for even a platonic relationship will probably result in a contribution to your household expenses . . . a possible bar to seeking additional dollars from your former mate, and a good reason for your ex to seek a *reduction* in your support.

If, on the other hand, your ex-spouse wants to move in with a lover, encourage him or her to do so. Another income in the household means that your ex-mate should have more discretionary funds available to pay you support. If your former mate instead allocates his/her dollars to support the love-in, you can (in negotiations or on the witness stand) point out the court's probable feelings about a choice that unwise. As soon as your former mate's love has settled in, begin asking for a larger sum to help you meet monthly expenses for yourself and/or any children.

The second reason to encourage (or at least endorse) such a pairing is that cohabitation can lead to marriage, and then the whole amount of your ex-mate's new spouse's income may swell the pot into which you can dip for additional support. While most divorced people *do* wed again, the Census Bureau recently indicated that your wait for your ex-spouse to marry could prove shorter if you're an ex-wife—five out of six divorced men remarry, while only three out of four former wives elect to marry again.

If you expect to receive spousal support but want to be able to live with (or marry) a prospective lover without incurring a costly modification downward, then make sure that your marital settlement agreement (and later judgment) provides that such support will not diminish or terminate if you cohabit or rewed.

If you foresee a need for additional support funds (and it's always wise to assume that you will), keeping careful records can aid you in collecting overdue sums, in gaining more money via modification, and in receiving a larger sum than you otherwise might obtain.

To succeed in each of these goals, *first,* keep a careful record of all child and/or spousal support received. Make your own chart and head its categories:

Date ordered paid	Amount ordered paid	Date paid	Amount paid	Any monthly balance due	Total balance due

Carefully log in each check, money order, or dollar bill you receive. No matter when you receive funds, credit them to the earliest payment missed. For example, if your support is due each month, and your ex-mate hasn't paid since April first, but you get a check in July, then apply it to satisfy the April payment. While the chart is laid out so that you'll always know the total sums overdue, don't worry about the total overdue balance until you're ready to collect. Whether you file an abstract of judgment, seek an earnings withholding order, or ask the court to find your former mate in contempt, you will need to supply the total overdue sum only at the time you fill in the necessary papers for the procedure you choose. (You may need to show the payment schedule and all missed payments on a contempt action in your state, and for this, you can probably use the figures in just the way you've compiled them on your chart.)

Second, gather whatever evidence you can to show that your ex-spouse now enjoys an increased earning ability and/or that your ex-mate's roommate contributes a substantial share of that household's expenses, helping to defray your former mate's living costs.

Third, establish your increased financial need by filling in the figures on the chart that follows. Save and organize necessary documentation (like receipts, canceled checks, bills marked "paid") to prove that your expenses have in fact risen. Also, add on to this chart any legitimate but unusual or unexpected expenses that you've incurred since the divorce.

Whether you seek to obtain a support increase by prevailing in a court hearing or by negotiating with your spouse, presenting a completed version of the following chart will aid you immeasurably in pursuing additional dollars by either path.

SUPPORT MODIFICATION CHART

YOUR TOTAL INCOME

	Prior monthly amount (sum at date of last agreement or court order)	Current monthly amount
Salary or job earnings	______	______
Commissions	______	______
Overtime	______	______
Income from Amway, Avon, Etc.	______	______
Dividends	______	______
Income from annuities	______	______
Interest from savings, credit union	______	______
Interest from investments (bonds, stocks, limited partnerships, syndications, etc.)	______	______
Interest from personal loans	______	______
Profit-sharing funds	______	______
Bonuses, business contest proceeds	______	______
Rents or other income from property	______	______
Trust income	______	______
Earnings from any inheritance	______	______
Earnings from royalties, patents, license fees, permits, drilling rights, easements, etc.	______	______

	Prior monthly amount (sum at date of last agreement or court order)	Current monthly amount
Earnings from testimonials, endorsements	______	______
Recovery from lawsuits or claims	______	______
State disability, insurance proceeds	______	______
"Constructive income" from barter	______	______
Public assistance (welfare)	______	______
Child support	______	______
Spousal support	______	______
Social Security	______	______
Scholarships or grants	______	______
Unemployment insurance	______	______
Other (specify)	______	______
Medical or other insurance	______	______
Aid received from employee union	______	______
Monies from retirement or pension funds	______	______
Animals raised for breeding/sale	______	______
Total	______	______
YOUR DEDUCTIONS		
Income taxes (state and federal)	______	______
Social Security	______	______

	Prior monthly amount (sum at date of last agreement or court order)	Current monthly amount
Disability and unemployment	_______	_______
Retirement plan, voluntary	_______	_______
Retirement plan, involuntary	_______	_______
Union contributions, voluntary	_______	_______
Union contributions, involuntary	_______	_______
Savings plan contributions	_______	_______
Charitable contributions	_______	_______
Total	_______	_______
Number of deductions claimed	_______	_______
Your total monthly spendable income	_______	_______

YOUR EXPENSES

YOUR HOUSING	Prior monthly amount	Current monthly amount
Rent or mortgage payment	_______	_______
Pool loan payment	_______	_______
Home improvement loan payment	_______	_______
Repair, upkeep, and maintenance	_______	_______
Housekeeper, maid, cleaning crew	_______	_______
Security systems/private patrol	_______	_______

	Prior monthly amount (sum at date of last agreement or court order)	Current monthly amount
Insurance (if not included in house payment)	______	______
Home owner's insurance	______	______
Home taxes (if not included in house payment)	______	______
Pool, exterminator, other (specify)	______	______
Total	______	______
YOUR UTILITIES		
Water and Sewer	______	______
Electricity	______	______
Gas	______	______
Telephone	______	______
Garbage	______	______
Other (specify)	______	______
Total	______	______
YOUR FOOD		
Groceries	______	______
School lunches, milk	______	______
Meals outside home	______	______
Special dietary requirements	______	______

	Prior monthly amount (sum at date of last agreement or court order)	Current monthly amount
Other (specify)	______	______
Total	______	______
YOUR CLOTHING		
Clothing for self	______	______
Clothing for children	______	______
Laundry and dry cleaning	______	______
Alterations	______	______
Tailoring	______	______
Storage	______	______
Other (specify)	______	______
Total	______	______
YOUR MEDICAL CARE (AFTER INSURANCE REIMBURSEMENT)		
Doctor and dentist for self	______	______
Drugs and medical supplies for self	______	______
Orthodontia for self	______	______
Ophthalmology/optometry for self	______	______
Dermatology for self	______	______
Chiropractic care for self	______	______
Podiatry for self	______	______

	Prior monthly amount (sum at date of last agreement or court order)	Current monthly amount
Surgery for self	______	______
Therapy for self	______	______
Doctor and dentist for children	______	______
Drugs and medical supplies for children	______	______
Orthodontia for children	______	______
Ophthalmology/optometry for children	______	______
Dermatology for children	______	______
Chiropractic care for children	______	______
Podiatry for children	______	______
Therapy for children	______	______
Surgery for children	______	______
Medical and dental insurance	______	______
Other (specify)	______	______
Total	______	______

YOUR TRANSPORTATION

Car payment or leasing fee	______	______
Car repair and maintenance	______	______
Car insurance	______	______
Gas and oil	______	______

	Prior monthly amount (sum at date of last agreement or court order)	Current monthly amount
Environmental/personalized license plate fee and registration	_______	_______
Car washes and waxing	_______	_______
Parking	_______	_______
Auto club	_______	_______
Bus fare and/or parking	_______	_______
Other (specify)	_______	_______
Total	_______	_______
YOUR INSTALLMENT PAYMENTS		
Creditor:	_______	_______
Creditor:	_______	_______
Creditor:	_______	_______
Creditor:	_______	_______
Total	_______	_______
YOUR PAYMENTS MADE ON LUMP-SUM OBLIGATIONS		
Owed to	_______	_______
Owed to	_______	_______
Owed to	_______	_______
Owed to	_______	_______
Total	_______	_______

	Prior monthly amount (sum at date of last agreement or court order)	Current monthly amount
MISCELLANEOUS		
Babysitter	______	______
Child care	______	______
School and school supplies for self	______	______
School books for self	______	______
School and school supplies for children	______	______
School books for children	______	______
School tuition	______	______
School uniforms	______	______
Horseback-riding lessons, tack, etc.	______	______
Band/orchestra/choir involvement	______	______
Academic tutoring or special classes	______	______
Children's summer camp	______	______
Musical instruments	______	______
Family vacation(s)	______	______
Newspapers, magazines, and books	______	______
Cultural expenses	______	______
Country/health club memberships	______	______
Club dues and related costs	______	______

	Prior monthly amount (sum at date of last agreement or court order)	Current monthly amount
Uniforms for work	______	______
Hobby costs (including special clothes)	______	______
Barber/beauty shop for self	______	______
Cosmetics for self	______	______
Hair care for self	______	______
Personal hygiene for self	______	______
Manicure/pedicure for self	______	______
Barber/stylist for children	______	______
Cosmetics for children	______	______
Hair care for children	______	______
Personal hygiene for children	______	______
Membership dues (specify)	______	______
Savings deductions, other deposits	______	______
Child/spousal support paid to others	______	______
Cable television/special channels	______	______
Health insurance, self and children	______	______
Life insurance, self and children	______	______
Accident insurance, self and children	______	______
Children's allowances	______	______
Recreation and sports involvement	______	______

	Prior monthly amount (sum at date of last agreement or court order)	Current monthly amount
Lessons: tennis, golf, sailing, etc.	______	______
Entertainment for self	______	______
Entertaining at home/away	______	______
Hardcover and paperback books	______	______
Alcohol and mixes	______	______
Cigarettes, cigars, etc.	______	______
Incidentals for self	______	______
Entertainment for children	______	______
Incidentals for children	______	______
Video cassette recorder costs	______	______
Electronic games	______	______
Videocassette recorder repairs	______	______
Tape cassettes/rentals/repairs	______	______
Pet food, care, surgery, grooming	______	______
Livestock, work or hunting animals	______	______
Animals raised for breeding or sale	______	______
Family gifts	______	______
Phone answering service/machine	______	______
Credit card insurance/notification services	______	______
Personal floater insurance (furs, gems)	______	______

	Prior monthly amount (sum at date of last agreement or court order)	Current monthly amount
Costs of maintaining and repairing boats, planes, trailers, campers, motorcycles, dune buggies, other vehicles (including taxes, upkeep, slip or storage fees, maintenance and repairs, insur ance, registration)	______	______
Bank service charges	______	______
Safe-deposit box charges	______	______
Liability for lawsuits/claims	______	______
Other (specify)	______	______
Total	______	______
Your total monthly living expenses	______	______

YOUR EX-SPOUSE'S TOTAL INCOME

	Prior monthly amount (sum at date of last agreement or court order)	Current monthly amount
Salary or job earnings	______	______
Commissions	______	______
Overtime	______	______
Deferred salary due	______	______
Income from Amway, Avon, etc.	______	______
Dividends	______	______
Income from annuities	______	______
Interest from savings, credit union	______	______
Interest from investments (bonds, stocks, limited partnerships, syndications, etc.)	______	______
Interest from personal loans	______	______
Profit-sharing funds	______	______
Bonuses, business contest proceeds	______	______
Rents/other income from property	______	______
Trust income	______	______
Earnings from any inheritance	______	______
Earnings from royalties, patents, license fees, permits, drilling rights, easements, etc.	______	______

	Prior monthly amount (sum at date of last agreement or court order)	Current monthly amount
Earnings from testimonials, endorsements	______	______
Recovery from lawsuits or claims	______	______
State disability, insurance proceeds	______	______
"Constructive income" from barter	______	______
Public assistance (welfare)	______	______
Child support	______	______
Spousal support	______	______
Social Security	______	______
Scholarships or grants	______	______
Unemployment insurance	______	______
Other received (specify)	______	______
Medical or other insurance	______	______
Aid received from employee union	______	______
Retirement or pension funds	______	______
Animals raised for breeding/sale	______	______
Total	______	______

YOUR EX-SPOUSE'S DEDUCTIONS

Income taxes (state and federal)	______	______
Social security	______	______
Disability and unemployment	______	______

	Prior monthly amount (sum at date of last agreement or court order)	Current monthly amount
Retirement plan, voluntary	______	______
Retirement plan, involuntary	______	______
Union contributions, voluntary	______	______
Union contributions, involuntary	______	______
Savings plan contributions	______	______
Charitable contributions	______	______
Total	______	______
Number of deductions claimed	______	______
Your ex-spouse's total monthly spendable income	______	______

Fourth, remain close to people who've kept in touch with your former mate—if you want to reap money from the rumor mill, you've got to fertilize the news lines. Once you've got such a person in your clutches, buy the lunch and ply him/her with a drink or two. Ask how your ex-mate's doing in life. Is the job going well? Are sales up? How about a past or promised promotion? Does a move to another branch or department indicate an earnings jump? What kind of benefits is the employer now offering to benefit employees' children? Has your former beloved recently received an inheritance? A large cash or property gift? Entered a partnership with another on the side? Bought into an apartment complex, shopping center, or other income-producing investment as a syndicate member or a limited partner? If your past partner's a professional who offers services to business people, has he or she recently accepted any share in a money-earning project in lieu of a fee? A yes to any of these queries could dramatically increase the fund from which you draw your monthly support, and provide extra dollars for you.

Fifth, make a copy of the front *and* back of all checks you receive from your ex-spouse, regardless of why he/she made them out to you. Whether he once paid an after-divorce baby-sitter's fee, or she makes you a loan, slip that imprinted chit into a Xerox machine on your way to the bank.

Copying the check's front side will give you all the information you'll need to attach any funds in that account if support payments ever lag or cease in the future. Is the check personal, business, or corporate? Do other names appear on its face? Is the address close to your ex-mate's employment or home, or does it suggest a new business venture that you'll want to learn more about? Is this check drawn on a personal account, on a pension plan, or on a trust fund, money market, or investment vehicle of some kind? Does the source suggest an undisclosed asset in which you now should share, or a new source of earnings that could boost your support income? Is there more than one signature on the check? What is that person's relationship to your former mate? (A cosigner who works as your ex-spouse's banker, accountant, CPA, investment advisor, or money manager can prove a profitable source of additional information, should you need to subpoena income records for future modification attempts.)

Copying the back of your ex-mate's checks will force you to take note of whether your former spouse has imposed any limitation on your financial rights. Such limitations usually consist of a written line, added by the writer of the check, that states something like: "Endorsement by the payee constitutes acceptance of the face value as full payment of all related debts due." Making a copy and studying the back of each check therefore ensures that you don't endorse (agree to) a forgiveness of any balance then due. If such a phrase *does* appear on any check made out to you and you know that the face value on the check does not represent the total amount currently due you, then cross out the offending phrase before you endorse the check and deposit the funds.

Sixth, note the number of times that you're paid by money order, by travelers' check, by cash, or by trips, clothes, produce, or other forms of inventory that you know your former partner deals with in his or her business life. Such receipts could indicate that your ex-mate pays you by skimming funds from a business connection, from illegal earnings, or from his/her (or an employer's) business stock. Each of these instances suggests the possibility that your ex-mate is up to something the Internal Revenue Service or a law enforcement agency could find most interesting. Since most family-law courts don't care about a party's illegal or immoral activities (unless a custody award or child visitation right hangs in the balance), you'll probably gain little by threatening a return to court to obtain a higher support award. A spouse eager to avoid criminal charges or higher taxes, however, may prove most compliant in providing more support if you could show proof of behavior that would intrigue the police, the district attorney, or the IRS.

Such threats constitute a form of blackmail, of course, and you must gauge both the effect that such an action will have on your self-esteem and on your former mate. Some parties will not engage in such threats because they consider it demeaning to do so. Others refrain because an agency like the IRS might find them liable as well, if the couple has filed joint returns crammed with "discrepancies." A few people refuse to take this tack because they fear that a mate will respond with an emotional reaction or by withdrawing from negotiations. In one case, the wife's attorney kept suggesting that the tax authorities might prove interested in a husband's financial misstatements. Eventually the husband and his lawyer had heard enough. They filed an amended return, taking the wind out of wife's sails. "I refuse to deal with a blackmailer," husband's attorney explained.

In fact, this last suggestion raises the issue of whether to negotiate for additional support or whether to return to a more formal forum to present your case. Despite the many advantages of negotiating, a formal hearing does present advantages in some circumstances. The two lists that follow should help you decide which approach may prove more effective in your circumstances. While you weigh these factors, consider that you'll probably lose nothing by approaching your ex-mate and asking for additional support in an amicable manner. Base your request on facts, showing him or her your completed support Modification Chart and your objective evidence—gleaned from your detective work—of your former partner's higher earnings.

It might prove better to negotiate before or instead of going to court in these types of situations:

1. Circumstances haven't changed enough to justify a new court order (your expenses remain about the same and/or your ex-mate's income hasn't risen much, if at all), but you can present several equitable reasons why support should increase. These could include the following:

- A realization that the support was inadequate from the first and should have totaled more.
- Events have failed to occur that you depended on (obtaining your CPA license, recovering fully from a past illness or accident, etc.).
- An informal change in sharing physical care of the children, so that you have them (and their expenses) more than you bargained for.
- Health or business setbacks have limited your expected earnings following divorce.
- You've been forced to help pay community debts that were not included in your MSA (and therefore never appeared in your judgment's terms).
- You've failed to manage your budget as well as you thought you could at the time of the divorce.

2. You need more funds but haven't really lived up to your part of the MSA or judgment terms. You need "clean hands," as the courts phrase it, to ask a legal forum for justice that will benefit you. In other words, as law books remain fond of pointing out, "You must do equity to expect equity." So you must try to get more funds out of your ex-mate while avoiding an appearance in court. While your former love may not know that you're dealing from a position of weakness, the court will not rush to protect (or benefit) a party who has not delivered on his or her promises.
3. Your MSA or your judgment contains terms relating to support that now appear vague, legally unenforceable, or otherwise detrimental to you.
4. Your judgment does not include terms pertaining to support at all (they were overlooked, or appeared in an agreement that was not transferred to your judgment and therefore were not included in your final terms).
5. Your former mate makes more money, and you've tried to obtain objective evidence of the source and amount, but all you've gathered is some evidence that the source is illegal or that your former partner isn't declaring all the funds. While a court might ignore such vague accusations, or suggest that another judicial branch consider them, you hold some out-of-court power by indi-

cating that you will inform on your ex-mate, thus causing him or her hassles with the district attorney or a visit from the IRS.

6. You're aleady looking ahead to a future modification attempt, and you'd rather have any obtainable-now figure entered into the court record via agreement and without any evidence of the circumstances surrounding your mutual decison. If no surrounding facts appear in the record, you'll probably be able to obtain more support funds in the future (assuming that you can show a party's increased ability to pay) without showing any change of circumstances since the date of the agreement you are now negotiating.

On the other hand, it could prove better to go to court in the following situations:

1. Your ex-mate obviously is enjoying an increased income—but you can't get your hands on any real proof. Court procedures provide for subpoenas, depositions, interrogatories, and other methods of discovery and of soliciting such evidence (under oath) from your former love or from third parties with inside knowledge.
2. You know that your former mate's now living with a lover who contributes to his/her household expenses (thus freeing up more cash with which to pay you support), but you cannot get your former partner to admit to the live-in arrangement or persuade him or her to admit to receiving any monies contributing to household costs. In such a case, you might have to subpoena the lover's pay records, checkbook register, a household ledger, or other evidence of shared living costs.

Whenever you consider seeking additional support, altering a payment schedule or amount, or shifting custody or varying a visitation schedule, consider your timing and weigh every potential pitfall before you commit yourself to a course of action. Be realistic about the probable chances of reaching your goal. Make a savvy forecast, keep your expectations and requests reasonable, and you'll gain many of the dollars you need while saving yourself trauma, frustration, and time.

12

Good Tips for Gains Anytime

THIS BOOK of advice about surviving—and profiting from—your divorce has presented chronologically the process of preparing for a separation and the dissolution of a marital community, the parting itself, and covered numerous postdivorce financial issues. You may wonder how there could remain a whole chapter of information worth skimming through. Some of the suggestions contained in this last chapter could have appeared appropriately in each previous segment of this book; because you can use these tips to great advantage from the first intimation of trouble in your marriage to the final divorce decree, I am grouping them here.

The counsel you'll find in "Good Tips for Gains Anytime" comes from divorcing people, legal journals and case reviews, judges, family-law commissioners, and other lawyers in the family law-field. Apply what you find here liberally, for this advice can carry you successfully through your divorce, into life after the decree, and into a healthy, productive, and profitable new marital partnership.

Let's consider reconciliation in all its shades and ramifications. An offer to reconcile may spring from you or from your spouse at almost any stage of your proceedings. If you agree, do so with some knowledge of how a reconciliation will affect your property, your support rights, and the extent of your obligations. If you receive such an offer in the first weeks or months after you part, *beware* of the motives underlying a partner's outstretched hand. Your mate's offer may be sincere, so give him or her time to work out a viable relationship on terms you both want. While you're cooperating, however, bear in mind that a reconciliation can bring about the following:

- Negate informal property divisions and debt allocations that you've worked out between you (a particularly harmful effect if these arrangements would have been profitable to you).
- Eradicate any need or cause of action for support.
- Erase the terms of any temporary custody allocation, or compromise any action you may have brought to obtain child and/or spousal support.
- Negate any restraining order that you have obtained to exclude your spouse from the family home, or to protect yourself or the children from physical violence or psychological trauma dished out by your mate.
- Alter a separation date, so that you might have to share assets whose value is increasing and that you previously held in your name alone.
- Convince the court that it should not grant your request for a divorce, or persuade it to order a delay in any initial filing, interim order, or final decree.
- Provide an unscrupulous mate with an opportunity to run up community bills (payable by both of you) before the real separation occurs.

If reconciliation possibilities arise *after* you've signed a marital settlement agreement, or after the court has divided your property and debts but not yet issued a final decree, draw up a short agreement between you explaining that the reconciliation will—or will not—affect the terms settled to date. If those terms promise a favorable property division for you, you'll want to ensure that any reconciliation does not erase your gains. If the terms previously set allocated only a miserly share of assets to you or provided for inadequate support, consider a writing that formalizes your mutual wish that your reconciliation nullifies the terms of any agreement or judgment already reached.

It may turn out to be especially useful to obtain such a writing if the term of your prior agreement dealt with real property. If the terms of the new agreement ratify your rights, you'll certainly want to have this signed document notarized and filed with the county recorder to overcome any presumption that your reconciliation erased any of your sole ownership gains. If the new writing erases former terms that were unfavorable to you, then you'll also want it signed, notarized, and filed to regain ownership rights that had slipped away. Lastly, if your latest pact gives you more assets or rights, arrange for your signatures to be notarized and file this document immediately. What if you choose not to add such a new agreement to the county recorder's files? A mate who changes his/her mind about remaining married to you could play a "reconciliation charade" just long enough to void (or persuade you to void) a prior agreement allocating an asset solely to you, then sell or trade "your" property and pocket the price.

If you do truly reconcile, remember to tell *both* attorneys, as either one may routinely apply for a final divorce decree in your case. If the final decree went through, not only would you become cohabitants (instead of marrieds), but any gap before you remarried could cause expensive snags in your later rights. For example, any assets, rights, or earnings that your partner accumulates in the period before you wed again could qualify as separate property, in which you can claim no share. This period will also cause a gap in the insurance coverage for a "legal spouse" until a remarriage can occur. Finally, you could suffer economic loss if your fiancé(e) were to take the opportunity to demand more favorable property treatment in exchange for saying "I do."

Here's another valuable tip: learn well from the best teacher you'll ever meet—experience. If you observed your current spouse doing rather flaky things during a divorce from a previous mate, guard against your playing the patsy this time around.

One woman psychologist mourned: "When Peter was married to Evelyn and seeing me, I know that she never suspected he was planning a divorce. In fact, she'd come into the office and boast about how attentive Peter acted at home. I should have remembered that. About three years after our wedding, Peter began showing more consideration to me, his second wife. He helped out with chores, suggested entertaining more, bought me little gifts, and encouraged me to share my most intimate thoughts and dreams. When he arranged a weekend away for our fourth anniversary, bought me a mink, and set up a candlelit, midnight supper just above the high-tide line, I thought our marriage would last forever. Instead, I was served with divorce papers the following Monday morning! To top it all off, Peter admitted that he'd fallen in love with a nurse in his office . . . just as he'd romanced me while I worked as a therapist on his psychiatric staff. His pattern never varied, but I never saw it staring me right in the face."

Another woman said, "During his divorce, Martin hid community assets from his second wife in my bank account. Now that he wants a divorce, he's dating some other woman and doing the same damn thing to me!"

In short, don't expect your leopard to alter his or her spots. If he sequestered property during an earlier parting, he'll probably try to do it again. If she asked a girlfriend to keep her new furniture before her last divorce, she'll no doubt consider something like it this time, too. Instead of gnashing your teeth over such perfidy, remember the twists in those old tricks and follow them to recoup the treasures you'd otherwise lose.

Even if your mate's never experienced divorce, take a cue from his or her business and personal dealings with other people over the years. Did you watch, participate, or benefit when he/she

—secreted earnings or profits from the IRS?
—misrepresented an asset's worth to a potential buyer or lender?
—finagled deals for personal profit?
—risked and/or lost others' assets for personal gain (or worse, for a thrill) via gambling, betting, cardplaying, etc.?
—misappropriated business or corporate assets for personal use or profit?

While wed to this wheeler-dealer, you probably overlooked these illegal and/or immoral acts. Now, however, you stand to suffer as one of your spouse's victims. Rather than panic, remember his or her favorite tricks and work out ways to foil those plans, or to put properties beyond his/her grasp.

Use your intuition at every possible stage of your separation and divorce. Such instincts can operate as personal early warning systems. They let you know when something's amiss, or someone's not the ally he or she once seemed. While men often admit to hunches, most do not use them to full advantage because they discount such feelings instead of acting on them. Both sexes need to remember that intuition has been described as "reason in a hurry." Intuition comprises perceptions, impressions, and sensitivities that nudge you into an awareness for your own good. Pay attention to your psychic seismograph. Let it lead you away from economic and emotional harm, and toward potential benefits. To show how profitable psychological twinges can prove, consider these scenarios!

Unhappy in her marriage, Lorrie asked for a "leave of absence" from Denton and requested that he finance her six-month stay in a nearby beach community. In her delight at his agreement, Lorrie discounted her intuitive fears that, because of his miserly approach to their family budget, Denton would later regret consenting to these terms. In order to protect herself Lorrie lunched with an attorney friend and asked what she could do to maintain her right to support and her share in any communal property while she "found herself." Though she feared for her financial future,

Lorrie failed to follow through on suggestions that she photocopy important records showing ownership vestings and asset worth before she packed her bags. Within a month of her departure, Denton resented underwriting Lorri's vacation and began bemoaning these "wasted dollars." Within two months, he had moved the business account for his design firm to another bank, opened a new account in his own name to receive his earnings checks, hidden papers showing title and vesting to several antique automobiles, and padlocked his personal and business files. He then cancelled Lorrie's health and medical insurance (obtained and maintained through his company). During the third month, Lorrie suffered severe back pain and learned of a malignant tumor that required immediate (and expensive) surgery. It didn't improve her condition or state of mind to learn that she could expect no financial assistance from her health insurance carrier. In the fourth month, Lorrie and Denton decided to divorce, but she soon learned that none of their records were readily available to her. While Denton could not prevent Lorrie from obtaining necessary asset and vesting information from other sources, he could—and did—add considerably to her cost and delay in discovering, evaluating, and proving her share of their property. If Lorrie had followed through on her initial instincts, she could have quietly compiled her own file of asset information, asked service suppliers (like the insurance carrier) to notify her of any proposed changes, and obtained an informal but signed agreement spelling out Denton's agreement that their living apart would not affect his financial obligations during this period of time.

In a more positive example, Phillip used an intuitive leap to the right conclusion to swell his assets during divorce. He and Betty were holding friendly, frequent negotiation sessions when she asked for a postponement of an upcoming meeting so that she could take a short trip. A few days later, she returned to their small California town driving an electric blue Ferrari. Two weeks later, Phillip noticed a $500 withdrawal from their joint account had been made by Betty before her departure date. A few discreet inquiries among their friends revealed that Betty had recently toured Las Vegas and hit the jackpot at one of the casino's jumbo slot machines. Combining these facts, Phillip concluded that Betty had parlayed a community property grubstake (savings from their joint account) into a $46,000 piece of property. He checked with his attorney and learned that, while perspiration after separation is the separate property of the "sweating" spouse, the accumulations that flow without additional effort from community property remain community in character. In short, the court that eventually heard this issue agreed that little—if any—separate skills entered into Betty's playing a slot machine. The justices concluded that Betty's after-separation luck would not change the nature of this win; that it really sprang from the no-skill use of community property funds. As a result, Phillip received (in addition to his negotiated share of their communal assets), the sum of $23,000 to ease his entry into single life.

Another useful suggestion is to weigh all offers to settle as objectively as possible. If you insist on clutching to your breast every sentimental knickknack of your marriage years and will share nothing with your spouse, you will feel many of these items torn away in court by a judicial stranger. In truth, the mementos of wedded bliss often act merely as constant reminders of happier times. They will taunt you from the half-light of memory with guilt and remorse, blaming you for letting a marvelous marriage slip through your grasp. If you cannot seem to give up the items or the memories, seek counseling. Some powerful but hidden feelings may be preventing you from accepting this ending as inevitable. As long as these emotions rule your reason, your refusal of even fair settlement offers will cost you high legal fees, your spouse's cooperation, and your self-respect.

Cooperate by sharing information about your earnings, and about the assets, debts, and property of your marriage. If you're an employee, your spouse can check your earnings quite easily, and a court could question your credibility on all other issues if you fib about income. If your mate's at all aware, he or she will have a pretty valid idea of what you have accumulated during marriage, so there's little profit (and much potential cost) in fudging your net worth. In almost every circumstance, your mate or his/her attorney can seek information from a third party—like a CPA, the IRS, an employer, an employee, a business partner, or a banker—who feels no compulsion to misrepresent your financial health. In the meantime, if your information-frustrated spouse has to pay for formal discovery techniques like interrogatories, depositions, and notices to produce, he or she will almost certainly ask for a court order forcing you to pay some or all of such costs. If you formally agree to reveal information but in reality hamper such investigative efforts, your mate's lawyer can seek sanctions against you and/or any lawyer who advised such delaying tactics. Therefore, you could end up paying for your attorney's game-playing, the fees your mate incurred while his/her lawyer pursued the hidden facts, *and* some healthy court-imposed sanctions for your lack of cooperation. In fact, in the California case of *Marriage of Wright*, an intractable husband who secreted assets had to pay $20,000 in legal fees to his wife's attorney, who had to invest extensive time uncovering the community's true worth.

Even while still wed, you can benefit from the next suggestion: build a support network of caring, nonjudgmental friends. This will enhance and protect your feelings of self-worth, help you through difficult emotional periods, aid you in your career, and help you retain your sanity during your divorce. To make such a network as beneficial as possible, undertake to do the following:

- Forge these friendships with people not counted among your spouse's acquaintances, business associates, relatives, or your mutual friends.
- Choose at least a few of these pals for their honesty and judgment. (You'll sometimes need a comforting soul; but your practical-minded friends will probably prove the ones to pull you through.)
- Screen your network for individuals who have a vested interest in the outcome of your divorce, for their interests could prove adverse to yours. (A friend who secretly craves your mate could undercut your negotiations in order to ensure that your marriage really ends.)
- Keep enough people in your network to "spread the agony"—even caring friends get "used up" and tired of hearing about your triumphs or your pain.
- Use some discretion, even if you yearn to "tell everything to everybody"—some people may harbor spiteful feelings toward you and may use inside information against you or damage your career or reputation.

Prepare sensibly and early for living alone. Work out a budget and determine exactly how much income you'll need. How much of this sum can you supply, and what amount will have to come from other sources (a spouse, a boarder, a second job, the children)? If you plan to leave the family home, seek housing nearby so that you can stay in touch with the children and can keep an eye on your former residence until a final sale. When weighing the cost of adequate housing, remember that you'll need extra bedrooms, sufficient floorspace, and perhaps local diversions (like a swimming pool or recreation area) if you want any children's visits to prove pleasant. If you'll be working from your new domicile (preparing tax returns, baby-sitting, counseling, running a small public relations agency), make sure that these activities will not contravene any regulations concerning land use, parking, noise, or crowding.

Keep exercising your negotiating muscle. Most of us accept what we see or hear without question if the information appears reasonable. We almost never attempt to change another's attitude, answer, or response if we feel that it's offered in good faith. During a divorce, however, keep in mind that two people may (and often do) hold totally different opinions on a single issue. This does not mean that you cannot effect a compromise, or alter that party's point of view. To reach such a result, however, you must practice the art of negotiation. Start early by attempting to change details that don't matter much to you. For example, you might bargain with your baby-sitter over when he/she wants to go home, how much allowance your children should receive, or where a friend wants to dine. Visit your local library and bookstore to review the numerous books now available on developing these skills. If you aim for win-win solutions, in which you *both* benefit, it will take less skill and persistence to persuade even a reluctant spouse to see things your way.

The next suggestion involves a crucial aspect of profiting from a divorce, for it asks you to *act,* rather than *react,* throughout proceedings leading to a final decree. Don't waste time and energy analyzing your spouse's reasons for behaving as she or he does. Wondering why Ben suddenly wants custody of Fifi the French poodle or why Henrietta begins dating husband Henry's best friend almost always proves a waste of time and a diversion of energy. If a development seems to have a legal ramification, your lawyer can fill you in; if not, then you'll do much better noting a spouse's behavior and determining what you can do about it to reach your personal goals. Instead of fantasizing about a mate's secret thoughts, list at least three options open to you that will bring you closer to an outcome that you desire. We panic when we see no alternatives, but we forge better agreements when we can see and propose several means of gaining what we want.

As soon as you begin actively attempting to achieve a certain outcome, you will free yourself from the tyranny of a mate's moods, whims, and threats. Merely by filing first, for example, you can set the hearing schedule, choose the forum, set the tone of later appearances, and escape the power of a spouse who forever threatens to file. You can *always* negotiate and/or continue to make settlement offers to the other side . . . even on the courthouse steps. When a spouse realizes that an outcome appears inevitable because of your efforts, he or she may opt for settlement well before trial.

In fact, by giving up an overly active concern for your spouse's secret desires, you will free energy to uncover and pursue all the common property, a much more profitable pursuit than musing over a mate's motivations. Many people find that mixing assets and emotions can prove a costly proposition, but anger rechanneled can fuel investigation and negotiation activities.

Finally, switching energies will help you prepare better for your future and will help you cope with any convictions of blame you still feel. Many people wage one-party campaigns against themselves to retain a blame element, heaping guilt upon themselves. Don't be one of them.

If you recognize the wisdom in this advice but cannot stop blaming yourself for a parting, or you keep mulling over the reasons behind a spouse's actions, consider getting therapy. You can obtain needed input with little outlay by joining a therapy group, or by finding a clinic offering a sliding-fee scale. If seeking counseling would make you uncomfortable, think about starting a discussion group for people undergoing divorce. Sharing your fears, frustrations, and angers with others who feel your pain can lessen your emotional burdens *and* provide you with practical, inexpensive solutions to the problems that most of you will face.

Develop a *plan*. Even a fantasy can prove the first step toward a plan, but a realistic plan will require much hard work. Make sure that your goal is one so deeply desired that you'll find the strength to carry through. If you fantasize running a hospital ward, find out what it will take to obtain your R.N. degree and some management experience. If you crave a travel agency of your own, interview agents and schools and outline a learning schedule that you can handle.

Use some of that freed-up energy to develop several ways of completing your plan. The more avenues you see leading to your goal, the greater the likelihood of your achieving what you've set out to do. In order to increase the number of avenues, work at sharpening your "option outlook." Learning to spot (or create) alternatives can help you avoid feeling panicked and trapped. You might start by asking yourself, for example, to think of three ways to increase your income without losing your sanity. As an alternative, imagine that you fell ill and could not work. Think of at least two ways in which you could support yourself, with or without help you could reasonably expect from others. After you've fantasized a few catastrophes and imagined several "escape options" for each, you'll feel increased self-confidence in your coping skills.

Go easy on the decision making before, during, and for some months after your divorce. Decisions relating directly to your legal proceedings will require all of your factor-weighing energy for a time, so don't take on more problems than you need. The ending of a marriage requires time for mourning and regret. While you're riding these emotional waves, you're not going to operate on an even keel all—or even much—of the time. You may feel vulnerable, wounded, and weak. You may find some people or actions attractive that you normally wouldn't care for. Self-destructive actions may suddenly begin to undercut many of your hopes. For this period of time, you may feel incapable of making even simple decisions or of reasoning through even simple problems.

During this time you may also appear easy pickings to someone eager to capitalize on your distress. You may inadvertently attract people who want to take advantage of your temporary imbalances by draining you emotionally, by insisting on physical intimacies before you're ready, or by proposing financial deals that you're in no condition to consider rationally. To avoid these emotional and physical pitfalls, some people cling to rigid rules when they face a stressful situation. If, for example, you insist on three dates before you indulge in physical intimacy, you may find that your "policy" will protect you from involvement too soon, or save you from an emotional investment in an inappropriate partner.

To sidestep financial traps, some divorcing parties find it useful to create a "board of advisers" whom they consult before making any decision involving funds above a set amount. If you can't call on such a group of advisers, consider asking a trusted, levelheaded friend to act as an "escrow officer" by holding liquid assets for you with the understanding that you must solidly justify any financial request. You might also want to place any large lump sums in a savings and loan's certificate of deposit. This will put those dollars beyond your immediate reach, for you will have to complete necessary paperwork and pay a penalty for early withdrawal.

Use the holidays (especially the Christmas season) to gather crucial information that will profit you later on. Encourage your mate's feelings of sentiment and sharing to spur him to give you gifts that can finance the tougher times ahead (but ask for your own savings account, for example, rather than a sable cape). Copy all records that you or your spouse has already gathered to support your upcoming tax return, and duplicate past tax returns as well. Collect and copy all the bank statements sent toward year's end that show interest earned on your accounts. Copy profit-sharing printouts or letters announcing your spouse's pension interest at the close of that calendar year. Note all year-end bonuses and copy any paperwork involved. Duplicate any transmittal information churned out when your spouse decides to sell stocks, bonds, or other securities for a year-end gain or loss. Copy the information supplied by any tax shelter plans that your mate invests in to lighten the bite of the IRS.

Any time you settle on terms involving future payments to you, make sure that you follow this suggestion: obtain adequate security for the performance of your mate. It is unfortunate but true that obligations determined in a divorce action often go unpaid as a result of either malingering or an accident to your ex-mate—or even his/her death. Ensure your right to receive funds or other type of payment by arranging for adequate protections. Such security can include the following:

- Life insurance payments if a spouse's death cuts off child and/or spousal support funds.
- A charge against the paying party's estate that will survive the death of the obligor.
- Payments directly from a pension plan, that don't flow through your ex-spouse.
- Survivor's benefits on an annuity or pension plan.
- A performance bond that will pay if your mate does not.
- Joint tenancy in a property, which will revert directly to you if your spouse dies.
- A lien on receivables (payable to your spouse) that you can impose if his/her payments fail.
- A trust or other fund that pays you directly while remaining beyond your spouse's control.
- An annuity plan that furnishes you adequate support if your mate falls ill, disappears, refuses to work, or passes away.

Indulge yourself. Julie bought herself a longed-for piece of sculpture to mark her parting. Janet mailed invitations to her "coming-out party" during her first month as a live-alone. Arnold stocked up on all the detective novels he'd never allowed time for and spent three weekends in a row in bed with the telephone turned off. Hal visited a therapist once a week to help himself understand his feelings and fears.

Deal openly and forgivingly with your pain. If you deny it, your agony can poison other relationships, sabotage your best intentions, and even destroy a new marital partnership.

Use this formal break to cast off old emotional baggage that you've been carrying for years. Here's your chance to start anew and put behind you old behavior patterns that used to diminish or demoralize you.

Give yourself at least two years to completely regain your emotional equilibrium. If you recover sooner, hooray! But don't berate yourself for relapses or for being a slow healer.

Finally, recognize that you may no longer *like* your former love, but that you *can* rise above such negative emotions for the single purpose of completing your divorce—a highly personal process that in fact could rank as the biggest business deal of your life. Arrange your dissolution of partnership as coolly and knowledgeably as you can, and profit from your divorce!

Index